THE TOURNAMENTS
AT LE HEM AND CHAUVENCY

THE TOURNAMENTS AT LE HEM AND CHAUVENCY

SARRASIN
THE ROMANCE OF LE HEM

JACQUES BRETEL
THE TOURNAMENT AT CHAUVENCY

TRANSLATED BY
NIGEL BRYANT

THE BOYDELL PRESS

© Nigel Bryant 2020

All Rights Reserved. Except as permitted under current legislation
no part of this work may be photocopied, stored in a retrieval system,
published, performed in public, adapted, broadcast,
transmitted, recorded or reproduced in any form or by any means,
without the prior permission of the copyright owner

The right of Nigel Bryant to be identified as
the author of this work has been asserted in accordance with
sections 77 and 78 of the Copyright, Designs and Patents Act 1988

First published 2020
The Boydell Press, Woodbridge
Paperback edition 2022

ISBN 978 1 78327 459 8 hardback
ISBN 978 1 78327 710 0 paperback

The Boydell Press is an imprint of Boydell & Brewer Ltd
PO Box 9, Woodbridge, Suffolk IP12 3DF, UK
and of Boydell & Brewer Inc.
668 Mount Hope Ave, Rochester, NY 14620–2731, USA
website: www.boydellandbrewer.com

A catalogue record for this book is available
from the British Library

The publisher has no responsibility for the continued existence or accuracy of
URLs for external or third-party internet websites referred to in this book, and
does not guarantee that any content on such websites is, or will remain, accurate
or appropriate

Contents

Introduction	vii
The Romance of Le Hem	vii
Performance in the Festival at Le Hem	viii
Sports Report from Le Hem	xviii
The Tournament at Chauvency	xxi
Love	xxii
Demigods and Martyrs	xxvi
Editions, Manuscripts and Further Reading	xxx
Sarrasin, *The Romance of Le Hem*	1
Jacques Bretel, *The Tournament at Chauvency*	61
Index to *The Romance of Le Hem*	123
Index to *The Tournament at Chauvency*	127

Introduction

THE ROMANCE OF LE HEM

The Romance of Le Hem is a detailed account of a festival of jousting held in October 1278 at Le Hem, now the village of Hem-Monacu, on the banks of the Somme to the east of Amiens in north-eastern France.[1] It was written by an eyewitness, the otherwise unknown Sarrasin, based on 'the notes I took'.[2] That he intended from the outset to write the account is suggested both by his taking of detailed notes and by the maiden Forteche, while watching the jousts alongside him, urging him to 'record the good and omit the bad. All good, true knights will love and cherish you for it.'[3] And immediately afterwards he is commissioned to write his book by the presiding 'queen', the sister of the lord of Longueval, with payment guaranteed by the lord of Bazentin, and Sarrasin pledges to deliver the completed work 'before the year is out'.[4] There is no reason to suppose that he was late.

---

[1] In the text the site of the event is several times named '*Ham sour Somme*' as well as '*le Hen*', '*le Han*', '*le Hem*' and '*le Ham*', but in his 1939 edition (pp. xlviii–lii) Albert Henry argues convincingly that these names cannot refer (as was once assumed) to the town of Ham-sur-Somme, about 30 miles further upriver. The close proximity to Hem-Monacu of the fiefs of many of the participants, and the fact that the two lords who organised the event, Aubert de Longueval and Huart de Bazentin, had no rights over Ham-sur-Somme while one of them held the land at what is now Hem-Monacu, make it overwhelmingly probable that Hem-Monacu was the site of the festival. The objection that the romance refers to a castle at 'Le Hem' and that no trace of one remains at Hem-Monacu, Henry answers by quoting a nineteenth-century report that since time immemorial the local inhabitants had recovered building materials – hewn stones and tiles – from an islet in the river where there had evidently been a major building, either a manor house or a fortress. He points out that the expansive, gently sloping ground between the village of Hem-Monacu and the river Somme (with the probable castle on the islet) would have been an ideal setting for the jousts.
[2] Below, p. 54.
[3] p. 50.
[4] p. 59.

So, invaluably, we have a detailed, eyewitness record probably written within weeks of the events described. But on first reading, Sarrasin's account may seem anything but down-to-earth and reliable. It may in fact strike the first-time reader as downright fanciful. Written in the verse-form – octosyllabic rhyming couplets – of many an Arthurian romance, it not only introduces early on a symbolic figure, the personification of Courtesy, giving guidance to the lords of Bazentin and Longueval in their organisation of their jousting festival, but rapidly interrupts proceedings to tell a story – for all the world lifted straight from a romance – of 'the Knight of the Lion' rescuing four damsels from the castle of an abductor. What on earth, one could be forgiven for asking, is going on? Is this really a serious account of what happened?

Yes, it is. Careful reading makes plain that every element of Sarrasin's text, however outlandish it may initially seem, records in a perfectly logical way the planned thinking that underlay the elaborate mixture of martial sport and theatre that constituted the festival at Le Hem. For theatre as well as jousting, and jousting in the context of enacted stories, were central to what occurred there. It makes *The Romance of Le Hem* an intriguing source of material for scholars not only of medieval chivalry and tournaments but also of performance.

Performance in the Festival at Le Hem

Guinevere and her court

When the lords of Longueval and Bazentin sit together and discuss the baleful effects of the king of France's ban on tournaments, and agree that they really should remedy these effects at whatever cost, Sarrasin in his account of their meeting has 'Lady Courtesy' waft in to inspire and direct their plans. This may seem to some modern minds pointlessly whimsical; but it is nothing more than the poet's way of expressing his admiration for the 'courtesy' – the generous, positive spirit – that underlay the two lords' decision. It might also be viewed as a rather charming way of giving a retrospective account of their inspiration and of the development of their vision for the event.[5]

What they plan for their festival – inspired, Sarrasin says, by 'courtesy' – is in very large part a performance. One of Longueval's sisters (never, sadly, named) is to travel to Le Hem as no less a figure than Queen Guinevere, escorted by 'Sir Kay the seneschal' and 'seven hundred knights, ladies and maids'; and, says Sarrasin, 'it was no secret – the whole surrounding country

---

[5] Two lines at the end of the passage suggest an additional layer of possibility: that in some degree 'Lady Courtesy' had in fact been Longueval's sister Marguerite. See below, p. 6.

heard the news'.⁶ Although couching his account in the phraseology of a romance, Sarrasin is in fact telling us what really happened: that the festival was conceived and proclaimed from the outset as an Arthurian spectacle. It followed, of course, that all who gathered to join 'Guinevere' and 'Kay the seneschal' were themselves immediately role-playing as the members of the Arthurian court; and Sarrasin simultaneously eulogises them and describes, as it were, their stage directions when he says that Guinevere's knights 'can't abide being idle' and are 'ever ready to joust, whatever the cost' while her ladies and maids are 'the fairest ever seen' and 'engage in pleasure and laughter all day long'.⁷

Soredamor [pp. 8–9]

Continuing in romance vein, Sarrasin's account now makes it clear, I would suggest, that, having arrived and assembled at Le Hem, those gathering at the festival were presented – probably on the evening before the jousting was to begin – with a complete piece of theatre. A young woman⁸ playing the damsel 'Soredamor' (a name borrowed from Chrétien de Troyes' romance *Cligès*) comes before them all – in their roles as 'Guinevere's court' – with a dramatic appeal for help to rescue her sweetheart from captivity. Reading Sarrasin's vivid description, it is not difficult to reconstruct exactly what was performed:

Enter the damsel 'on a struggling nag, accompanied by a dwarf who was leading her by the bridle. The queen was seated at supper, crown on head. The dwarf made his way through the hall to the top table, where Sir Kay spoke up…'⁹ Was the dialogue which follows – Kay's bumptious welcome of the damsel, and her appeal to the queen for help – scripted? Why would it not have been? If it was, then Sarrasin either borrowed a copy of the script and adapted and incorporated it into his poem, or recreated it as closely as he could from memory. As for the preceding back-story of what had happened 'a year to the day' previously, when a maiden named Alise had sought help from Guinevere's court and Soredamor's sweetheart had assumed the mission, only to be tricked into captivity by Alise, this could easily at the time have been delivered in dialogue between Soredamor and Guinevere, with the queen expressing, for example, her 'dejection at being without such a worthy knight' as Soredamor's beloved. If it was indeed couched in dialogue,

---

⁶ p. 7.
⁷ p. 7.
⁸ She is evidently related to Longueval's sister who is playing Guinevere, as Sarrasin says she seeks the queen's help because 'she was quite close kin' (p. 8). I would suggest (though it's a guess, of course) that this is playful understatement and that they were perhaps even sisters.
⁹ p. 8.

then Sarrasin's account is a mixture of quotation and précis of the scene he saw performed.

What is certain – and particularly interesting to see – is what followed Soredamor's appeal to the 'queen' and her 'court': in theatrical fashion Longueval's sister / 'Guinevere' paused... and then there was participation from the extras:

> Lady Guinevere was silent; but having pondered awhile she replied so that all the court could hear:
> 'Damsel Soredamor, you will have fine aid from me and from the knights of my court.'
> With that, some hundred knights flocked before the queen, all offering to assume the mission, whatever might befall them. But the queen promptly said:
> 'Sit down and eat, sirs: one alone will go with her.'[10]

Some hundred knights, Sarrasin tells us, flocked to offer their service. In other words, all those present at the festival at Le Hem, supping together before the jousting was to begin next day, understood exactly what their roles were; they knew their Arthurian romances; they knew how Arthur's knights would and should respond to a damsel in distress; and the modern reader can see and hear exactly how they ad-libbed.

And then, after 'Sir Kay' (sadly, we don't know who was playing him) has offered to be the 'one alone who will go with her', there is a splendidly dramatic turn as:

> A knight sounded a horn at the foot of the bridge, and the dwarf cried:
> 'Hear that horn-blast! Lady, lady, the one out there who blew it has brought the captive knight! Now we'll see if your court can truly help us! He's little respect for you if he dares to come so near!'
> 'By my life!' said Kay, 'I'm ready to go if the queen gives me leave!'
> 'Sir Kay,' the queen replied, 'I pray you wait till tomorrow.'[11]

We can of course never know for sure, but this has all the marks of a scripted scene, and fine theatre it would have been – and how very rewarding for all those present, not merely an audience but thrown into active roles in an Arthuresque adventure. In modern theatrical terms it was a promenade performance.

The Knight of the Lion, Part One [pp. 10–18]

To judge from the logic of Sarrasin's account, this promenade performance continued next morning outside on the tourney-ground, where the

---

[10] p. 9.
[11] p. 9.

crowd gathered in the stands and saw 'Sir Kay' ride out to meet the knight. At this point it may well strike the first-time reader as anti-dramatic and mystifying (bordering on incompetent) that Sarrasin promptly breaks the flow by launching into an apparently unconnected adventure about 'the good Knight of the Lion' (a figure meant surely to remind the audience of Chrétien de Troyes' 'Knight of the Lion', Yvain) and 'four of the queen's maidens'. What's more, it proves to be a long digression. But it is entirely necessary in order to make sense of what is to occur later on, during the day's jousting. For just as the resolution of Soredamor's plight is to be played out mid-jousts, so is the resolution to the Knight of the Lion's story, and I think it highly probable that Sarrasin is setting the story down for the reader at this point because everyone who'd been present at the festival had already heard and understood it – as they would have needed to if they were to appreciate what they went on to witness later in the day. I would suggest therefore that the story of the Knight of the Lion had been told to 'the queen's court' – i.e. everyone attending the festival – as part of the previous evening's entertainments, along with the performance of the Soredamor scenes. And indeed, it may be significant that Sarrasin says he will 'recount it ... just as I heard it told'.[12]

What form the 'telling' took will be a matter of great interest to any reader keen to reconstruct the performance of romances. As Sarrasin relays it, it is strikingly full of dialogue, crying out for performance by multiple voices in addition to a 'narrator'. It is possible that one of those voices may have been (participating in true festival spirit) the count of Artois, for the Knight of the Lion is none other than the count, as is revealed towards the story's end.[13] And it is interesting to note that, at the moment of revelation, Sarrasin tells us simply that he 'was revealed to be the count'.[14] Which count? This translator has needed to insert a footnote for the modern reader, but Sarrasin had no need to identify him because the audience for which he'd written his book already knew: they'd been there and seen him. Likewise, the modern first-time reader is entitled to be baffled by the first reference to him as 'the knight who'd brought the lion'.[15] Which lion? Sarrasin's audience, having been present at proceedings and now reading or hearing his book as a souve-

---

[12] p. 10.
[13] Nancy Regalado has noted that 'Robert d'Artois had taken the lion as one of his emblems well before the tournament at Le Hem, adopting a lion's head for his seal in 1274 in place of the Artois coat of arms'; and she interestingly wonders: 'Did Robert d'Artois and the minstrels in his household organize and perform the whole episode of the Knight of the Lion – tale and interludes – as his contribution to the feast?' Nancy F. Regalado 'Performing Romance: Arthurian Interludes in Sarrasin's '*Le Roman du Hem*', in *Performing Medieval Narrative*, ed. Vitz, Regalado and Lawrence (Woodbridge, 2005), p. 114.
[14] p. 15.
[15] p. 16.

nir of the great occasion, already knew: they had already had the delightful experience of seeing the count accompanied by (if not an actual lion, which is surely stretching practicality) a man in a lion's suit and mask, bounding and cavorting and at one point acting as 'a most courteous beast, sitting calm and quiet before the queen with its muzzle on the table'.[16]

Anyone keen to reimagine the possible performance of this fine adventure may well consider that its final scene – the arrival at court of the knights defeated by the Knight of the Lion – would have been ripe for full enactment, involving as it does the dramatic entrance of the knights and the lion followed by the rich, mocking jibes of Sir Kay.

And how interesting it is that Sarrasin concludes this section by telling us that they 'took their seats for supper, where those young knights errant were the object of keen attention! And as soon as supper was over the queen promptly bade a start to dancing, which lasted well into the night.'[17] This, I would suggest, is confirmation that the enactment of the Soredamor scenes and the telling / performance of the Knight of the Lion's adventure, both of which were preparing everyone for what was to be enacted on the tourney ground next day, were part of the entertainments (along with supper and dancing) of the evening before the jousting festival began.

Sir Kay's Jousts [pp. 18–26]

And next day the jousting did indeed begin. But it was by no means the end of performance. Centre of attention first is the lord or knight in the role of 'Sir Kay', waiting for his opponent to appear and expressing his frustration at being denied the first joust which he considers his by right. It seems to me most likely that the dialogue involved in this initial comic scene – for a scene it is – was mostly planned and scripted. The absence of his opponent sets up the following exchange between 'Guinevere', 'Kay' and a lady in the stand:

> The queen now called on Sir Kay to use his lances, for time was pressing on and knights from many lands had come to win renown: she told him to get on with it! You never heard a madman or a drunkard react as Kay did then! The knights who'd heard the queen's order couldn't help laughing; nor could the ladies leaning at the windows of the stand. And when one of them cried:

---

[16] p. 18. That it was a costumed actor rather than a real lion is suggested by Sarrasin's memory of the moment when the Knight of the Lion jousts with Longueval and is met with 'a blow that alarmed the lion, awed by the mighty crash!' (p. 36). This suggests to me a memorable bit of acting rather than a distressed beast.

[17] p. 18.

> 'What are you waiting for, Sir Kay? Something from one of us?'
> Kay called back: 'Lady, we're short of two people here: you need a lover by the look of you, and I need an opponent! I hope they're both sent from Hell!'
> 'You've always been like this, Sir Kay!' said the queen. 'And you'll never change! You take yourself so seriously! You've no need to be so vexed – the lady meant her question kindly.' Then she called straightway for her barons to advise her.
> 'Sirs,' she said, 'we've knights arriving from far and wide, and it's high time we began proceedings. God grant me good fortune in what I'm about to propose: to give our guests from foreign parts a chance to join the ladies, I wish to offer the following condition if you'll agree: have it proclaimed at once that if a knight and his mount both fall but the knight stays in his saddle, he can have the squires and pages help him up again.'
> 'They won't say no to that!' said the lord of Raineval.
> 'And let whichever knight's first ready go and joust, if he can find an opponent. And let the heralds remind all comers that the ladies are here and watching!'[18]

I see no reason to suppose that any of this was unscripted except, perhaps, the taunting question from one of the ladies and Sir Kay's wicked retort, in which case they were sharp ad-libbers as well as good deliverers of script. The lord of Raineval might have felt free to interject, too, but the queen's material is surely pre-planned. It was entirely necessary to stage this initial scene in order to give the lord of Longueval – one of the festival's two organisers, of course – the honour of the first joust (and all the attention), rather than Sir Kay.

And when that first joust is done, the 'scene' concludes with, I would suggest, yet more scripted material:

> Sir Kay came hurrying to the queen and said: 'Lady! Lady, they've done me shame, and you even more than me! You know I should have the first joust at your court! Strike me blind if I'll stand for this! And let's be honest: what a modest and mannerly start they've given us!'
> 'Yes, Sir Kay, without a doubt you'd have shown the way much better! You and your opponent would have scattered the field with shards!'
> 'I would indeed, lady! I'd have been fearless!'
> 'There's nothing to stop you doing so yet, if you're still so inclined.'
> 'You unhorsed so many,' said the ladies, mocking, 'when the queen was taken to Gorre: you know how well that ended!'
> Sir Kay, shame-stricken, went very quiet![19]

---

[18] p. 19.
[19] p. 21.

It may, of course, all have been ad-libbed, but if so they were remarkably good improvisers. The final barb about Gorre, referring to a humiliation suffered by Kay in Chrétien de Troyes' *Lancelot*, is particularly interesting: whether scripted or not (and it may indeed have been a brilliant ad-lib from one or more of the ladies in the stand, though scripting is far more likely, as it's too neat a conclusion to an otherwise unfinished exchange), it shows the assembly's rich familiarity with Arthurian romance – specifically with Chrétien's work, even though this festival is taking place a century after his death.[20]

That is not to suggest, however, that *all* the banter between Kay and the ladies was scripted. A short while later, as Kay's long-awaited opponent finally appears, Sarrasin records what sounds like a witty impromptu exchange between 'Kay' and a dwarf and those watching in the stands.

> The ladies didn't hold back but called right out to Kay, saying:
> 'The tardy knight and the hardy knight are going to meet! So make sure you keep your vow, Sir Kay! You said at the start that you and your opponent would scatter the field with shards! He's come to take you on, so you'd better get strewing! No knight should break his word to ladies!'
> Sir Kay was mortified to hear the ladies' taunts. 'Would to God,' he said, 'no woman under heaven had a tongue! A curse on yours! You're so quick to sound off with scorching jibes!'
> 'Don't let them get to you, Sir Kay,' said the dwarf, who was a nasty piece of work. 'Behind their soft caresses women have claws! They always speak their mind and have their way. Woman is a very dodgy dish!'
> This cheered Kay no end: he thought he'd been well avenged! But one of the queen's maids, Forteche, said:
> 'I tell you, dwarf, you'll do yourself no favours by slagging off the ladies! You'd do better to hold your tongue. Sir Kay can say what he likes – he's always having a go at us.'[21]

Once again, that last remark shows the audience's familiarity with Kay's character in romances. And if this exchange was impromptu, equally 'unscripted' is Kay's joust, the competition being clearly in earnest and its outcome uncertain:

> Sir Kay the seneschal, to answer the ladies' mockery, went in so close that they crashed together, chest to chest, both man and horse, sundering stirrups and breast-straps; though neither rider lost his seat, the impact was so terrible that everyone was certain they'd been killed. The queen

---

[20] Everyone fully understood Kay's character, too: 'not merely in all of Chrétien's romances but throughout the entire Arthurian tradition… [Kay's voice is] one that truly drips with sarcasm and irony. Kay is *the* sharp tongue; his words and tone cut through all that courtly palaver.' Evelyn Birge Vitz, *Orality and Performance in Early French Romance* (Woodbridge, 1999), p. 144.

[21] p. 24.

was aghast – she loved Sir Kay dearly – and sent a worthy, valiant knight to see how the two knights were. But their attendants had already helped them to mount two palfreys, so the queen's alarm was quelled.[22]

Since the result of this joust was apparently unrigged, and if the barbs directed at Kay had indeed been impromptu, it may follow that the next dialogue was improvised, too, as Kay rides up to the stands and calls out:

> 'Where is Madam Haughty, who bade me strew the field? If it weren't unseemly to bicker I'd soon say something that I'll keep to myself. But let me give her this much: she wouldn't have all that bling about her neck, or be so decked with all that get-up, unless she had a lover. She's made me mad, my lady!'
> 'She wears it for her husband's sake!' the queen replied. 'There's no reason to think otherwise!'
> 'Let's hope to God you're right!' said Kay.[23]

Reconstructing further, I would suggest, however, that his following, final speech was pre-scripted to provide a perfect exit and conclusion to the 'scene'. It's a speech which entirely captures Kay's acerbic character in Arthurian romances (and introduces, incidentally, a theme that is to be much developed in *The Tournament at Chauvency*):

> 'I tell you, ladies, anyone who upsets me rues the day! And anyone who trusts you women will get it in the neck! You act all proper and upright but if any man tries hard enough you'll always fall in a trice! Then again, no service we offer will satisfy you unless it involves a battering or a wound! By the apostle Peter, you women want our love for you to be equal to our love for God! You want men to well and truly pay before they win your love! God send you all a wretched day!'[24]

It's as well that it does capture Kay's character, as that seems in some ways to have been the point of the whole sequence, setting up his bumptiousness for a possible fall (which, with genuine jeopardy, doesn't happen); for it's curious that Kay's joust does not in fact provide a conclusion to the Soredamor story, which – unlike the Knight of the Lion's adventure, as we are about to see – is left surprisingly unresolved. His opponent does not seem to have been representing the knight who'd blown the horn at the foot of the bridge; he does not bring Soredamor's captured lover; Soredamor does not reappear. Unless Sarrasin strangely misunderstood and mis-recorded what occurred, the memorable and hugely entertaining character Sir Kay, rather than Soredamor and her captured lover, was the focus of this part of proceedings.

[22] p. 25.
[23] p. 25.
[24] pp. 25–6.

The Knight of the Lion, Part Two [pp. 34–7]

After these sequences the festival of jousting continued in earnest with a series of jousts between the knights attending, and it was a while before the audience was treated to another performed interlude: the resolution of the Knight of the Lion's adventure. But then:

Enter the four maidens he'd rescued, escorted by the knight himself (the count of Artois). After a splendid, and surely scripted, scene in which Kay cruelly mocks the damsel 'Long-Suffering' who is sent by the knight to seek the queen's permission for him to join her household, the man dressed as the lion also reappears in a fine theatrical moment as

> the knight bade his lion move, and his four maidens set off in pairs, singing more sweetly than the Sirens, and with the lion at their head they arrived at court. Everyone flocked to meet them amid fanfares of trumpets and drums, and they rode through the gate into the lists in perfect array. The ladies in the stand saw the Knight of the Lion and had eyes for no one but him and his lion and his maidens. The knight, sporting armour like wings, rode into the lists ready to joust, lacking nothing.[25]

A great entrance indeed, and it's no surprise when Sarrasin reveals that the knight who now enjoyed the honour of riding forth to joust with the count of Artois / 'Knight of the Lion' was festival organiser Longueval, once again taking pride of place. It is very striking that at no point did the audience at Le Hem evidently need any explanation of who these figures were or where they'd been or what they'd done: they were fully aware of the back-story, having heard and seen it told and performed the night before. And once the count and Longueval have run their courses in the lists, the whole adventure of the Knight of the Lion is brought to a perfectly resolved conclusion – in, I would again suggest, a clearly scripted piece of theatre – as

> he quickly dismounted and helped the maidens from their palfreys and led them straightway to the queen, who was seated aloft in the stand. He greeted her most courteously and said:
> 'Your knight comes as called, lady, and will gladly do whatever you command. Armed as you see me, I am at your service.'
> 'A thousand thanks, sir,' she replied, 'for the honour you have done me. Go now and disarm and come and sit with us and watch the jousts. If you wish to take the maidens with you they'll go and serve you willingly: you've well deserved it. And may those who've caused them grief get *their* deserts!'
> 'I promise you truly,' said the count, 'they were fairly treated as prisoners and suffered no impropriety. And it's led to a happy outcome for the knight their captor. That's all there is to tell.'[26]

---

[25] pp. 35–6.
[26] pp. 36–7.

The Duke of Lorraine's Joust [pp. 37–8] and the Maiden and her Cruel Lover [pp. 38–41]

After this dramatic interlude, which so satisfyingly resolved what the audience had seen the previous night, how delighted they must have been when it was followed by two further pieces of theatre, both of them complete surprises. The first involves an unexpected and marvellous piece of stage machinery, evidently some form of float, providing an attention-grabbing entrance for the duke of Lorraine. 'Queen Guinevere' turns everyone's attention from the Knight of the Lion and

> away to the right, where they could see what looked like a chapel in the air, wondrously beautiful and gliding through the air towards the tents. Everyone was trying to work out what it was! It was the duke coming, imprisoned inside! Which duke? Tell me! It was the duke of Lorraine, placed there with the condition that he could in no way be released but by four maidens! He pressed on till he reached the lists, where his prison was broken open by the queen's fair maids. Then he was armed most richly: his caparisons, surcoat and fine mail sleeves were without a doubt worth more than five hundred livres tournois.[27]

The duke's subsequent joust (about which Sarrasin interestingly chooses to say little 'because the duke contributed no largesse to the feast') is soon followed by yet another theatrical interlude, as

> a beautiful blonde-haired maiden approached the queen, riding, I remember, a scrawny white nag without a saddle. And this maiden, fair and white-skinned, had a lance propped on her shoulder and was carrying a sword. And a wicked, foul-natured dwarf was riding behind her on another skinny nag, this one piebald, and at every step was beating her about the shoulders and arms with a many-knotted scourge. Ahead of her rode her lover – it was he who was bringing her in this cruel fashion: he'd turned against her – for no other reason than her admiration of the queen's good knights![28]

Her plight, straight out of a romance, is a scripted (and Arthurian) cue for more jousting, as the poor, abused maiden appeals to 'Queen Guinevere', saying:

> 'I'm suffering all this pain and shame because of you! A dozen weeks ago we were at home talking of one thing and another till the subject turned to knights, and my lover said he'd like to know if your knights were as valiant as was reputed far and wide. I said that in the whole wide world none finer could ever be found, and he was so outraged by this that without a moment's pause he put me straightway in the saddle! No damsel was ever so basely treated! Have pity on me, queen, for he's

[27] p. 37.
[28] p. 38.

sworn an oath that I'll endure all this till one of your knights has jousted with him. I promise you, the first to challenge him will set me free!'[29]

Not for the first time, the knights at the festival are effectively being cast in the roles of Arthur's knights, and one of them comes forward to answer the maiden's plea. This knight, perhaps significantly, is a 'local', Wautier de Hardecourt – Hardecourt-aux-Bois being only a couple of miles north-west of Le Hem; and no doubt roared on by plenty of local support he out-jousts the cruel lover. There is a strong sense that the outcome of this joust (unlike Sir Kay's earlier on) is rigged: while good old Wautier smashes one lance down to his fist and lands an awesome blow with his next, it's suspiciously convenient that the cruel lover, having said that 'if he failed to unhorse the knight he would forgive the girl all ill will and seek the queen's pardon',[30] twice misses his blow completely. Much cheering no doubt all round. And of course the rigged defeat of the lover is necessary to make sense of the prepared (and once again surely scripted) scene that concludes the interlude, as the knight admits his fault and begs forgiveness of Guinevere, the maiden makes a dramatic choice of whether to return to her cruel sweetheart or stay with the queen, and Sir Kay – by now a leading player in the festival – adds a typically offensive comment.

Sports Report from Le Hem

Well-conceived, accomplished and entertaining as these performed interludes appear to have been, and contrived though the outcomes of some of the jousts necessarily were, it is abundantly clear from Sarrasin's account that there was nothing contrived or playful about the vast majority of the one hundred and eighty jousts which he tells us took place. They were in earnest. Throughout his 'little book' Sarrasin gives us eyewitness evidence of the formidable risk and violence involved in a sport succinctly described by one of the watching commoners as 'proper dangerous!'[31]

In the very first joust we see 'Guinevere' – Longueval's sister – imploring God to protect her brother from harm as he charges to meet the castellan of Arras, and according to Sarrasin

> such were the blows they exchanged that five hundred thought a thunderbolt had struck! Stumps flew higher than any man could throw: of the castellan's lance not half a yard remained, and his opponent's was shattered likewise, reduced to powder! They were driving their horses so straight and swift that people were saying:
> 'If they collide they'll kill each other!'[32]

[29] p. 39.
[30] p. 40.
[31] p. 27.
[32] p. 20.

Introduction xix

If this sounds suspiciously like the florid hyperbole of descriptions of jousts found in romances, we may wish to reconsider how hyperbolical the writers of romances actually were. For as his poem goes on, Sarrasin's descriptions become no less violent and more and more convincing. When, for instance, Robert de Montigny jousts with Guillaume d'Annois,

> they weren't playing at it! They charged full tilt and clashed full on, meeting body to body and horse to horse. It pained me to see such a fearful crash, and the ladies watching from the wall thought they were finished and were dreadfully upset. Everyone was convinced they both were dead, and some were stricken with grief.[33]

A notably sober, hyperbole-free description of injury and comment on the dangers is given when

> Mahieu de Warlincourt gave Mahieu de Vaudricourt a blow in the chest from which he suffered long, a blow witnessed by more than five hundred, and there were many in the lists who thought it had killed him; but hurt though he was, he broke his own lance down to his fist. From far off the queen could see him slumped unconscious in his saddle and she was most alarmed; but it's all part and parcel of jousting.[34]

Sarrasin's descriptions of the jousts are often impressive. His work has been criticised from a literary point of view – even his modern editor Albert Henry considers Sarrasin's literary talent 'very often inferior to Bretel's'[35] – and it would certainly be hard to argue that his verse is particularly elegant. But as reportage of a sporting event his work bears comparison with much modern sports journalism. Given that jousting is in its essence highly repetitive, one would expect the number of ways of describing each clash to be finite, and there is indeed an element of repetition in one or two parts of the work where Sarrasin's eagerness to record and credit every jouster turns it into something of a register. But for the most part Sarrasin does a good job of conjuring varied images, and if at times he is more intent on recording the score – the number of hits and broken lances – than he is on creating colour, he is no more or less resourceful than many a modern reporter of the equally repetitive action involved in, for example, cricket, baseball, tennis, track and field athletics or indeed the vast majority of sports, in which of course the score, and success and failure, can often be deemed of paramount importance.

That is not to say that his reporting is entirely impartial. He had been commissioned to write the report by the tournament's organisers, and since they and the knights of immediately neighbouring lands were competing

---

[33] p. 27.
[34] p. 38.
[35] *Le roman du Hem*, ed. Henry, p. xiii.

against 'outsiders' from further afield (Normandy, Flanders, the Île de France and elsewhere), the reader will note how Sarrasin, while giving polite credit wherever it's due, takes every opportunity to go overboard and eulogise the efforts of the 'home' side. The closer they are to the organisers themselves, the more fulsome the praise: see for example the admiration he pours on the young knight Renaut de Montauban (referred to familiarly as 'Basin'), even taking time out to mention a previous triumph he'd had jousting in Germany;[36] the reason for the eulogy becomes clear when one twigs that Montauban was a fief of one of the organisers, the lord of Bazentin, and there was close connection between the families through marriage.

But this can hardly be deemed a serious flaw. On an important level Sarrasin's work is a roll of honour, richly deserved by those with the courage to participate in such an awesomely dangerous sport. And he is recording the daring and skill of their jousts as a glorious souvenir for those who'd had the vision – and the largesse – to stage the event, a largesse not shared, he notes, by the non-contributing duke of Lorraine.

But for all the skill of his sports reporting, and fascinating though it is as a record for us seven centuries and more further on, Sarrasin's work would surely be rather less engaging if it were an unbroken list of individual jousts. Similarly, those lucky and privileged to be present at the festival at Le Hem might have been rather less entertained once forty jousts turned to fifty, turned to ninety, topped one hundred and finally reached nine score. The jousting does not, after all, build to a climax in a mêlée as it does in the tournament at Chauvency, where we hear one of the heralds remark that he would much rather see a full-blooded mêlée than 'attend on individual jousting'.[37] Perhaps Bazentin and Longueval thought a mêlée would be a step too far in flouting the king's ban on tournaments;[38] in any event, in the absence of such a climax they brilliantly conceived a whole range of textures, contexts and motivations for jousting, interrupting the individual contests with delightful, witty and colourful theatre.[39]

---

[36] p. 30.

[37] Below, p. 97.

[38] Juliet Vale has observed that 'Sarrasin anticipates three days of martial activities but seems to recount only two' and suggests that 'the organisers might originally have hoped that they would have been granted licence to tourney and planned a third and final day devoted to a full-scale [mêlée] tournament, although in the event they had to content themselves with jousts'. Juliet Vale, *Edward III and Chivalry* (Woodbridge, 1982), p. 13.

[39] This – and indeed the mixture of banqueting and theatre and sport throughout the festival at Le Hem – is entirely consistent with the very nature of medieval feasting: Christina Normore has written of its 'multimedia' character and of 'the immersion of medieval audiences in the interactive world of banqueting'.

But the theatrical interludes were not there just to provide variety, to entertain. As Maurice Keen observes,

> theatre is a serious activity. The object of the best theatre is not only to entertain, but also to instruct and uplift. In the context of the tournament, the element of theatre had a serious purpose beyond that of lending colour to the occasion. It was a way of bringing it home that what was going on was more than a great social gathering centred on an exciting sport: that it was at the same time a celebration of the values of chivalry... By parading in Arthurian or other romantic dress, the participants were reminding themselves of the example that the great figures of the chivalrous past had set.[40]

Theatre is indeed a serious business, and so is fiction – especially if, as we shall see, no real distinction is made between fiction and history. Everyone participating at Le Hem was effectively in the world of Arthurian romance, trying to emulate the paragons of chivalry in literature on whom, it seems, they modelled their values and behaviour.

The festival was planned and scripted with great imagination and purpose for (and/or by) the two lords, and Sarrasin records it in detail, fulfilling his commission well.

The Tournament at Chauvency

Most readers will, however, probably judge *The Tournament at Chauvency* to be, if not in a different league, an even more accomplished piece of writing – and sophisticated, too: it may be written in the same form, the same octosyllabic rhyming couplets as Sarrasin's poem, but Jacques Bretel's vocabulary is exceptionally rich and he uses it in ambitious and sometimes idiosyncratic ways, which on occasion caused the scribes of the surviving manuscripts to struggle. Bretel, of whom no more is known than of Sarrasin,[41] records the tournament held seven years later, in 1285, some 150 miles south-east of Le Hem at what is now called Chauvency-le-Château, near the modern borders with Belgium and Luxembourg; and he does so with a flair and skill

---

C. Normore, *A Feast for the Eyes: Art, Performance and the Medieval Banquet* (Chicago, 2015).

[40] Maurice Keen, *Chivalry* (New Haven and London, 1984), p. 99.

[41] All one can infer with any reasonable confidence is that Bretel lived by the pen (at the beginning of the poem he walks from the count of Salm's castle and into the woods to 'seek inspiration, composing some little couplets about love'), and that (according to himself, at least!) he was held in a fair degree of esteem: ladies and damsels seem to know and welcome him and one herald tells him that 'knights, heralds, minstrels all speak well of you – as do I! I've been wanting to meet you.' (p. 91.)

that paint even more vivid pictures than Sarrasin's, conjuring character and atmosphere, sound and scene and action, in sometimes arresting fashion.

Few medieval accounts of events have such thrilling immediacy. Bretel sat, he tells us, in a prime place – 'I had an excellent position, sitting on the fourth step of the stand, and I loved having such a full and perfect view'[42] – and the reader sees and hears the action as if sitting at his shoulder: sees the colours and blazons on shields and apparel, even sees the state of the ground; hears the exactly recorded battle-cries, the horses neighing and whinnying, the clarions, trumpets, horns and drums, the mimicked accents of German and Picard. And the reader eavesdrops on conversations, too: Bretel reports exactly what he heard passing between heralds and ladies, between the ladies discussing the day's proceedings, and even between lovers. At the risk of being charged myself with hyperbole, I think it might be said that some passages in Bretel's fine work are as close as one could hope to get to time travel.

Love

Given the apparently real and authentic detail found at every part of his work, in which we share in every turn of his head and hear precisely what he heard, it may surprise some modern readers to realise how Bretel and the participants and all those watching at Chauvency perceived and understood what was happening. Why did they think the tournament was taking place at all? The reader may note that the very first word of Bretel's poem is 'love', and so, quite deliberately, is the very last. The fact is that love is the main and ever-present theme – not only of Bretel's poem but of the event itself.

A familiar trope in Arthurian romance is that 'all deeds of prowess are undertaken and accomplished for ladies and maidens, from whom all worth, honour and valour pass into the body of a knight',[43] and it would be easy to imagine that a trope, a romantic literary trope, was all it was. But it is striking that all involved at Chauvency see the proceedings in terms of that very trope. As two knights lie sprawled semi-conscious from their joust, Bretel reports the heralds berating the ladies and maidens in the stand with the idea that:

> 'It's for you these knights make their eyes reel and fly from their brains! The joy of your precious love is dearly bought! Those who risk their bodies and souls for you are lying there in such a state that neither head nor foot is stirring. It's for your love, women, that they lay their bodies on the line. Their toil and suffering never cease: they strive all day and lie awake

---

[42] p. 85.
[43] *Perceforest – the Prehistory of King Arthur's Britain*, trans. Bryant (Woodbridge, 2011), p. 259.

all night in agonies of desire! A blight upon your own health, women, if you show no pity for these knights suffering for your sake!'[44]

A short while later, when two more knights lie stricken, another herald goes further, telling the ladies:

> 'They're in danger of death – all for the sake of winning your love! You should at least relieve their suffering and help them recover – those knights who truly, sincerely love you – with looks of gentle favour. It would inspire them to even greater valour: the brightest clerk ever made by God couldn't edify a knight in sixty years as a lady could in a fortnight! Love is such a mighty force that none can refuse His urgings; all obey Love's commands, as you can plainly see in these two lying on the ground, who hold Love in such adoration and esteem, and are so intent on winning honour, that they yearn for nothing else. And why is Love preeminent? Because Love is the driving force of courage and prowess, of courtesy and largesse. When Love takes a man in His alluring way, He fires his heart with desire to excel in all worthy deeds. No one can rue being stricken by Love; and if any man finds himself suffering woe, if Love then smiles upon him he'll find one blessing makes up for a hundred pains! Such is Love's reward!'[45]

Time and again the watching ladies and maidens are reminded of their responsibilities: the encouragement and hope they can offer through their 'exhortations to courtesy and valour' can 'make a courtly knight of the callow youth... can turn the reluctant into proper knights... Just by responding kindly you can make the craven bold – just by saying "I love you, dear" you can make a rough fellow right chivalrous!' In fact, 'honour and disgrace are dependent on God and on you, ladies!'[46]

It may of course be that these addresses by the heralds were formulaic and routine, publicly reciting what custom required them to say. But the idea of love as the inspiring force for a knight's endeavour is expressed in private, too, by a lover to the object of his devotion, overheard and quoted by Bretel:

> 'I love you more than anyone alive, with a love that grows and intensifies with every passing day, forcing me – I cannot help myself – to love you with all my heart. And this at least is my recompense: that you are the source and inspiration of whatever honour I accrue; for if my body performs deeds of any worth, it's for love of you that it labours.'[47]

An especially memorable expression of the idea comes not during the jousts, in which individual knights compete for honour and praise, but immediately

---

[44] p. 69.
[45] p. 74.
[46] p. 83.
[47] p. 101.

before the ferocious battalion-against-battalion mêlée that concludes the action at Chauvency. This, too, Bretel tells us, is to be fought

> in the cause of love. Hauberks rent and split asunder, horses killed, mail hoods cloven: that's the way that kisses are earned, and courtly liaisons, and fond looks, and sweet words issuing from lips to touch the tender heart, intoxicating true lovers with the delights of dulcet speech.[48]

Is this, one might be inclined to wonder, just the male view of proceedings? Are the ladies unwillingly lumbered with these amorous strivings? Not according to Bretel. On the evening after the mêlée (which, he tells us, the women had been very eager to see, having not seen one before), he sits and listens to them talk among themselves, and

> in carefree spirit they were immersed in conversation about the feats of prowess they'd seen before their very eyes, and the fear they'd felt at the mayhem of the hot and frenzied mêlées, the violence and the injuries, the broken arms and slashed faces, the mighty blows of fist on nose! That's what true lovers are forced to endure if they seek to win honour and praise and the joys and rewards of love: it's what Love demands in return for the pleasures He sends! That's what I found the ladies discussing when I joined them.[49]

All parties, it seems, accept the idea that deeds of arms and love are essentially connected. Even a cynical, sarcastic remark from a herald, quoted by Bretel, reinforces the notion:

> One lady spoke out declaring she'd given her love to Waléran of Luxembourg, while another proclaimed she'd given her heart and undivided love and everything she possessed to the noble knight Wichart!
> 'Well let's hope you mean it!' said a herald who heard them. 'They've paid in full, so complete the transaction! Love and a rapturous welcome await them! Since you're so enamoured, no wonder they break their necks!'[50]

A reader may also note how many knights in the festival at Le Hem had charged into their jousts crying 'Love!' This essential connection of arms and love may explain why – bizarrely, perhaps, to the modern mind – the knights at Chauvency approach their jousts singing.

> At the head of them all I saw a knight eager to enhance his honour and prowess. He came, singing, to the end of the lists, and all those with him sang as one, most joyously and beautifully.[51]

---

[48] p. 106.
[49] p. 120.
[50] p. 86.
[51] p. 89. The fact that only single lines or couplets from the songs are quoted in the manuscript raises interesting questions. Is it a sign that the songs cited were

And not only the individual jousts are prefaced by songs. So too is the mêlée. The event at Chauvency was truly a '*tornoi*' – a tournament – rather than a '*feste*' as at Le Hem, because it involved a mêlée: a contest between two teams of knights using sharp weapons, simulating a proper battle. The event at Le Hem was a festival of jousting, with attachments to blunt the lance-heads (and no swords used), and thus perhaps circumvented the ban on tournaments; but Chauvency lay in Lorraine, beyond the French king's jurisdiction, so the ban did not apply. And as the knights prepare at Chauvency to engage in the mêlée 'there wasn't a lance or spear to be seen, but swords and maces, daggers, bludgeons, clubs'.[52] This is serious martial business, so how remarkable it is that Renaut de Trie, armed with 'a sword of no great length but notably broad-bladed', rides to join in this brutal battle singing a love song:

> Alas! How shall I live? Love won't let me carry on!

And how do the watching ladies greet the knights' arrival at the mêlée? By singing a song of their own 'to cheer and inspire the amorous':

> No coward will ever have a fair sweetheart –
> The brave will take them all![53]

And when darkness finally brings an end to the 'deafening welter of fervent deeds of arms', how do the knights leave the battleground? They ride away singing. 'High in spirits but battered, cut and bruised, covered in wounds on body and face as is the way after combat, all the knights were merrily singing a sweet and pleasant song:

> I hold my sweetheart by the hand – step forward any I offend!'[54]

This juxtaposition of violence and tenderness, of fearsome physical injury and joyful love-song, gives a startling insight into the medieval temperament.[55]

---

well known and instantly recognisable to Bretel's audience? Were they cues for a reader-aloud to sing a full verse (or more)? In some cases were the refrains, and only the refrains, sung by the tourneyers as they rode into combat, rather in the manner of a football chant?

[52] p. 105.
[53] p. 105.
[54] p. 115.
[55] The essential connection seen between deeds of arms and love, and the insistence on the sufferings one is compelled to endure in return for love's rewards, may also explain why at the end of the poem, in his 'sermon' about love, Bretel can (without any apparent irony) include as exemplars of true lovers the adulterers Guinevere, Lancelot and Tristan, and speak of the 'host of boons that come from Venus, who to Paris, Priam's son, made the gift of Helen, the cause of such great suffering for the Trojans' (below, p. 119). Love is not just a demigod (see next paragraph) but a mighty, indeed all-powerful lord whose

Demigods and Martyrs

Equally startling, perhaps, is the quasi-religious approach to it all. In passages already quoted it is very noticeable that Love is frequently referred to as if 'He' were a god, one who sends rewards to His devotees if they earn them through their chivalrous efforts and suffering, and one whose quasi-divine laws it's possible to break, requiring the payment of due penance:

> If you've transgressed against Love and His commands, either in word or deed, promise to make amends; and by way of penance, abstain from boastful or offensive speech.[56]

Prowess, too, and 'Her son Courage' appear as personifications[57] akin to deities from the pagan pantheon, abstract expressions of qualities and aspects of the psyche. These objects of veneration for chivalry, these supreme values, impose rigours upon knights that are every bit as onerous as those demanded by any order of religion.[58] Indeed, the distinction between religious devotion and devotion to arms is decidedly blurred: when the young knight Conradin Warnier is nearly killed in his joust, Bretel goes to see 'that martyr to arms who had suffered much and exposed his body to torture like the crucified Christ'.[59] Knightly, martial endeavour is perceived as a sacrifice, and Bretel quotes a minstrel from Looz whose words, he says, were 'eloquent, polished and apt – not one ill-chosen or wide of the mark', as he declared that:

> 'A heart that can make such a sacrifice truly cherishes honour and dreads shame. When a knight strives to excel with every ounce of bone and flesh and blood, and once he has his helm on head would never shirk or show the slightest fear of death or wound, imprisonment or ruin, that knight loves, trusts, respects and fears God truly.'[60]

---

demands override all others; it is interesting to see the extent to which, in the fourteenth-century romance *Perceforest*, humans' relations to their emotions are seen in feudal terms: all people, it is implied, should be subjects of the lord Love and they owe him total loyalty. See *Perceforest*, trans. Bryant (Woodbridge, 2011), pp. 11–15.

[56] pp. 119–20.
[57] p. 67.
[58] This is a point made half a century later in the book of chivalry usually attributed to the Geoffroi de Charny who was killed at the battle of Poitiers defending the *Oriflamme*, the royal battle standard: 'the good order of knighthood,' it reads, 'should be considered the most rigorous order of all'; what is required of religious orders 'is all nothing in comparison with the suffering to be endured in the order of knighthood', and 'in this order one can well save the soul and bring honour to the body'. Charny, *A Knight's Own Book of Chivalry*, trans. Elspeth Kennedy (Philadelphia, 2005), pp. 95–6.
[59] p. 75.
[60] p. 75.

And this is a God who, in Bretel's eyes, clearly approves not just of the knights' martial efforts (the field on which they fight their mêlée he describes as 'holy ground')[61] but of their joys in singing and entertainment: as they sing and dance with the ladies and maidens in the evening between the days of jousting, 'so intense was their merriment that they pleased God and His saints. And how could they have failed to please Him? For by the Virgin, never in my life have I seen any people in such blissful, high, elated spirits.'[62] How, by implication, could any king or churchman question the worth of tournaments and even think of banning them? They are glorious expressions of a whole set of values, the commitment to which are a means both to a martyr-knight's salvation and to the joyous rewards of love.[63]

The question might be raised, of course, whether the participants in the tournament at Chauvency and the Arthurian festival at Le Hem were adopting and acting out the values proposed in literature or whether the literature expressed established values. I would suggest that the former is the case: life was imitating art. Half a century before these tournaments, the biography of the great knight (and exceptional tourneyer) William Marshal treated Marshal and his deeds as heroic in the manner and on the scale of the *chansons de geste* or the romance of Alexander (of which its audience, to judge by the obliqueness of some cross-references, had a detailed knowledge); it did so not simply because such works were the model and the idiom for recounting the deeds of a great achiever, but because they were the model to which Marshal had aspired in his life. A century after the events at Le Hem and Chauvency the biography of the famed French commander Bertrand du Guesclin is written precisely as a *chanson de geste*, making Bertrand and his fellow knights heroes in the epic tradition, new Rolands, worthy of mention in the same breath as Alexander. Knights were expected to emulate their forebears in epic and romance – for true forebears they were: du Guesclin's biographer for one speaks of figures from epics, such as Lion of Bourges, as if they were from the real past. Literary influences were soon to be powerfully

---

[61] p. 104.
[62] p. 79.
[63] Richard Kaeuper has well observed that knights 'largely appropriated religion... They absorbed such ideas as were broadly compatible with the virtual worship of prowess and with the high sense of their own divinely approved status and mission... [but they] downplayed or simply ignored most strictures that were not compatible with their sense of honour and entitlement. For in one of its essential dimensions chivalry rested on the very fusion of prowess and piety; it functioned as the male, aristocratic form of lay piety... The worship of the demigod prowess – with all the ideas and practices of the quasi-religion of honour – was merged with medieval Christianity.' Richard Kaeuper, *Chivalry and Violence in Medieval Europe* (Oxford, 1999), p. 47.

at work, too, in the founding of orders of chivalry: Edward III's Order of the Garter was created, says the chronicler Jean le Bel, in imitation of the Round Table and to establish a direct connection with Arthur, who was clearly considered historical:

> King Edward's noble heart inspired him not only to restore and improve the castle at Windsor, which King Arthur had built and where the Round Table was first established in honour of the worthy knights of that time, but also to create a counterpart to that Round Table for the greater honour of his own knights.[64]

Two years later King John II of France's order of chivalry, the Company of the Star, with its 'Noble Maison' at Saint-Ouen, was almost certainly modelled not just on Edward's Garter but also on the 'Franc Palais', the chivalrous order founded in the romance of *Perceforest* (which purported to be the 'pre-history' of King Arthur's Britain). Chivalry transcending time as it did, classical as well as Arthurian literature was brought to bear, with the Burgundian Order of the Golden Fleece being inspired by the story of Jason and the Argonauts, whose adventures were depicted on a tapestry long owned by Duke Philip the Good, a bibliophile whose library was particularly well stocked with works on Alexander.

How unsurprising it is, therefore, to see the tropes of Arthurian romance, the attitudes and values of the world of medieval literature, being assumed and enacted at Le Hem and Chauvency. The participants, and those watching, were modelling themselves and their behaviour on figures regarded as their real forebears.[65]

And how lucky we are to have the record of such an enthusiastic witness. 'Such a fine time I was having,' says Jacques Bretel, 'that it's nothing but a pleasure to record and recount.'[66] He loves every minute – though the picture isn't all sweetness and light: he has an intense dislike of most heralds, whose wrangling and spouting he constantly decries, along with their dishonesty. He almost comes to blows with one, after calling him a leper. Another he describes as a 'sneering snake', another has 'wrecked the life and reputation of many a man to acquire his wealth', and a band of them, preparing to snap up arms and harness scattered during a joust, he likens to

---

[64] *The True Chronicles of Jean le Bel*, trans. Bryant (Woodbridge, 2011), p. 153.
[65] In the words of Nancy Freeman Regalado, they were 'enacting an ideal way of being in the world'. N. F. Regalado, 'Picturing the Story of Chivalry in Jacques Bretel's Tournoi de Chauvency (Oxford, Bodleian Library, MS Douce 308)', in *Tributes to Jonathan J. G. Alexander: Making and Meaning in the Middle Ages and the Renaissance*, ed. Susan L'Engle and Gerald B. Guest (London, 2006), p. 342.
[66] p. 75.

> a flock of crows – hungry for trinkets, not carrion. Not even Herod, the embodiment of greed, was a hundredth part as grasping as a herald out to grab what he can. But I'll say no more – it's better to speak of the good than of that lot: would to God there were just two heralds in all the world who knew enough to do the job for the whole pack of them (not that they'd ever see eye to eye) … A curse on the lot of them: always on the take, giving not a thing, and full of lies and pomposity.[67]

Whether prompted by professional rivalry or not, the candid, outspoken hatred expressed here makes the reader all the more inclined to trust Bretel, who tells us his purpose is to celebrate courage:

> I'll never stop saying what my heart bids me say, honestly and ungrudgingly. There's nothing wrong in celebrating courage – and it can be uplifting and inspiring – so I hope I'll gain approval for doing so: courteous words deserve courtesy in return! That'll encourage me to continue speaking well of the good and keeping kindly quiet about the bad.[68]

In this he is following the example of the watching ladies: at one point he goes to the stands

> and sat with the ladies to discuss and identify who was who, which of them was especially worthy, and who was from foreign parts and who was one of ours. I was in the right place to hear all this and was happy to learn from what they said; for these ladies, who know what makes a good knight, and who purge and improve the less worthy through their gentle guidance and charming company, spoke passionately and with honest decency, extolling the virtues of the good and keeping quiet about the bad.[69]

Such 'honest decency' makes Bretel's account a convincing one, his judgements worthy of trust. As for the sounds and pictures he has left us, many are so extraordinary that a reader can fully believe there is nothing glib about his line: 'I've never seen anything so wonderful in all my life.'

---

[67] pp. 76, 80. Sarrasin, too, comments on their grasping nature, below, p. 22.
[68] pp. 89–90.
[69] p. 107.

EDITIONS AND MANUSCRIPTS

The most recent editions of the two poems are:

Sarrasin, *Le roman du Hem*, ed. Albert Henry (Paris, 1939).

This is an edition of the only surviving manuscript: fonds français 1588 of the Bibliothèque Nationale, Paris.

Jacques Bretel, *Le Tournoi de Chauvency*, ed. Maurice Delbouille (Liège and Paris, 1932).

Three manuscripts survive, and fragments of a fourth. Delbouille bases his edition on MS 330-215 of the Bibliothèque de la ville de Mons, but makes corrections and fills lacunae by reference to the text in the famous manuscript Douce 308 of the Bodleian Library, Oxford[70] – notably the end of the poem, from line 4335 ('A pithy speech hits home...' [p. 118]) onwards, the last two folios of the Mons manuscript having been lost. That is not to say that the Oxford text is without its errors and omissions, and Delbouille took the Mons manuscript as his base because Douce 308 has itself two significant lacunae: from line 1007 ('So said the herald...' [p. 74]) to line 1568 ('...collars around their necks' [p. 82]) and from line 2021 ('...and God-given grace' [p. 88]) to line 2182 ('...Bauffremont and Rosières' [p. 90]). With neither manuscript version being complete, this translation follows the fullest possible text, as established by Delbouille in his edition.

---

[70] 'A complete kit of secular chivalry, for it contains a literature of recreation and edification that links a romance, a chronicle, and a moral allegory featuring chivalric exploits to elegantly refined pastimes of singing, dancing, and conversations about love.' Regalado, 'Picturing', p. 343. The gathering together in Douce 308 of the Alexander romance *Les Voeux du Paon* (the historical past) with courtly songs, questions about love and Bretel's *Tournoi de Chauvency* (the present) and with apocalyptic prophecies and a final showdown between the forces of God and the forces of the Antichrist in Huon de Méry's *Li Tornoiemens Antecrist* (the future) is possibly significant: it may say much about how the event at Chauvency and the place of love and chivalry in the world were perceived.

Further Reading

Barber, Richard, *The Knight and Chivalry* (revised edition, Woodbridge, 1995).
Barber, Richard and Barker, Juliet, *Tournaments: Jousts, Chivalry and Pageants in the Middle Ages* (Woodbridge, 1989).
Chazan, M. and Regalado, N. F. (eds.), *Lettres, musique et société en Lorraine médiévale: Autour du Tournoi de Chauvency (MS Oxford Bodleian Douce 308)* (Geneva, 2012).
Cline, R. H., 'The Influence of Romances in Tournaments of the Middle Ages', *Speculum 20* (1945), pp. 204–11.
Crouch, David, *Tournament: A Chivalric Way of Life* (London and New York, 2005).
Jones, R. W. and Coss, P. (eds.), *A Companion to Chivalry* (Woodbridge, 2019).
Kaeuper, Richard, *Chivalry and Violence in Medieval Europe* (Oxford, 1999).
Keen, Maurice, *Chivalry* (New Haven and London, 1984).
Leach, Elizabeth Eva, 'A Courtly Compilation: the Douce Chansonnier', in *Manuscripts and Medieval Song: Inscription, Performance, Context,* ed. H. Deeming & E. E. Leach (Cambridge, 2015), pp. 216–41.
Leach, Elizabeth Eva, 'Which came first, the demandes d'amours or the jeu-parti? Evidence from the *jeu-parti* subsection of Oxford, Bodleian Library, MS Douce 308', *Music & Letters* [forthcoming]
Normore, Christina, *A Feast for the Eyes: Art, Performance and the Medieval Banquet* (Chicago, 2015).
Regalado, Nancy F., 'Performing Romance: Arthurian Interludes in Sarrasin's *Le roman du Hem*', in *Performing Medieval Narrative*, ed. E. B. Vitz, N. F. Regalado & M. Lawrence (Woodbridge, 2005), pp. 103–19.
Regalado, Nancy F., 'Picturing the Story of Chivalry in Jacques Bretel's Tournoi de Chauvency (Oxford, Bodleian Library, MS Douce 308)', in *Tributes to Jonathan J. G. Alexander: Making and Meaning in the Middle Ages and the Renaissance*, ed. Susan L'Engle and Gerald B. Guest (London, 2006), pp. 341–52.
Sandoz, E., 'Tourneys in the Arthurian tradition', *Speculum 19* (1944), pp. 389–420.
Vale, Juliet, *Edward III and Chivalry* (Woodbridge, 1982).

For the heraldry in *The Tournament at Chauvency*:
http://www.armorial.dk/tournaments/Chauvency.pdf
http://wappenwiki.org/index.php/Tournoi_de_Chauvency

The Oxford MS (Bodleian Library, Douce 308) of *The Tournament at Chauvency* is now available online:
https://eeleach.blog/2015/10/01/douce-308-complete-images-now-online/

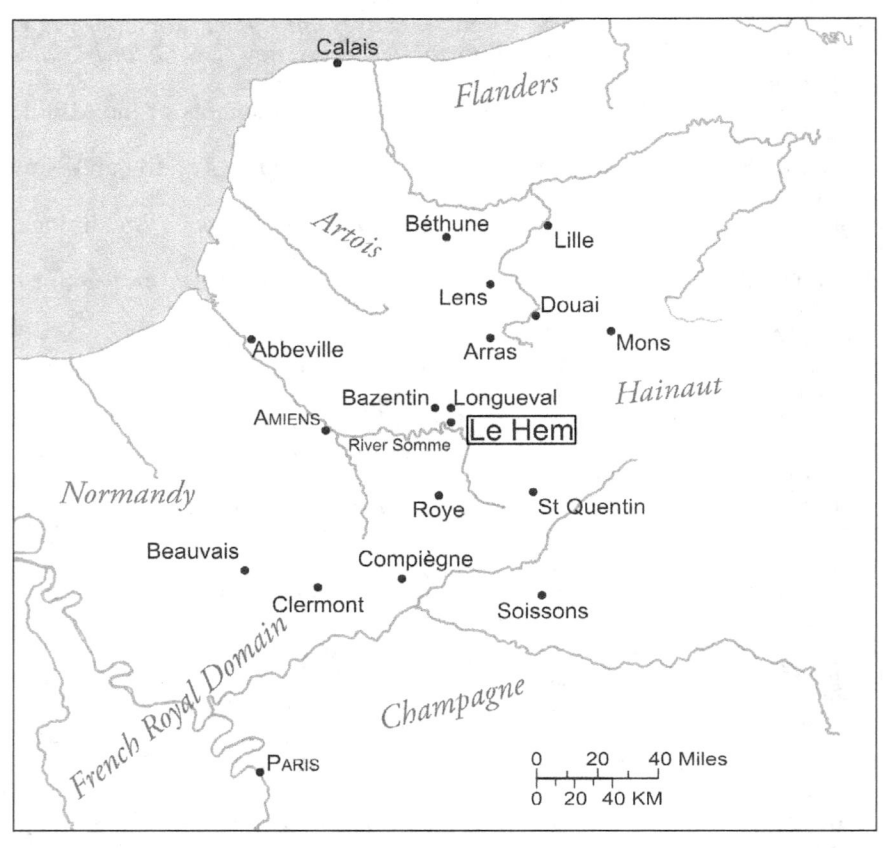

Le Hem: The Surrounding Lands

SARRASIN

The Romance of Le Hem

Sarrasin[1] can't hold it back: he has to speak of the flower of chivalry who used to rove through France. Hearing this romance will surely bring to mind the king of Sicily, Charles,[2] who is held in awe and dread but is also humble and courteous: meek as a lamb towards God but fierce as a lion towards those who provoke and wrong him. All who ever cross his path admire him for his loyalty and fear him for his awesome might: he can exact fearsome retribution, and also knows how to bide his time till he sees the perfect moment.

The men of his day were fine beyond words – I saw them. Fauvel de Suzanne,[3] lord of Provence, was alive then: he ever strove against Indolence; it had beset him since his youth but he resisted it so manfully that Prowess came to dwell in him and he crushed all wicked vices till none in him remained. I saw Sir Robert de Ronssoy[4] in Paris in his day: a brave, upstanding, cultured man, courtly and endowed with many virtues, entirely committed to good deeds. He was admired for his looks as well as for his goodness (even in places he'd never been – just as sometimes we've no idea that a maid's in love with us!). That's why all men should strive to do good and to order their lives in such a way that they're held in true esteem.

King Charles, at that time[5] a count, sought honour at all points, and pursued a career that has made him the worthiest man known today – I'm sure no thinking man will disagree. Outstandingly brave he was, and generous and most loyal: his house was always filled with minstrels and with

---

[1] The MS reads 'he'; owing to a missing folio (which contained the end of the works of the Picard poet Philippe de Rémi and the start of *Le roman du Hem*), a small but unknown number of the opening lines are lost. In them the author must have named himself.
[2] Charles of Anjou (1227–85), count of Anjou and Provence, brother of Louis IX ('Saint Louis'). He had been crowned king of Naples and Sicily in 1266.
[3] Robert Fauvel de Suzanne, who had died in 1260. The castle of Suzanne-en-Santerre was just downriver to the west of Le Hem.
[4] Ronssoy is a few miles east of Le Hem.
[5] i.e. before 1266, when he was crowned king of Sicily.

heralds, and he was ever open-handed towards good and valiant knights. He was the constant upholder of Prowess, Largesse and Valour, which now are left impoverished, naked, and avert their gaze from worthy men. We should scorn indeed all those whose counsel to the king is such that his realm is now left desolate, with Prowess banished. All through France Sir Ease is having a high old time, indulging his every whim – off with his hounds and his hawks and then drinking, eating, sleeping. Idleness, his constant companion, comforts and supports him all the way; Idleness is the finest lady ever born – so says Sir Ease, for She panders to his every fancy: has him lie abed all the morning long and wave away all demands upon his time. A great dissembler She is, surpassing in guile all others, along with her daughter Shame. It seems to me that Largesse, Prowess and Courtesy have lost the battle in France, which should be of grave concern to the king and all his good companions.

And if you'll hear me now, I can no longer hold back the truth: men used to journey to France from every land to take part in tournaments, but now I see the French dismayed by the loss of such valuable trade – so many people profited from it, by God they did! Worthy men heading for the tourney-grounds would share their wealth with all who could provide ably for their needs. But one day King Philip[1] came to Compiègne (or Creil) where many a knight in dazzling array performed deeds of arms galore before him. No king of France has ever been known to get involved: since Noah boarded the ark no one has known a king of France to take part in tourneys – it's unheard of; I don't think it's ever happened and I don't think it ever will. And let me tell you, so that it may be placed on record for future generations, that it was twelve hundred and seventy-eight years after Christ's Incarnation – that's the exact date, absolutely – and the king in question was the son of good King Louis; and rightly or wrongly, he placed a ban on tournaments,[2] much to the dismay of many folk. Jongleurs above all had profited daily, and so had the heralds and the lorimers, the blacksmiths and the saddlers. Even those with the cushier jobs were cursing the king for banning tourneys!

'Damn all those behind this ban!' said the sellers of fine wines and rabbits and partridges and plovers!

'Amen!' said men of every trade. 'God see them damned indeed!'

---

[1] Philip III of France, r. 1270–85.
[2] It's not at all clear from Sarrasin's phrasing, but the ban had been placed on tournaments by Philip's father, Louis IX ('Saint Louis'); Philip III had maintained the ban but did lift it on more than one occasion. Whether one of those occasions was the festival at Le Hem is not certain, and indeed the count of Artois, who is to play a leading role at the festival, was under excommunication in 1278 for having participated in tournaments, so his presence (prince of the blood royal though he was) would presumably not have offered protection from royal wrath.

Many humble men who'd made good money now found themselves impoverished; they'd have lived well and prospered if tournaments had gone on as before.

There were others, too, who didn't give a thought to this but regretted the ban just as much. And who were they? It's knights I mean: it has to be said, they lost out more than anyone – I've no doubt of that, it's the gospel truth. These days you see them in the towns engaging in endless wrangles and disputes, when no amount of money would keep them there if they had tournaments to go to! It's doing nothing for their reputation! Some who were always committed to fine deeds and to laying their bodies on the line have lost every scrap of respect: they've all turned into litigants! Base fellows are becoming knights and knights are little better than minstrels. I say this to them all: a knight should be devoted to excelling in arms or he's not worth the name. But they do quite the opposite. They start out brave and valiant, and still think themselves so when they're idle. But here's what *I* think: talking big doesn't make you brave – a knight gains nothing by being a windbag: a gale blows out at a few drops of rain. And let me tell you: a knight of dubious qualities is viewed with suspicion in any court – so take care, good sirs! God grant that all noble men conduct themselves well and as they should, and place themselves beyond reproach!

And God grant, too, that the king comes to see how his kingdom is the worse now that tournaments are held in the Empire[1] but suppressed, alas, in France. King of France, it would be better for you that Flemish cash, and English, too, and coin from Cologne beyond the Rhine were spent in France than kept away by your ban! What's more, if tourneying were freely allowed, you'd soon see men off on crusade! But tourney and crusade are both on hold, and they'll stay that way as long as God and the king decide. [188]

It was because the world's in such a state, going to pot with no tournaments, that one day I saw two knights – from Artois both, and both brave and valiant and courteous, of high worth indeed (and if I praise them it's with good cause) – looking utterly woebegone. They were talking together like the good friends and neighbours that they were.

'Truly, lord of Bazentin,'[2] said the lord of Longueval,[3] 'I'd be glad to get something off my chest – it's bothering me no end. The times are out of joint indeed – they stink! Honour and Prowess are sorely wanting, Largesse and Courtesy are vanishing. I tell you straight: I wish the king would get on

---

[1] i.e. the Holy Roman Empire: Sarrasin would have been thinking of the Low Countries and the German states.
[2] Huart de Bazentin. Bazentin is about five miles north-west of Hem-Monacu (Le Hem).
[3] Aubert de Longueval, Bazentin's close neighbour.

with it and give us leave to take up arms. We've been idle too long! Damn all – the king excepted! – who're happy that it's so! It's breeding conceit and immorality, with daily feuds and ructions. All this inactivity's creating nothing but misery!'

'I know what you have in mind,' replied the lord of Bazentin. 'You were beating about the bush a few days ago – you didn't quite come out with it but I knew what you were getting at. Whatever it costs me in shame and trouble (though God forbid it should!), you can count on me to support your plan, no matter what. You'll see! Embark on whatever you please – damn anyone who fails you! As long as I can put my fiefs in hock – Bazentin, Montauban and Ribécourt – I'll back you all the way, to my dying day.'

Sir Aubert de Longueval gave him a thousand thanks, saying: 'God preserve me, good lord of Bazentin, if you'd given me two hundred pounds of silver I couldn't be more grateful! It seems we're in agreement, sir: you see the world now reeks of pride and greed and envy. This is hardly a life at all! We need to support each other now. All thought of crusade has long been set aside, and there's no tourneying being done – no one knows quite what to do! My plan is to stage a festival of jousting – I wouldn't care how much it cost as long as you're behind me.'

'I promise you faithfully,' said the lord of Bazentin, 'it shall be announced without delay! Here's what we'll do: we'll have it proclaimed in both our names – no other name shall be given – to take place at Le Hem.[1] It'll be cried abroad in every land. And I promise you, the hardest part will be the first: knights will have to joust three times if they want to gain entry – till they've run three courses they'll not get in!'

Lady Courtesy[2] broke in on their conversation then. She arrived with a downcast air, having come to court in threadbare state and been shunned by those who should have been on Her side. If those two knights had known the help She was about to give them they'd have given Her warm greeting; but seeing Her looking so poor and bereft they asked Her to leave them to talk for a while if She didn't mind. But at this She sat down between them and revealed exactly who She was and Her present state – how She and Her son Largesse[3] were held in contempt. With that the knights leapt to their feet, mortified at the shameful disrespect they felt they'd shown in not rising and giving Her finer greeting; the fact was they'd not recognised Her in Her poor and tattered state! They begged Her pardon.

'In faith, good sirs,' She replied, 'I freely forgive you. Everywhere I go I keep seeing those who've served me as I would wish – spending their fortunes and risking ruin – earning little credit for it: they're

---

[1] '*Ham sour Somme*': see Introduction, p. vii, note 1.
[2] As with 'Idleness' and 'Shame' on previous pages, Sarrasin is introducing a symbolic figure, an abstract personification. See also note 3 below, p. 6.
[3] '*Doner*': literally 'Giving'.

spurned by everyone! We're kindred spirits, you and I, and I'll never let you down: work through me and I'll be a valuable support. You two are sharing your hearts, your bodies and your wealth with me. It's a fine idea to stage this festival, truly: it'll be a splendid, noble affair, free of quarrel, dispute and strife, and word of it will spread to every town and city from here to Constantinople!

'I pray you, let it be proclaimed in Britain, the land of which the story of the Grail tells us King Arthur was lord. Among its many wonders there are hanging stones still at Salisbury, placed there by magic by Merlin in his day.[1] And there you'll find fine jousters, fierce and tough and mighty. Lancelot, who proved himself supreme among knights, and the great knight Gawain and the rest of the Round Table, the finest in the world, they were all born in Britain – though when the Trojans conquered it they gave it a different name and called it England.[2] There you'll find valiant knights indeed; there you'll find many fine jousters: they're bold, the knights of England. So I say again: announce your festival there without delay or second thought! The lord and king of that realm is brave, generous and courtly: King Edward is his name;[3] and let us pray that God preserve him, for he's worthier than words can say.

'And throughout Flanders and the Empire, and in Hainaut and Brabant, and all through France[4] and the land of Champagne, you'll see grand companies of knights in fine array – there are many held in fond esteem, and it's only right to give credit where it's due: being brave and valiant they'll never miss a call to arms: they'll answer any summons in an instant. So send swift word to Normandy, Auvergne and Berry!

'Have your festival proclaimed in God's name on Saint Denis's Day;[5] tell all who crave renown in arms and joy in love to present themselves that day before Queen Guinevere! And no knight fighting in such a lady's name should have a hare's heart: in the thick of combat he needs to prove his worth and lay his body and his charger on the line, boldly crying "Love!" to the ladies!

---

[1] A reference to Stonehenge; for Merlin's legendary involvement in erecting the stones, see for example Robert de Boron, *Merlin and the Grail*, trans. Bryant (Woodbridge, 2001), pp. 90–1.

[2] As told by Geoffrey of Monmouth in *The History of the Kings of Britain* and by Wace in *Brut*. But Sarrasin has the story confused; according to Geoffrey of Monmouth and Wace, Brutus of Troy (Brut) changed the island's name from Albion to Britain, renaming it after himself.

[3] i.e. Edward I. The prestige of Edward and his English knights was due not least to their being widely identified, as in this passage, with their supposed Arthurian forebears: Edward fully grasped this and exploited it.

[4] i.e. the French royal domain – largely what is still referred to as the Île de France – as opposed to, for example, the duchy of Normandy or the county of Champagne.

[5] 9 October.

'And listen now, heed my advice: it would be only right and proper that, to show the queen due honour, each knight should bring with him a lady or a maiden; for the queen has none – she's never left her land with a smaller escort, truly: she's only seven hundred ladies, maids and knights, well short of the three thousand that she used to lead.[1]

'Strive to the full to receive her splendidly – her and everyone: make sure you've no shortage of food and wine and everything befitting such a feast. You'll have to provide them with fare for all three days, and so you shall! On the first two days you'll provide for the ladies and the knights and all who gain entry to your feast – and none shall enter and set eyes on the girls and ladies, so many and so fair, until they've jousted! But on the third day all who've come from far and wide shall enter: take care that no door or gate is barred to anyone who chances to arrive, for the sight of the wonders they'll behold will delight them all. Seven knights will appear, clad in mail and fully armed with helms and shields, and all seven will look identical. They'll present themselves in courtly fashion to the queen as she dines, and tell her exactly why they've come: to submit to her as captives in the name of the Knight of the Lion. After them will appear a maiden, escorted by a dwarf, and she'll ask the queen for aid; then you'll see knights flocking to offer help.

'Now make sure you plan impeccably, for you've embarked upon a glorious enterprise! Summon the ablest heralds and have them proclaim your festival, loud and clear, just as we've discussed: they can start around Varesnes and Noyon.'[2]

'Dear lady,' they said, 'God send you due reward for advising us so graciously: your guidance was much needed.'

And they knelt before Her and begged Her in God's name not to leave them. She promised to return without fail with the lady of Cayeux, who would enhance the feast indeed.[3]

'May God, the king and lord of all, bless you, dear lady!'

Then these two worthy knights mounted their palfreys, and had the great event cried abroad by many a herald, far and wide, announcing to all that the lords of Longueval and Bazentin had chosen to stage a great and

---

[1] Since he evidently knew *The Story of the Grail* – he has already referred to it and is about to do so again – Sarrasin may have had in mind an episode in the First Continuation of Chrétien de Troyes' *Perceval*: when Guinevere leaves the city of Orquenie to go to the Castle of Marvels, 'in her company were five hundred girls, not counting the ladies and the damsels who numbered more than two thousand'. *The Complete Story of the Grail*, trans. Bryant (Woodbridge, 2015), p. 82.

[2] South of Le Hem, between Saint-Quentin and Compiègne.

[3] This is Longueval's sister Marguerite, wife of Guillaume de Cayeux (Cayeux-sur-Mer, in Ponthieu). It is possible that these lines are a playful, coded way of saying that 'Lady Courtesy' was in fact, in some degree, Marguerite.

splendid festival to which a host of people from many lands might come. Their only fear, I saw, was that there would be too few! And they had the castle of Le Hem magnificently decked, ready for many a lady and many a man to come and dance their rounds. [471]

Sarrasin's fond wish is to compose a poem about this festival, using his ability and knowledge to the full. You've heard the story of the Trojans,[1] and the fine romance that Chrétien wrote about Perceval and the adventures of the Grail,[2] full of delightful passages. You've been told many times of the Round Table, and how they were such outstanding, chivalrous knights that the prowess and might of valiant King Arthur and his knights should be celebrated in every court. So now, I pray you, prepare to hear more fine words! Listen now, and I'll tell you without further ado about the most glorious event ever known to have been staged in France or Frisia!

It was proclaimed far and wide, in many foreign parts, and word of it reached Britain, that land of marvels; and I promise you, from there came knights of the finest quality, who never shrink from seeking out great adventures, and are ever ready to engage in joyous sport with strong, stout lances.

The queen's company escorted her to Le Hem. Among them was Sir Kay the seneschal. The queen was the most refined and cultured lady living – any who hear her name invoked need fear no ill or fever; it was Queen Guinevere who was coming to the gathering at Le Hem – and it was no secret: the whole surrounding country heard the news. In this, as in all other matters, God forbid I tell a word of a lie. The queen's escort was by no means large: just seven hundred knights, ladies and maids, though they were truly the fairest she'd ever assembled – with one exception: we'll tell you about her in due course.[3] But let me tell you now about the queen, ever a friend to the good, and anyone in peril on the sea should invoke her name. She is a lady of beauty and honour, and wherever she goes she takes a charming, delightful escort who engage in pleasure and laughter all day long. Her knights can't abide being idle: they're ever roaming distant parts in search of great adventures. And when they escort Queen Guinevere on her travels they never rest: they press on day by day from land to land. And when she goes abroad it's not in the manner of some young maid: she

---

[1] A reference again to the story of Brutus, as told by Geoffrey of Monmouth in his *History of the Kings of Britain* (c. 1135) and by Wace in his *Roman de Brut* (c. 1155). Brutus, great-grandson of Aeneas, lands in Britain with fellow Trojans, builds a new Troy on the banks of the Thames and becomes Britain's first king.

[2] Chrétien de Troyes' last (unfinished) romance, *Perceval, the story of the Grail* (early 1180s).

[3] This is never properly explained, but I take it to be a reference to the one known as 'Long-Suffering' who is to be cruelly mocked by Kay below, p. 35.

takes all she can to provide for her company. So as she made her way to Le Hem for Saint Denis's Day the train of wagons and gear she brought was beyond all counting. Let me tell you in brief that she was accompanied by some hundred knights, ever ready to joust, whatever the cost.

But the queen was greatly troubled, for it was exactly a year to the day since a lady, Alise, had come to Carduel complaining about Brien of the Isles,[1] a knight who was robbing her of all her land and wanted to marry her against her will: she'd begged the queen to have pity and lend her aid. And God bless the lady Soredamor:[2] her sweetheart – a handsome, brave and courteous knight – had offered Alise his help within the month, and how he came to regret it! For as soon as he reached her house she wickedly deceived and tricked him and had him locked in prison! Neither the queen nor any of the knights of her court knew anything of this, and they were downcast and dejected at being without such a worthy knight at Le Hem. Alise was keeping him imprisoned because he wouldn't be her lover; she could look at him whenever she wished but that was all: he would rather have been torn limb from limb than let anyone but his beloved Soredamor have joy of him.

After learning he'd been imprisoned – and why! – Soredamor didn't dally for so much as two days before setting out to seek the queen, for she was quite close kin. She found her at Le Hem. She rode through the gate on a struggling nag, accompanied by a dwarf who was leading her by the bridle. The queen was seated at supper, crown on head. The dwarf made his way through the hall to the top table, where Sir Kay spoke up courteously, saying:

'God keep you, girl. Where have you come from?'

The damsel's response was: 'God and all the saints preserve my lady and all the assembled company!'

Whereupon Kay said: 'By my life, damsel, I wouldn't have greeted you if I'd known you were going to be so rude as to ignore my question! A knight who risks his skin for you deserves to have his head shaved! Offering help too readily – to you or anyone, come to that – is never a good idea! Don't think I'm unwilling to serve you if you wish, but I want to know what's in it for me!'

'Sir Kay, Sir Kay,' said the queen, in the hearing of all, 'you're always so harsh and bumptious, so ready to speak out of turn. Let the

---

[1] '*Bruiant d'Uel*': Brien of the Isles is a knight, usually of Arthur's court, who appears in several romances, firstly though fleetingly in Chrétien de Troyes' *Erec*. He is almost always a dangerous figure; he is, for example, an enemy of Lancelot and betrays the king in *Perlesvaus* – see *The High Book of the Grail: Perlesvaus*, trans. Bryant (Woodbridge, 2007), pp. 252–5, 272.

[2] Another name borrowed by Sarrasin from Arthurian romance: Soredamor is the title character's mother in Chrétien's *Cligès*.

damsel tell us why she's come and then do as behoves you and hold your wicked tongue.'

The girl, still sitting mounted in the middle of the hall with her dwarf, said: 'Good queen, I have come to complain about Alise, the lady of Hebrison, who's holding my sweetheart imprisoned because he refuses to grant her his love. Four times I've crossed the sea, from Scotland and from Northumberland, and at last I've found you here. I ask if there is a knight in your court who'll come with me, armed and mounted, to rescue my beloved. Good queen, you've always granted help to ladies, maidens, knights and all who were in need: you've never turned any away. Gracious queen, you are praised and renowned in all lands near and far both for your words and for your actions, for not a soul who asks for aid – knight, damsel, lady – leaves your court without it. Now tell me, noble queen, I pray you, how my request will be met.'

Lady Guinevere was silent; but having pondered awhile she replied so that all the court could hear: 'Damsel Soredamor, you will have fine aid from me and from the knights of my court.'

With that, some hundred knights flocked before the queen, all offering to assume the mission, whatever might befall them. But the queen promptly said:

'Sit down and eat, sirs: one alone will go with her.'

Then Sir Kay piped up: 'This is mine by right, my lady! Your lord King Arthur granted me the honour – which I have earnestly fulfilled – of always having the first joust, whatever the occasion, and so I shall tomorrow, if it please God. I'll follow the girl and the dwarf wherever they may go, and rescue the knight held captive by the lady.'

Just then a knight sounded a horn at the foot of the bridge, and the dwarf cried: 'Hear that horn-blast! Lady, lady, the one out there who blew it has brought the captive knight! Now we'll see if your court can truly help us! He's little respect for you if he dares to come so near!'

'By my life!' said Kay, 'I'm ready to go if the queen gives me leave!'

'Sir Kay,' the queen replied, 'I pray you wait till tomorrow. The damsel and the dwarf will stay with me tonight if they've no objection.' And she summoned one of her ladies, saying: 'Come: I entrust my kinswoman to you.'

The dwarf said he'd burn in Hell if she was in anyone else's keeping. And so they stayed that night till dawn next morning.

Sir Kay rose early, as soon as he saw day break. He armed and mounted without delay and went and waited in the lists till a knight appeared, spurring hard, mounted on a great, strong, swift and spirited charger, and planted himself at one end of the tourney-ground. The queen and all her people came and took their seats in the stand: she couldn't wait to see Sir Kay the seneschal's joust. [715]

But if you'll be patient just a little, I'll tell you first of an adventure, harsh and cruel, which befell four of the queen's maidens: Ydone, Aiglentine, Cardonelle and Alixandrine.[1] Many a knight was daunted by the prospect of their rescue, but the good Knight of the Lion succeeded in the task. That fine lord had earned the name on two counts: his courage and his largesse. Let me recount this stirring adventure, just as I heard it told.

These four girls were taken captive in the forest, and were in constant distress until the Knight of the Lion came. Those maidens, born so fair, were kept imprisoned for just a week short of a month. Let me explain who took them captive, and how and why.

It happened, I recall it well, one Monday in September. They went out riding as they so often did, unaccompanied by any men. It was early morning, and the weather being so calm and fair they went bare-headed, without any kerchiefs, dressed in simple white shifts. As they rode along, without a care in the world, they looked ahead and saw a cross in the middle of their path; on it was hung a sheet of parchment proclaiming the adventures to be found at a nearby castle, where seven knights were ever ready to joust against all comers. The girls sat still and listened till they heard cries in the distance, whereupon they tarried no longer but headed straight for the castle.

The gatekeeper welcomed them most courteously, and they, well-mannered girls that they were, returned sweet greeting and politely asked if he might arrange for them to speak to his lord.

'Nothing would induce me to refuse!' he replied. 'God forbid!'

And he ran to his lord and told him there were four maidens at the gate, charming and fair indeed, who wished to speak with him. Hearing this, every last man and woman present went to meet them, delighted and rejoicing at this God-sent gift. They led the girls, still mounted, into the hall, where the lord very courteously helped them dismount and had them served most graciously, and entrusted them to the care of ladies of the castle. Everyone was gazing at them eagerly – and little wonder. All was swiftly prepared and the lord took them to wash their hands, serving them very readily and honouring them most gladly. He enquired nothing of them till they'd eaten; then he said:

'If you don't mind my asking, damsels, where did you sleep last night? And I'd gladly know, if I may be so bold, where you're going dressed like this?'

Cardonelle was first to reply, with the leave of the other three; she said: 'The finest, wisest, most courtly lady in the world is heading for Le Hem to attend the festival announced by the two knights. They've invited my lady the queen and are making eager preparations to receive her in noble

---

[1] The first is named at this point 'Marote', the last of the four 'Plaisans'; their names are later changed to Ydone and Alixandrine.

fashion, truly. If I told you about the festival and what's in store, you'd think I was making it up! No one's heard of the like since the days of good King Arthur! Queen Guinevere has sent us to find ladies to attend, and now we've come to your land to ask that you and your company come without delay and join her court; before she leaves Le Hem you'll find jousting there in which you can test yourselves if you're so inclined. We saw a notice just outside, fixed on a cross, declaring that anyone seeking a joust would have it at this castle, but it would be a shame to detract from the great festival by trifling here! I mean no disrespect, but you'd do better to leave this be and come to Le Hem! Many a brave and valiant knight will be going there to joust before the ladies: no such event is any good without women! There'll be plenty at Le Hem! So tell me your mind: will you come or not?'

The lord of the house replied most courteously, saying: 'You've delivered your message admirably: she's a gracious lady indeed who has such a messenger! But neither you nor I can go to Le Hem just now – I'm afraid you're forbidden to leave, as are we all.'

[Cardonelle, bewildered,][1] asked him, on her companions' behalf, kindly to explain why neither he nor anyone who came there could leave his own castle.

'God forbid, damsel,' he replied, 'that I should lie to you. Many a mighty, spirited knight has come and competed here, but none could ever vanquish me: if any could, he could take me and you and everyone here as his captives wherever he wished. That's the position, truly.'

'Ah, sir! Proclaim this at Le Hem! That's where our lady will be – she'll be grieving and bitterly worried that we're so late arriving!'

'We'll send there in the morning, without fail,' said the lord.

'No, sir – tonight, in God's name!'

'Very well, damsel.' And he summoned a squire and entrusted him with the message.

The squire fulfilled his errand ably, and the very moment Queen Guinevere heard the news she begged the Knight of the Lion to go and set the girls free. And so he did: he set off as soon as the queen said the word, delaying not an instant. [883]

It was a Tuesday just as dawn was breaking, and he was riding all alone, without a squire, mounted on a great destrier, strong and swift, worth a hundred pounds by the look of it. He was armed, I remember well, with everything befitting a knight, lacking nothing, and I truly believe he was as worthy a knight as could ever be. But he was far from happy: his search was proving fruitless; his lady Queen Guinevere had sent him to scour many a land to find the girls imprisoned in the castle – without any proper

---

[1] An unresolved rhyme indicates a missing line in the MS.

cause, as you've heard – and on and on he'd searched as the queen had bidden. He'd set out on the feast of Saint John,[1] with instructions from the queen to take the girls to Le Hem if he could find them; and she'd said that if he succeeded in rescuing them, she would reward him with whatever he reasonably asked, saving her honour and her rights. He'd suffered baking heat and freezing cold in his search for the girls, and now, in the very week of the feast of Saint Denis,[2] he'd come to where chance had led him and was roaming on at random.

'Alas!' he said. 'This is no good! No honour's going to come my way! Dear lord God, send me guidance in my mission now – I've been toiling so hard and long.'

Then he looked ahead and saw a squire, all alone, coming towards him on a miserable-looking nag, skinny and clapped out, managing no more than a trot. The knight rode on to meet the youth – and straightway asked if he'd kindly tell him why he was covering his face.

'Sir,' the squire replied, 'I'm guessing you're one of the queen's knights and eager for news of the four girls, for the queen will soon be in need of plenty of girls and ladies. This very day I've been in the castle where the girls are being kept. Shame on all the knights of the court for not coming to their aid!'

The knight grabbed hold of the squire's reins and said: 'You're not leaving till you tell me where they are!'

'Sir,' said the squire, 'their captors won't let you have them in a hurry! But you look a true knight, so I'll gladly tell you why I've covered my face. The lord of the Castle of the Wood lives straight ahead – that's where I'm going now. He's holding Ydone and Aiglentine, Cardonelle and Alixandrine: all four are in his castle – and so are seven new knights ever ready to joust. I promise you every word I say is true. Many a strong and spirited knight has come and tried his strength against them, and if one were found who could vanquish all seven he'd be free to take the damsels away. I have to ride like this – I want to go unnoticed!'

'Tell me, friend, in God the holy Father's name, where I can find these knights.'

'God save me, sir, I'll gladly tell you all I know. They're at the castle – the most handsome ever seen, it is: I can testify to that – I stayed there last night. Let me tell you briefly what I can: take that path to the right and stick to it and you'll see a cross with a horn[3] hung upon it – but

---

[1] To make sense of the dates, this must refer to the feast of Saint John of Meda, 26 September, as the tournament at Le Hem was due to take place on 9 October (Saint Denis's Day: above, p. 5).

[2] i.e. when the tournament at Le Hem was about to be held.

[3] The MS reads 'shield', which may be right, but it makes more sense to assume that it's the horn that is about to be mentioned below, p. 13.

it's not for me to tell you the rest: there's a message fixed to the cross explaining everything. If you'll promise me just one favour, I'll let the damsels know you're coming to save them.'

'I give you my word, dear friend,' said the knight, 'with all the loyalty God has bestowed on me, I'll grant you the favour – but you'll not know my name unless circumstances demand.'

'I commend you to God, kind sir: I'll go and take my message. Go carefully now: you've undertaken a mighty challenge. God grant you honour and praise!'

With that the squire set off and rode to the castle: he couldn't wait to deliver his news. He found the girls, all four together, in a garden where they'd gone to relax and forget their woes. As soon as he saw them he went and said:

'God save you, damsels, be of good cheer and have no fear: you'll be freed this very night! I've just met a knight who told me he's been searching for four girls for many days! He swore he wouldn't tell me his name, but gave his solemn word he'd repay me with a favour if I came straight here and brought you the news!'

'Go quickly, dear friend: mount and slip out of the gate and see what arms he bears and hurry back and tell us! And say we'd dearly love to know his name if he'll tell you – and if it please God, thanks to his mighty valour we'll be able to rejoin our lady the queen!'

'I tell you, damsels, he looks so strong I'm sure he's up to it! And he's splendidly mounted and wants for nothing in the way of arms. I'd say he's as worthy a man as could be! I'll go and learn whatever I can, and as soon as I'm back I'll tell you what I've found!'

Without exchanging a word with anyone he went and recovered his nag where he'd left it tethered in the wood. The trusty youth mounted quickly and headed off to find the knight. Back he rode to the cross and found him there, and hailed him and told him how the four damsels had sent him back.

'And, before God, they ask if you'd consider sending them your name?'

'No indeed, my friend. Just go and tell Aiglentine that I've come on the queen's behalf and am not in the best of spirits.'

'What about your arms, sir? Tell me of your device.'

'I do believe, my boy,' he said, 'you're trying to catch me out! If you want to describe my arms, they're gold – I'll tell you more if you'll sound this horn.[1] Gold arms I have, yes, emblazoned with red cockatrices.'[2]

'Oh, come off it!' said the squire. 'You're having me on! Shame on you: palming me off with nonsense! I don't believe there's a man on earth who bears such a shield! But I bring news from the castle that'll cheer you no end: the damsels held captive there have a shield with them in which is set

---

[1] i.e. the horn hung on the cross – see above, p. 12, and note 3.
[2] '*Coquefabues*': mythical beasts.

a precious stone, and as long as you bear it you need fear nothing. I'm not joking! They want to send it to you if you'll accept it, to help you when you do battle. Every man I know would be delighted by the gift!'

The knight calmly replied that he wouldn't accept it till he'd rescued the damsels if he could.

'If that's all I'm going to get from you,' said the squire, 'I'll go back!' And he set off swiftly into the wood and was lost to view. [1101]

The knight now read the message fixed to the cross; then he gave the horn such a ringing blast that the whole castle shook, and he was about to follow what was written and head for the castle when he saw a squire riding towards him. Up the squire rode to meet the knight, who had his shield braced and helm laced, ready to joust if given a lance; the squire came right up and planted one beneath his arm before galloping back to the castle. The knight followed at a steady pace[1] till he arrived before the gate, where he saw a knight bearing white arms emblazoned with a red castle – he sported this device on all his gear. Without any hauteur or discourtesy he politely asked this knight, the lord of the house, to deliver the four girls to him: there was nothing he wanted more, for Guinevere had sent him to find them and he'd searched many lands and now knew they were imprisoned there. I'll give you the lord's reply in short: he didn't ask but *ordered* him to surrender as his prisoner forthwith! He could forget about this errand for his lady!

'It would need a lot more knights than just yourself!' said the lord.

The knight was incensed by these scornful words.

But let me tell you now about the squire. Returning to the girls he told them all that had happened, from first to last.

'By my eyes,' said one, 'let's go up to the battlements! Be assured: this is the knight who'll rescue us – he'll give all of them here a proper battle! Let's go up to the tower's top and see how he performs!'

All four ran swiftly to the top of the tower and saw that their rescuer knight was an impressive sight indeed! Raring for a joust, he was riding forward to face the castle's lord, who'd pay dearly by the looks of things if his hauberk had any flaws! The girls cried out:

'In fierce combat a man's true worth is seen! Now God save me, sir knight, you've four people rooting for you who may soon be in your care!'

And he looked up then and saw a host of ladies and damsels, many of them young and fair, and heard the four girls calling to him, begging him in God's name to think of them.

'Damsels, come what may I'll do my utmost – as you're about to see!'

And with that he launched his horse into a charge, and it was clear to all who saw him that he knew how to wield a lance and set his shield. No

---

[1] '*l'ambleüre*': faster than a walk but slower than a canter.

knight was ever so handsomely clad – and the destrier on which he sat was anything but lame! He was as ready as could be to joust, with lance aimed straight at the face of the foe. The lord of the castle came eagerly, full tilt, to meet him, and they exchanged such blows that both their lances shattered. All those watching were awestruck by the clash, but thanks be to God neither knight was harmed, and they rode back swiftly to their starting-lines. The lord's men sent to ask the knight how he was; he said he could happily take such blows till All Saints! Then he turned and saw a squire ride through the gate; he was bringing him a great, stout lance.

'I'm sent to tell you,' said the squire, 'that in time of need you find out who your friends are!'

'Indeed! Then tell me, my dear man: it's a friend, is it, who's sent me this?'

'Those girls up there, atop the tower to the right, don't know who you are but have great faith in you.'

'Hand me that lance, then, boy, and send my greetings to the girls – and may God send them the right result: that I can escort them back to court!'

Before the squire set off he saw the knight brace and set his shield once more and then spur his steed into a charge that devoured the ground; his foe, the moment he saw him, charged to meet him as fast as his horse could go, making the earth tremble. Their lances shook to their very tips as they sought with all their might to unhorse each other – that's how they were playing it, yes indeed! And as they met they exchanged such blows that they almost knocked each other senseless, and smashed their lances to their very fists.

Cardonelle cried, with clasped hands: 'Tell us your name, sir!'

But he cried back: 'Not I!' But he did at least make a bow to her.

Then he rode straight back to his starting-line and found a boy who gave him a sturdy lance and said that the girls were imploring him not to fail. The moment he heard this he set off again in another charge, and the lord of the castle came at him with all the speed he could summon. But I promise, without a word of a lie, that as they spurred to meet each other, no one heard their thunder above the tempest that now beset the castle – you never heard such a wondrous storm. They met, and dealt one another such awesome blows that any man, sage or fool, would rue the day – too late! They made the castle echo with the fury of their clash, and it left them both so stunned that they didn't know where they were. They'd each dashed the helm from the other's head, so neither party had shame or censure; and being now bare-headed – as they both reeled, barely conscious – the knight was revealed to be the count.[1]

---

[1] Robert II, count of Artois, 1250–1302, nephew of Louis IX of France ('Saint Louis').

'Our knight deserves nothing but praise!' said Aiglentine. 'He's come on behalf of Queen Guinevere and I'd say he's a fine knight indeed – I do believe it's the count of Artois that's come to rescue us!'

All four ran down to find out if the knights were alive or dead. A squire rode from the castle on a strong, swift mount and was relieved to find them still in one piece. He was a good and trusty youth: he recognised the count of Artois but didn't let on! He left him and went straight over to his lord and told him he'd been jousting with the count. His lord made no reply – mainly because he hadn't heard a word: he was still stunned from the blow!

And meanwhile the castle was still being battered by thunder and lightning – such a storm that they were all convinced the place would be reduced to rubble: the tiles on the roofs were cascading down. There'd never been trouble like this at previous jousts, and plenty of them had been pretty tough! But the Knight of the Lion[1] had brought the castle's adventures to an end.

No one stayed inside: men and women alike came flocking forth – except the four captive girls, for the lord had kept them so strictly confined that they didn't even dare enter the courtyard without his leave. As if awaking from a dream, the knights returned to their senses. All the people of the castle had come running, and now helped them both, making sure they didn't topple and fall. The count was doing all he could to avoid being recognised, and the youth was savvy and discreet and came to his lord once more and, seeing he'd raised his head, told him:

'I promise you, sir, you've unknowingly jousted with the count of Artois! That's who he is, I know for sure! He's come here to reclaim the girls, and so he will: he's won them from you – you should return them to him without demur.'

The lord of the castle laughed and went straight over to the count, who was covering his face with his hand and calling for someone to bring him his helm for God's sake! But the lord said:

'If it please you, sir, you can take lodging with us here tonight; but before God, if I may be so bold and you've no objection, I'd be glad to know your name.'

The count replied: 'My father's name was Robert.'

And the lord said, most courteously: 'You're the count of Artois – you've no need to conceal it from us! I've already opened your castle to you: these keys are yours – I surrender them. And you may take me to such imprisonment as you deem fit: it's only right and proper since you've vanquished me in combat. Tonight you may sleep in the pavilion you see before you, or in the castle if you prefer. We all surrender to you – with

---

[1] Literally 'the knight who'd brought the lion': he has a lion with him, as becomes clear below, p. 17.

our lives spared, and our arms and our loved ones. We submit entirely to your will. If you decline to keep us here, you can send us to court – we'll leave at once.'

They entered the castle then, and the count was received with all courtesy and respect. But he was upset to see before him, on their knees, their faces wet with tears, the four damsels he'd come to find. Despite his lofty station he knelt likewise, still in his armour and wet with blood and sweat, and said he wouldn't stand till they'd forgiven him for having been so slow! They begged him to have pity, crying:

'Sir, set us free! We've been in this tower too long!'

He said he'd never leave without them. At this they were beside themselves with joy, and little wonder. Then they set about helping him from his armour with gracious care. And the seven knights of the castle came and craved his mercy, and promised to go to court at once and surrender in his name; if the queen requested a ransom for their release she'd have it – whatever sum she demanded, and more! The count replied that he'd gladly allow them to go to court, but forbade them to say a word about him, for he'd done nothing worthy of report. They disagreed!

The servants whose duty it was to set the tables did so swiftly, but I've no wish to tell you all that they ate and drank. After supper the girls took the count to their chamber,[1] where they celebrated more than words can say, dancing and rejoicing in a little private party, knowing they'd be leaving in the morning. While the count was making merry a knight came bringing wine, napkins, ginger; and the count took Cardonelle in his arms and sat down with the girls around him in comely fashion and they spoke of many things. Then fairly soon they took to their beds and slept till morning. [1407]

But early though the count rose, everyone in the castle was already up and their horses were out of the stables and saddled. It would take a fair while to describe the leave-taking, but the count, captor of the castle, departed in the highest spirits; as noble and handsome as the grandest of birds,[2] he set off with the girls. The seven knights for their part made for Le Hem to surrender as captives, and the count bade his lion[3] go with them, which it faithfully did. But they didn't all go together: the count, I think, travelled separately, with his girls. If I knew the details of their journey I'd gladly tell you, but I don't know the count of Artois's route.

As for the lord of the castle, he left there on Saint Denis's Night, eager to make his way to the queen. The seven knights, fully armed and clad in

---
[1] The MS reads 'their beds', implying that they escorted him to the chamber where they'd slept during their imprisonment.
[2] Literally 'the one I compare to the pheasant'.
[3] See note 1 above, p. 16.

mail, arrived at the palace – which was no mean sight, ablaze with the light of many torches – and were greeted by stares from the knights of the court as the lion, ever at their horses' feet, came bounding in ahead of them. Sir Kay the seneschal was getting his speeches ready! Their lord came before the queen at the high table, and the lion, a most courteous beast, sat calm and quiet before her with its muzzle on the table. The lord of the castle greeted the queen and said:

'My lady, we have come straight here to submit as your prisoners on behalf of the Knight of the Lion.'

The queen accepted them, but required them to remove their helms; they unlaced them at once so their faces now were visible. Then Sir Kay, in the hearing of all, was quickly in with:

'Look at you, all meek and mild! What havoc you'd wreak in battle! If all your companions are the same what a terrifying bunch you'd be! Ha! You're strapping enough to look at but I wouldn't like to bet on what's inside!'

Then he had a go at each in turn, saying to one: 'You look a right softie! It's tragic: seven of you, so tough and hard that you were beaten in battle by a single knight! Be honest now: why are you here? Have you come to ask for wives? You'd never be able to master one unless she was well compliant! That big, red-headed fellow, he'd be cuckolded in no time! As for that one, the only thing he'd keep a grip on is a pitcher of wine! That skinny one's knackered from travel by the look of him, and fatty over there, loaded with flab, he looks a proper pussycat!'

Kay thus aimed a barb at each of them, which didn't please the queen. And then, with the knights still mounted before him, he said: 'My lady, have pity on these valiant knights! They might come in handy if you're desperate!'

'Whatever happens, Sir Kay,' she said, 'I mean to retain them in my household, though I greatly fear they'll be ill disposed thanks to your spiteful words. You want to put everyone down.'

The queen had them escorted to a tower to be disarmed. Then they returned and took their seats for supper, where those young knights errant were the object of keen attention! And as soon as supper was over the queen promptly bade a start to dancing, which lasted well into the night. How could it be other than joyous in the company of that noble queen, endowed with all possible honour? [1517]

But I'll return now to the stand[1] where the queen had taken her place on high to see which knights knew how to aim and land a blow! Kay had sent several times to find out if his adversary had armed. It wouldn't be his fault if he failed to have the first joust, but he'd be vexed and aggrieved if

---

[1] i.e. where Sarrasin had suspended the story, above, p. 9.

anyone else did! It mattered to him desperately that he retained his right![1]

You'd have seen knights arriving now, fully armed, their horses all caparisoned. The entrance to the jousting ground was opened and a host of knights rode in. Everyone was massing there to watch – you never saw such a crowd at any market: so great was the press at the barriers that they broke in many places!

The queen now called on Sir Kay to use his lances, for time was pressing on and knights from many lands had come to win renown: she told him to get on with it! You never heard a madman or a drunkard react as Kay did then! The knights who'd heard the queen's order couldn't help laughing; nor could the ladies leaning at the windows of the stand. And when one of them cried:

'What are you waiting for, Sir Kay? Something from one of us?'

Kay called back: 'Lady, we're short of two people here: you need a lover by the look of you, and I need an opponent! I hope they're both sent from Hell!'

'You've always been like this, Sir Kay!' said the queen. 'And you'll never change! You take yourself so seriously! You've no need to be so vexed – the lady meant her question kindly.'

Then she called straightway for her barons to advise her.

'Sirs,' she said, 'we've knights arriving from far and wide, and it's high time we began proceedings. It's no great matter if Kay doesn't have the first joust – even if he jousted last he still wouldn't lose his right. God grant me good fortune in what I'm about to propose: to give our guests from foreign parts a chance [to join the ladies],[2] I wish to offer the following condition if you'll agree: have it proclaimed at once that if a knight and his mount both fall but the knight stays in his saddle, he can have the squires and pages help him up again.'

'They won't say no to that!' said the lord of Raineval.[3]

'And let whichever knight's first ready go and joust, if he can find an opponent. And let the heralds remind all comers that the ladies are here and watching!'

This was announced in ringing tones by the one called Corbiois,[4] his cry so loud and clear that it was heard by all. Then you'd have seen a stir indeed, as all the knights hurried to arm at their starting-lines. And there was Sir Kay, who'd been fully armed and ready since break of day! If his adversary didn't appear, he wouldn't be striking the first blows!

---

[1] Granted by King Arthur, as Kay said above, p. 9.
[2] By jousting and running no fewer than three courses, the condition imposed above, p. 4.
[3] Raoul des Préaux, lord of Raineval (Mailly-Raineval, south-west of Le Hem).
[4] A herald, presumably so named because he was from Corbie, just east of Amiens.

There was nothing reserved or slow about Sir Aubert de Longueval. Armed and ready, mounted on a handsome horse, he picked out a knight, a fine, experienced jouster, and issued a fearsome challenge. If you want to know his name, it was Baudouin, the castellan of Arras. And let me tell you, he hadn't come to Le Hem with any lack of self-assurance: every man from his land was there emblazoned with his arms! They'd come two by two and hand in hand, arriving very early that Tuesday. The queen and her maidens – many of them fair indeed – had already taken their places in the stand, and the castellan like a true knight gave the queen most courteous greeting and then all the others in turn. But I shan't wear my brain out and repeat their every word! Suffice it to say that the castellan decided to go and arm at his grand lodging, and I can assure you he promptly went and was promptly back. And there was the lord of Longueval, fully armed and astride his horse, waiting for him at the far end of the lists. His mind was on one thing and one thing only – and it wasn't the price of corn! There he was, shield braced, mounted on no mean destrier; and to test his steed he swept into a gallop past the ladies, but he'd no wish to delay the joust and was quickly back at his starting-line. The castellan likewise galloped past the stand and back again. Their attendants now handed them all they required, and then, as soon as they saw that each other was ready, they charged as fast as their mounts could bear them. They came to meet right in front of the queen – who had no ill feelings towards one of them: he was her brother![1] She raised her hands to heaven, begging God to protect him from harm. Such were the blows they exchanged that five hundred thought a thunderbolt had struck! Stumps flew higher than any man could throw: of the castellan's lance not half a yard remained, and his opponent's was shattered likewise, reduced to powder! They were driving their horses so straight and swift that people were saying:

'If they collide they'll kill each other!'

The queen beckoned a knight who was mounted but simply clad, wearing no armour, and he came swiftly to her call: he was a knight of many fine qualities, Gilles de Neuville[2] by name.

'In God's name, sir,' she said, 'go and beg them on my behalf not to clash! Send each of them my love.'

'God curse me, lady,' the knight replied, 'if I say any such thing! They'd think I'd lost my wits if I forbade them to seek honour and urged them to such shame! I'll take no such message!'

---

[1] This makes clear that 'Queen Guinevere' is being played by Aubert de Longueval's sister (possibly the sister who, records suggest, was later to marry Huart de Bazentin).

[2] One of several members of a family competing at Le Hem; Neuville is just south of Arras.

The castellan rode smartly back to his starting-line, but before he'd even reached it his opponent was ready, lance in hand. The queen was on tenterhooks, wanting to stop any risk of collision; but the castellan took his lance without more ado and thrust in his spurs, and the lord of Longueval was spurring to meet him: there was going to be a clash, an awesome one!

'God preserve him!' said the queen, and she turned away: she couldn't bear to look. But God had the power to preserve indeed, and saved them both from harm. They shattered their lances but rode on past and then turned back once more. As they grasped their third lances the queen was filled with fear and implored the Saviour to keep them from hurt and woe. What more should I tell you? They'd both jousted splendidly, beyond all reproach; and now, with their third lances, they dealt each other such mighty blows that the ladies were awestruck, and prayed for them! They passed so close that they buffeted each other, but rode on without hurt.

Sir Kay came hurrying to the queen and said: 'Lady! Lady, they've done me shame, and you even more than me! You know I should have the first joust at your court! Strike me blind if I'll stand for this! And let's be honest: what a modest and mannerly start they've given us!'

'Oh yes, Sir Kay, without a doubt you'd have shown the way much better! You and your opponent would have scattered the field with shards!'[1]

'I would indeed, lady! I'd have been fearless!'

'There's nothing to stop you doing so yet, if you're still so inclined.'

'You unhorsed so many,' said the ladies, mocking, 'when the queen was taken to Gorre:[2] you know how well that ended!'

Sir Kay, shame-stricken, went very quiet! [1731]

Then the Deaf Knight of Seuni[3] appeared, spurring a caparisoned charger; he saw the lists clear before him, truly, and his adversary at the far end ready and waiting. They charged full tilt to meet each other, landing mighty blows that pierced their shields and brigandines[4] alike. This joust was be-

---

[1] Literally 'would have seeded the field'.
[2] The MS has the puzzling '*quant la roïne entra u car*' ('when the queen entered the cart'). This is clearly a reference to Chrétien de Troyes' *Lancelot – The Knight of the Cart*, but either the scribe failed to recognise the place-name Gorre or, far more probably, '*car*' is a confused allusion to the cart in which Lancelot famously is forced to ride and '*la roïne*' is perhaps a scribal aberration for '*Lancelot*'. Speculation aside, the essential point of the ladies' jibe is that in Chrétien's *Lancelot* Guinevere is abducted to Gorre by the wicked Meleagant, and Kay, who'd been escorting her, is with humiliating speed defeated, wounded and imprisoned.
[3] '*Li Sours de Seuni*'. Both knight and place-name are impossible to identify.
[4] The brigandine was body armour, usually a coat of heavy cloth or leather, with metal plates riveted to the fabric.

tween the Deaf Knight of Seuni and Mahiu de Warlincourt,[1] a fine horseman indeed, and was avidly watched by the ladies and maidens leaning on the balustrades above.

Two more knights then came forward. Now, no good deed should be kept hidden: it should be proclaimed loud and clear, for all to hear; but Envy often ties men's tongues, to the detriment of many. (And as for heralds, they tend to say they're less inclined to broadcast deeds if nothing's given in return! They'd sing the praises of quite a few about whom they keep quiet for want of anything coming their way! Are heralds in the business of selling reputations? Not at all – that wouldn't be right or proper. But they more readily report fine deeds from court to court when they've been given a handsome gift or two!) As I say, two more knights were on their marks before the ladies, and everyone beheld them with delight, for they were as splendidly armed and mounted as could be. The ladies in the stand were calling down to the crowd below:

'Who are those two, sirs?'

And Gilles from Neuville in Artois, ever courteous, called back to them: 'One is the son of the rightful lord of Hangest.'[2]

'Which one?'

'The one with the chequered shield. So now you know! He'll succeed his father as lord. And the one facing him is Jehan, lord of Clères.'[3]

Hangest was clutching the fine lance he'd been handed – big and stout, superbly made: shame on him if he failed to put it to good use! And he stretched his back to sit tall and straight upon his charger, looking perfectly the part in every way. And his adversary – whom I rate highly – took up his lance likewise and they charged to meet each other. Hangest, lance in rest, headed for him, straight and true, the eyes of the queen and the ladies all upon him. The chequered knight charged nobly, lance aimed high. But why go into long description? He broke all three of his lances, which impressed the queen most highly, and because he'd jousted so well he earned the admiration of the queen and all who'd watched him. Some were running after him crying:

'Well done indeed!'

Without more ado two valiant knights came forward now and took their positions to joust, each sporting a kerchief or sleeve[4] of which they were well worthy. I'll tell you their names if I may: one was Boisset[5] and

---

[1] Warlincourt-lès-Pas, south-west of Arras.
[2] Jean III, son of Jean II, lord of Hangest (Hangest-en-Santerre, south-west of Le Hem).
[3] An 'outsider': Jean II, lord of Clères in Normandy between Rouen and Dieppe.
[4] i.e. a token from a lady.
[5] Mentioned elsewhere but never clearly identified.

the other was Simon de Lalaing.¹ Both were such a splendid sight that many of the ladies and damsels that day dreamed that one or other was jousting for love of her! Well might they so fancy! The lists now cleared, with people scurrying everywhere, as the two knights left their starting-lines and charged at mighty speed. Boisset, fired by love, was going all out! And Simon wasn't holding back – he headed for him straight and true, knowing he was watched by many a lady, but with his thoughts fixed on one alone and set on doing the business! He aimed his lance at Boisset and struck him high up close to the throat, and Boisset made no mistake and gave it to him in the teeth. Splinters of their shattered lances flew into the crowd.

'Such knights are worthy of esteem indeed,' said the queen. 'They certainly have mine! They're masters of their business.'

They'd smashed all three of their lances beyond all further use.

Now Dreux de Morlaine[2] came swiftly forward on a black destrier, fully armed and shield set: all he needed was a lance. His destrier leapt beneath him the moment it felt his spurs, and Guy de Neuville,[3] true to form, was at the other end, lance in hand, and charged from his starting-line with all the speed he could summon. Sir Dreux, I promise you, headed straight for him, brave and bold, fearing him not at all, in so tight a line that everyone said:

'They're going to collide!'

Sir Guy, for sure, held his line dead straight and didn't veer at all, and when it came to delivering their blows neither held back: unflinchingly they smashed their lances right down to their fists. Sir Dreux, behind his firm-braced shield, rode on and smartly turned. In the event he went through all three of his lances but made not the slightest impression on Sir Guy, who neither buckled nor fell; and it was the judgement of many present that both knights had done well.

I'll describe the jousts just briefly: if I were to give a blow-by-blow account of each I think you'd find it tiresome. But as for Sir Gieffroy de Clères,[4] the next to joust, it almost cost him, for his shield was useless: Sir Guillaume de Beauvais[5] dealt him a blow so fierce that he wouldn't have been without his brigandine for all the world – the lance would have gone clean through him. Sir Gieffroy in return aimed high at his head and caught him in the throat with a force that broke his lance, great-

---

[1] *'Monnars de Laleng'*. This is probably a rendering of Simon de Lalaing. Lallaing is in the county of Hainaut. Simon de Lalaing is a participant also in the tournament at Chauvency.
[2] 'Morlaines': probably Morlaine, just north of Beauvais.
[3] His relationship to Gilles de Neuville is uncertain.
[4] Presumably a relation of the Norman lord Jean de Clères, above, p. 22.
[5] Guillaume II, castellan of Beauvais.

ly impressing the queen and her fair and illustrious company. They'd performed admirably, and were highly praised by the ladies who said they'd struck excellent blows. [1895]

Meanwhile Sir Kay the seneschal was there below the stand, armed and ready, as tormented as could be that his opponent wasn't there: he feared his luck was thoroughly out. But then he turned his horse a touch and saw his jouster coming! Kay couldn't contain himself, and yelled:

'At last! The knight *par excellence*!'[1]

His opponent heard him loud and clear, and was well aware he was waiting for him and had been waiting ages; he understood exactly what he'd said. The ladies didn't hold back but called right out to Kay, saying:

'The tardy knight and the hardy knight are going to meet! So make sure you keep your vow, Sir Kay! You said at the start that you and your opponent would scatter the field with shards! He's come to take you on, so you'd better get strewing! No knight should break his word to ladies!'

Sir Kay was mortified to hear the ladies' taunts. 'Would to God,' he said, 'no woman under heaven had a tongue! A curse on yours! You're so quick to sound off with scorching jibes!'

'Don't let them get to you, Sir Kay,' said the dwarf, who was a nasty piece of work. 'Behind their soft caresses women have claws![2] They always speak their mind and have their way. Woman is a very dodgy dish!'[3]

This helped to calm Kay down: the dwarf had said it loud enough to be heard by the queen and all the ladies in the stand. It cheered Kay no end: he thought he'd been well avenged! But one of the queen's maids, Forteche, said:

'I tell you, dwarf, you'll do yourself no favours by slagging off the ladies! You'd do better to hold your tongue. Sir Kay can say what he likes – he's always having a go at us.'

'Gillart,' Kay said sharply to the dwarf, 'if you've any sense you'll speak in a way to please the queen whenever there's a chance.'

'By my life,' the dwarf replied, 'you know yourself there's no fun in that! You're a fine, bold knight but you're hardly a model courtier: if you see a chance to mock or put someone down there's never any stopping you – no one can see your next jibe coming!'

Said Kay: 'I'll not have you as a witness, charging me with heresy! I'm no different to other men: I like women – it's only natural! God rot those who speak ill of them, and good luck to all who court them!'

---

[1] More literally 'Here's the one who'll be the measure of us all!' Kay's sarcasm is doubly strong because it's the very cry that announces Lancelot's arrival at a tournament in Chrétien de Troyes' *Lancelot*.
[2] Literally 'women have the fur of a bear'.
[3] Literally 'woman is a cheese full of nasty stuff'.

With that the banter ended, and Sir Kay grabbed hold of a lance and went to test his horse. The good Aubert de Longueval offered him a destrier if he found his own mount wasn't up to it, but Sir Kay thanked him and said he'd swap him for no other – he seemed a fine steed. Everyone present assembled now to watch Sir Kay's joust. Those in charge of the lists set a track right close to the stand so that the ladies above had a perfect view of both knights. Let me tell you a little about Sir Kay's opponent: he was a strong knight, tall, well built in every limb, brave, gallant and full of valour; and he was perfectly ready and gripping his lance, with which he was aiming to deal fine blows. Sir Kay delayed no longer, but charged at him full tilt. And his adversary, Jehan des Jestes,[1] was no sluggard or faint-heart: he came well and truly at him – Kay thought, and rightly, that he was aiming in a dead straight line, right for him, and either he or his horse would die before they were done! Both knights were of the same mind: such was their resolve that they were charging headlong at each other – right there in the fullest view of more than three thousand ladies, knights and other folk.

'They're going to collide if they don't watch out!' said those who saw them closing. But they didn't swerve an inch. Why? Because they wouldn't stoop so low! Their first lances hit home as they exchanged almighty blows. Sir Kay the seneschal, to answer the ladies' mockery, went in so close that they did indeed collide, in a clash so fierce, being the strong and strapping knights they were, that the ladies leaning along the wall were sure they both were dead. They crashed together, chest to chest, both man and horse, sundering stirrups and breast-straps; though neither rider lost his seat, the impact was so terrible that everyone was certain they'd been killed. The queen was aghast – she loved Sir Kay dearly – and sent a worthy, valiant knight to see how the two knights were. But their attendants had already helped them to mount two palfreys, so the queen's alarm was quelled.

Sir Kay rode up and greeted her and she rose to acknowledge him, for she was fond of him – though ever wary and cautious, too.

'Where,' he called, 'is Madam Haughty, who bade me strew the field? If it weren't unseemly to bicker I'd soon say something that I'll keep to myself. But let me give her this much: she wouldn't have all that bling about her neck, or be so decked with all that get-up, unless she had a lover. She's made me mad, my lady!'

'She wears it for her husband's sake!' the queen replied. 'There's no reason to think otherwise!'

'Let's hope to God you're right!' said Kay. 'I tell you, ladies, anyone who upsets me rues the day! And anyone who trusts you women will get it in the neck! You act all proper and upright but if any man tries hard enough you'll always fall in a trice! Then again, no service we offer will satisfy

---

[1] Unidentifiable.

you unless it involves a battering or a wound! By the apostle Peter, you women want our love for you to be equal to our love for God! You want men to well and truly pay before they win your love! God send you all a wretched day!'

And with that Sir Kay was gone. [2071]

The count of Clermont[1] now came spurring into the lists like a man who meant business when he entered a tourney-ground! He asked the queen's leave to join her household if he ran three courses, and that one of her knights should come and face him. She delightedly accepted him, but was worried about the prospect of him jousting, being a man of such high status. She asked her counsellors for guidance, saying:

'Who should joust with this great man? Tell me. He's the king's own brother, and graciously wishes to join my household! I wouldn't have him joust against an opponent who's unworthy! I pray you, send him a knight he'll think worthwhile! In God's name, consider who it should be.'

'We decided that some time ago,' said the lord of Longueval. 'You could look through all your household and find none more fitting than the lord of Bazentin. Truly, by Saint Quentin,[2] there's no worthier knight at your court. Send for him, come what may.'

So he was summoned and duly came, armed and equipped with everything required. And the queen personally bade him go and joust with the king's brother, but implored him to do nothing untoward. Huart understood and thanked her deeply and proceeded to do as bidden.

The two knights promptly took their lances and set forth without more ado. Then you'd have heard the count of Clermont roar 'Montjoie!'[3] His destrier leapt forward and he charged, bearing his lance and shield most nobly, with aplomb. Huart, shield braced, saw the count approaching and cried 'Love!' – of which he was very mindful – and 'Montauban!'[4] Neither held back when it came to the thrust: they smashed their lances right down to their fists. They rode on past, shields firm-braced, and returned to their starting-lines. They seemed to have been born to joust: they were handsome, noble knights indeed. With shields set ready to face a blow, they charged once more without delay, with all the speed their steeds could summon, intent on delivering tremendous blows. Their followers were aghast at this second course: no mangonel, sling or catapult shoots faster than they galloped, truly

---

[1] This is Robert count of Clermont (1256–1317), sixth son of Louis IX ('Saint Louis') and brother of King Philip III. He was to be badly injured in a tournament in the year after this festival at Le Hem.

[2] Very much a local saint: martyred in the nearby town that bears his name and his body thrown into the Somme.

[3] The battle-cry of the French royal house.

[4] One of his fiefs (as he says above, p. 4), and the battle-cry of the Bazentin family.

– so said all who witnessed it. And with their third they charged in such a straight, tight line that if the track had been any narrower their mounts would have crashed together. But the queen had bidden all her knights not to collide, and to take special care in this case to cause no injury to the count, for he was brother to the king. He charged fiercely, valiantly indeed, impressing everyone; he broke all three of his lances on the lord of Bazentin, as they dealt and shared a succession of mighty blows.

And so it was that the count of Clermont earned his entry to the feast. He went and sat in the stand with the queen, and swore that if he saw any outsiders try to demean her or her men, they'd rue the day: he'd take them on, no matter what. [2169]

Then a herald came swiftly forward, crying: 'Clear the lists!' And all eyes turned to a knight named Sir Wistasse de Sisi:[1] he was preparing to joust against Ridel, whose father Sir Gilles[2] said most courteously:

'Ridel, God keep you and your opponent from peril! He's a worthy knight of great renown, and I promise you, you couldn't induce him to give up this joust for a hundred thousand silver marks!'

They braced their shields and charged at each other unswervingly. Sisi broke his lance as he landed a blow below the throat, and Ridel returned a blow that smashed his lance to shards. Straight back to their marks they rode; and with new lances they smartly returned with aim fixed at each other's helm and exchanged almighty, awesome blows.

'This game's proper dangerous!' said one of the watching commoners. 'God protect these knights and all the rest!'

If you'd been watching closely you'd have seen them aim their third lances straight for the eyes, but that's a lesser fault than striking and breaking lances lower down. Praise should go to all who perform well, and the queen praised Ridel indeed as he broke all three of his lances. Sisi had done well, too, with no cause for reproach of any kind.

Next up, as I saw myself, was good Robert de Montigny[3] against Guillaume d'Annois.[4] And they weren't playing at it! They charged full tilt and clashed full on, meeting body to body and horse to horse. I tell you, it pained me to see such a fearful crash, and the ladies watching from the wall thought they were finished and were dreadfully upset. It was a fearsome joust indeed. Everyone was convinced they both were dead, and some were stricken with grief.

---

[1] An unidentifiable knight from further afield – an 'outsider'.
[2] i.e. Gilles de Neuville, already mentioned twice; his son Ridel is another of the family competing at Le Hem.
[3] Probably Robert the son of Gui lord of Montigny, near Lalaing (Lallaing) in Hainaut, east of Douai.
[4] Annois is south-east of Le Hem, between Saint-Quentin and Noyon.

Sir Enguerran de Bailleul[1] now entered, blacker than iron, so clad that he looked like the very lord of Hell! Against him, in superb array, came good Pierard de Foucaucourt;[2] but his horse, good runner though it was, refused to confront the foe, for all Pierard's spurring – he was making every effort, as everyone around him could see. Sir Enguerran swore he wouldn't put up with this; he aimed to impress at every opportunity, and I do believe, so help me God, he was the son of the most admirable man between London and Rome, held in esteem by many people: the fine tourneyer and warrior Sir Wistasse de Tours, who was lord of Tours-en-Vimeu and had a great estate in Scotland, too.

Two knights now came forward in superb array. Their names for sure should not be hidden: one was Dreux du Plessier,[3] who didn't shrink from joining in – he was small and short enough as it was! The lord of Hamelincourt,[4] a giant by comparison, charged from his mark at once, crying 'Hamelincourt!' at the top of his voice, and Sir Dreux charged to meet him as fast as his horse would go. They came together unswervingly and met head on, horse and man together: their horses came off worst, too badly hurt to rise again – Sir Dreux's was stone cold dead. But neither knight suffered injury, much to their friends' relief. Their joust had been fine and mighty, and it would be very wrong not to praise them.

Next up was Dreux de Préaux,[5] a loyal knight of utmost vigour, mounted on a handsome horse indeed. Sir Robert d'Onival[6] rode to meet him without delay, and they charged full tilt and swapped huge and furious blows. They swept on past and then charged again, covering themselves so well with their shields that they did one another no harm.

Aigre,[7] a formidable jouster, took on Huon de Conflans,[8] and aimed not for his side but for his head or throat. Huon was crying 'Saint George!' with all the breath he could summon; Aigre, a fine horseman, was coming with lance levelled at throat or nose, no lower. Conflans was bent on jousting well, on doing his very best, and he didn't let himself down; and Aigre performed so well that of his three lances he was left with none – he broke them all.

---

[1] Bailleul-en-Vimeu, south of Abbeville. Enguerran, who had taken part in the Seventh Crusade under Louis IX, was the uncle of 'Jehan de Bailleul' – John Balliol, future king of Scotland – another participant at Le Hem: see below, p. 41.
[2] Foucaucourt-en-Santerre, a few miles south of Le Hem.
[3] Le Plessier-Rozainvillers, south-east of Amiens.
[4] South of Arras.
[5] A Norman knight, if this is the Préaux just east of Rouen.
[6] Possibly Onival near Ault, on the coast west of Abbeville.
[7] Sarrasin offers no further identification.
[8] Hugues III de Conflans (near Paris), later Marshal of Champagne.

Through the throng and into the lists rode the count of Guînes,[1] a truly good and valiant knight who loved to tourney, and a young knight – brave and impressive for his age – was sent to face him. The king is doing himself no favours or credit by banning tournaments! I promise you, Sir Simon de Béronne,[2] this young knight of many qualities, is a fearsome wielder of a sword. And he headed straight for the count, mounted on a black destrier. The count charged smartly to meet him crying 'Love! Love!'; I know no man of his standing who could have done his duty better. And both put on a splendid show, driving their horses on as true knights should and breaking their lances: their jousts earned the praise of many, I'd say.

Then a pair of renowned young knights promptly came to joust: one by the name of Guillaume de Blosseville,[3] and his opponent, charging straight and true, was named Jehan de Jumel.[4] He was a keen and strapping young knight indeed, determined to excel, and he turned his three lances into splinters.

Sir Wautier de Sorel,[5] astride a fine black destrier, charged Pieron de Bailleul,[6] and never since my days in swaddling-clothes did I see a knight charge better. They both played their parts to perfection, well and truly smashing their lances.

Dagart de Bourg[7] set himself and braced his shield: he it was who jousted next. His opponent held so tight a line that he almost crashed straight into him: Pierre de Morlaine[8] charged valiantly indeed, swift and brave, for his uncle Sollar was close at hand, urging him on. And he did as he was urged! He delivered a mighty blow and received the same, and broke two lances or even three; the thunderous blows he dealt Dagart could be heard from far away: Pierre played his part splendidly.

After this joust the lord of Montmorency[9] came to face the lord of Moreuil,[10] and I never saw a knight charge better. They dealt each other such mighty lance-blows on their shields that the shafts were smashed to pieces – both the first and the second. Then back came Moreuil, lance levelled, with all the speed he could summon from his mount; God bless

---

[1] Arnoul III, count of Guînes (south of Calais) until 1283 when, burdened with debts, he sold the county to Philip the Bold of Burgundy.
[2] A fief near Clermont in Auvergne.
[3] A Norman knight: Blosseville is near the coast west of Dieppe.
[4] South of Amiens.
[5] North-east of Le Hem.
[6] Difficult to identify with certainty, as there were several knights of that name at the time, but the likelihood is that he was related to fellow participants Enguerran and Jehan de Bailleul.
[7] An 'outsider', impossible to identify.
[8] Presumably related to Dreux de Morlaine, above, p. 23.
[9] Mathieu IV, lord of Montmorency (north of Paris).
[10] Bernard V, lord of Moreuil (south-east of Amiens).

me, anyone who saw how Sir Bernard de Moreuil braced his shield and charged should remember it well: horse and rider came as one, valiantly, full tilt, and he wasn't aiming to strike his opponent low but always high. He broke three lances, that's for sure – he'd jousted well, I'd say.

Next to joust were Sir Gui de Saleri[1] and the lord of Maignelay, Raoul by name,[2] whose devotion to honour and courtesy was insatiable. I can testify to how well he used his three lances: he smashed them down to his fist, and his opponent didn't disappoint. [2385]

Swiftly after, without delay, came Mahieu de Trie[3] to face Renaut de Montauban.[4] To my knowledge there weren't three knights more impressive at Le Hem: they were both fine figures indeed. Basin[5] is young and strapping and determined to excel in every way. Tall and strong and handsome he is, well built in body and limb, with a fine complexion and fair and curling hair, and eyes bright and shining, often sparkling, and a handsome forehead, nose and mouth: Nature, sweet and charming, has overlooked nothing; and he has a place, I assure you, in Prowess's house. And I'd praise him further in this respect: that neither in public nor in private will he proffer a word, good or bad, unless called upon. And now, with lance of fir-wood rather than ash, he came to meet Mahieu de Trie.

'Montauban!' he cried aloud, and Mahieu cried: 'Dammartin!'[6]

Basin dealt him a blow that almost knocked him senseless, but Mahieu returned a blow at the very top of his shield. Every one of their six lances found its target, and many watching were struck by the fact that experienced men deemed worthy and brave were more inclined to fail than young and novice knights like these. A most telling comment to this effect was made by Sir Gilles de Roizy:[7] Basin had jousted with him also, at Saint Sepurcre in Germany,[8] and there, in full view of everyone, Basin had dealt him so great a blow that he'd unhorsed him, valiant knight though he was.

'Oh, my life! Damn this for a lark!' Sir Gilles had said. 'Those who've never had a go before are experts from Day One! There's no honour to be had in this game!'

---

[1] An 'outsider', not possible to identify.
[2] Maignelay-Montigny, north-east of Beauvais.
[3] Son of the lord of Fontenay in the Norman Vexin.
[4] A young man related to Huart de Bazentin, Montauban being one of Huart's fiefs and the two families being closely connected through marriage.
[5] This is another name, perhaps informal, for Renaut de Montauban, suggesting that Sarrasin knew him well – hence the eulogy to come.
[6] Mahieu de Trie's uncle was the count of Dammartin (north-east of Paris).
[7] Roizy is north-east of Reims.
[8] '*A Saint Sepurcre en Alemaigne*': it is hard to identify this as a German place-name.

Basin performed excellently.

Then two more knights came spurring forward, eager to joust. Just like those before them, they set their lances in their rests and charged to meet each other. The name of one was Muis d'Avaine,[1] and his opponent was Pierre de la Malmaison.[2] He charged straight at him, and Muis d'Avaine, from the moment he set out, was aiming to strike him high. Neither party pulled out of the clash – they both broke their lances, well and truly. They rode on past, charged again at once and acquitted themselves superbly. The heralds were bawling:

'Hyencourt the brave! Muis d'Avaine, you're born of a line of worthy, valiant knights! Let no base acts or deeds be ascribed to you!'

He braced his shield and set it in place and threw caution to the winds; and his opponent, fearless, came boldly to meet him – or would have done if his horse had been as good as he'd have wished, but it was somewhat skittish. Muis d'Avaine was aiming straight for the eyes. And to come straight to the point, they acquitted themselves most nobly and before they were done they'd both smashed a helm or shield.

Then Le Foisseux de Moyencourt[3] sprang forward, and before he'd even been given his lance his opponent was at the ready: Pierre de Chennevières[4] by name, I believe. They thrust in their spurs and charged full tilt to exchange almighty blows. They shattered their lances and turned again, and of their second lances made stumps and shards and splinters. The ladies watching from above had all eyes on Le Foisseux, who handled lance and shield in masterly fashion and landed such a blow on his opponent's shield that he was left clutching just a stump of lance. It was the same with the third: they came together so close and fierce that they smashed their lances down to their fists. The ladies up above poured praise on Le Foisseux. And both of them had pierced their hefty shields and wounded one another.

Next to come forward were two who made a very fine show: Sir Jehan de Coulogne[5] and Sir Mathieu de Ver.[6] I tell you truly and in brief: they jousted well and strongly. [2503]

---

[1] Difficult to identify precisely, but the heralds' cry of 'Hyencourt the brave', soon to follow, makes it clear that he is a member of the Hyencourt family, Hyencourt being just south of Le Hem.
[2] An 'outsider', not possible to identify with certainty as there are several Malmaisons in France.
[3] Raoul, known as Le Foisseux, lord of Moyencourt, south-west of Saint-Quentin.
[4] An 'outsider': Chennevières is south-east of Paris.
[5] Just south of Calais.
[6] Probably Vers-sur-Selles, south-west of Amiens.

And now it pleases me to report a wondrous joust indeed, most awesome and perilous, between one named Bauduin de Saint-Nicolas[1] and another named Flamenc de Mons.[2] Flamenc it was who brought his opponent and his mount together crashing in a heap, felling them with a lance-blow right before the queen. But then low-life commoners, breaking into the lists for a closer look, caused Sir Flamenc and his horse to tumble, injuring and almost killing one of his pages. Causing this pointless fall did the wretches little good. But this shows why I say that no man should ever joust unless he's mounted on a good destrier – it's all too easy to be brought down.

Into the lists now came two young knights I wish to name: Sir Jehan de Moreuil and Mathieu de Montmorency.[3] They jousted, and I witnessed it, most properly and impressively. Sir Jehan made a splendid charge – I don't believe any knight so young jousted better at Le Hem.

Spurring forward now came Sir Pieron de Wailly,[4] who wasn't to be found wanting: he's a fine and strapping figure and most accomplished for his age. Who jousted with him that morning? It was Jehan de Saint-Martin.[5] They jousted well, I'd say.

Next came the lord of Chaulnes,[6] in fine array, most splendidly clad.

'Here's a handsome sight indeed!' said one of the ladies up above.

He was positioned close to the stand, just a stone's throw away, and Sir Jehan de Piere[7] was setting off towards him. Chaulnes would think he'd blown it if he failed to break his lance! Hearing the lady's admiring words he launched into a charge crying: 'Love! Love!' His opponent was charging, too. Jehan de Chaulnes broke three lances in short order and then withdrew.

Next to charge were Sir Nicoles Donchart[8] and Jehan de Fignières;[9] no matter how strong the lances they were given, they smashed and splintered every one, prompting the ladies to declare:

'A fine show by Fignières!'

Without more ado or any fuss two more now made their move: Nicolas de Barbançon[10] and Jehan d'Ytres,[11] who set his shield in expert style and charged to meet his opponent. Their lane was so narrow and their line

---

[1] A knight later recorded (in 1296) as being *échevin* of Bourbourg, east of Calais.
[2] Clearly a knight from Mons in Hainaut.
[3] These two are the sons of Bernard de Moreuil and Mathieu IV de Montmorency, who jousted earlier, above, pp. 29–30.
[4] Wailly-Beaucamp, near the coast north of Abbeville.
[5] A Norman knight from Saint-Martin-le-Gaillard, east of Dieppe.
[6] '*Chanle*': this is probably Chaulnes, south of Le Hem, a neighbour to Hyencourt.
[7] Unidentifiable.
[8] Unidentifiable.
[9] South-east of Amiens.
[10] A knight from Hainaut.
[11] North-east of Le Hem.

so straight that many greatly feared they would collide; and they came so close together that there was indeed a crash, their lances smashed and splintered, and from the impact of their mighty blows their eyes were full of stars.

Sir Robert de Moreuil[1] now appeared to face Jehan de Carrois.[2] In fine array and superbly equipped Sir Robert came to joust, and if his opponent's hauberk and gorget hadn't saved him, both head and shaft of Robert's lance would have gone clean through his throat, unstoppably. Sir Robert jousted splendidly.

And after him came the good castellan of Beaumetz.[3] I think he'd have won a lady's or a damsel's love that day if he hadn't had a wife: he looked so dashing astride his steed, and the ladies in the stand said he was a handsome figure in armour indeed. He gripped his shield by the straps and charged to meet Gerard de Chaulnes,[4] who was bearing on his helm, I believe, live birds inside a cage. Set tight in place beneath their arms both had a lance as stout as could be, but charging as fast as their mounts could bear them they exchanged blows so great that they broke all six of their lances. The ladies leaning on the rails beside the queen declared it a joust that wanted nothing: they'd charged quite perfectly. And those who really knew about combat all agreed that Sir Gerard de Chaulnes was a young knight of true promise. Nor should I fail to mention what Gilles de Neuville said: that if the castellan's life was not cut short he was bound to prove a worthy knight.

Two more followed and ran their three courses well: one was seen by his devices to be the son of the count of Guînes,[5] and I can testify to his worthiness to wear a kerchief or sleeve! He jousted, and with great success, against the lord of Aveluy.[6]

Through the gate and into the lists Sir Amaury de Saint-Cler[7] now came to face a shining, radiant angel[8] bearing the shield of Nevelon de Moislains.[9] This angel charged in noble fashion, fast and close and bold, yet ran his three courses in such a way that he didn't so much as bend a lance.

---

[1] Presumably related to Bernard and Jehan, who have both now jousted.
[2] Another 'outsider', probably from Carrois south-east of Paris.
[3] Robert de Beaumetz (east of Abbeville), castellan of Bapaume (north of Le Hem).
[4] '*Chanle*': presumably a relative of Jehan de Chaulnes (above, p. 32).
[5] Baudouin, son of Arnoul III (above, p. 29).
[6] Baudouin de Beauvoir, lord of Aveluy, north-west of Le Hem.
[7] An 'outsider', probably a member of the Chaumont family, lords of Chaumont and Saint-Cler in Champagne.
[8] i.e. a knight so dressed.
[9] '*Molains*': probably Moislains, a few miles north-east of Le Hem.

This was followed by a fearsome joust between two who were both named Jehan: Jehan de Lunes and Jehan de La Couture;[1] and both delivered such ferocious blows that they almost knocked each other senseless: they were the worse for wear for quite a while. Lunes charged with such abandon that he seemed to have no care for life or limb; and I well recall how the good youth La Couture was likewise so committed that they and their mounts came crashing down endangering limbs and lives alike.[2] God keep me from harm, it was a glorious joust to behold but a grim one for those who felt it!

Aimer de Neuville[3] charged on a rushing destrier to meet Sir Enguerran de Bailleul, who first jousted at Le Hem in the guise of a demon.[4] Both knights charged more fiercely than a pair of lions or leopards: they both performed superbly.

Sir Gui de Courtemanche[5] jousted next, with big, strong, stout lances indeed, I promise you. His opponent was Gilles de Chennevières.[6] Then Sir Gérard de Moislains[7] jousted with Jehan de Melles,[8] exchanging terrific blows. [2670]

And while the queen was there in the stand watching these fine and mighty jousters, she saw, coming from outside, four maidens, all of them dressed alike and mounted on ambling palfreys, and all of them such comely figures that I'm sure no lovelier were ever seen. All were dressed alike in summer garb, in white shifts with delicate pleats, most beautifully becoming. They were riding ahead of the knight who'd rescued them from the castle, and who'd given all four of them great brooches and clasps for their garments. This knight their escort drew rein outside the lists. He called to the damsel Long-Suffering[9] and she came to him clad, I well recall, in a mantle, with her head wrapped in a large kerchief; a tall figure she was, dressed in yellow and black. He handed her a letter with a mirror in the seal, and said:

'Go straight to the queen – she's seated up there in the stand. You'll easily pick her out among the throng. If Sir Kay sees you he'll escort you

---

[1] Both are unidentifiable.
[2] This is a conjectural reconstruction of a sentence in which an unresolved rhyme indicates at least one missing line.
[3] Another of the Neuville family jousting at Le Hem.
[4] Above, p. 28.
[5] 'Tordemence': probably Courtemanche, south-east of Amiens.
[6] An 'outsider', presumably related to Pierre, above, p. 31.
[7] Presumably related to Nevelon, above, p. 33.
[8] An 'outsider', perhaps from Melle in Flanders or Melles north-east of Tournai.
[9] 'Sueffre-Paine': this may be the woman referred to above, p. 7, when Guinevere's company of ladies and maidens is described as 'the fairest she'd ever assembled – with one exception: we'll tell you about her in due course'.

just so that he can make fun of you: if I were you I'd beware of responding in any way.'

So Long-Suffering set out and went straight to the queen. Sir Kay at that point was with a knight who'd taken a heavy blow and was being helped from his armour on his charger; but he was the first one to spot Long-Suffering and he went and waylaid her, saying:

'Welcome, my dear. Do tell me, are you the maiden for whom so many knights have died? Upon my soul, you'll not be leaving here without a lover if you'll pay heed to me! Your radiant beauty has beguiled me utterly!'

The damsel realised Kay was mocking her and stayed silent. She went to the queen and greeted her most courteously, and the queen, so good and gracious, rose to meet her.

'My lady,' said Kay, 'behold this object of men's prayers![1] She's bringing you a letter. Since she stepped inside the gate I've had three people grab her from me, driven wild by her beauty!'

'Hold your tongue, Sir Kay,' the queen replied. 'You've such a wicked way that everyone's wary of you. But thorns prick and sharp tongues stab – that's just how it is. No one's going to change your ways: they're too ingrained – you can't teach an old dog new tricks.'

The damsel resumed her errand, saying: 'Have this letter read, my queen; I need to be quickly gone.'

The queen took the letter and summoned a chaplain who read it word for word. And when she heard that the Knight of the Lion was asking to be rewarded with a place in her household she was beside herself with joy.

'Damsel,' she said, 'have your lord come to me, and God grant him honour!'

'Lady,' said the damsel, 'with full recognition of the rights of our court, my lord the knight is retained by you.'

'God be praised!' said the queen. 'And may He keep him always!'

The girl left then, and returned to her lord and told him: 'Where you sent me, sir, dukes and counts are present, and I was conducted to the queen by a knight who sought my love, though I think it was meant contemptuously. The queen, most graciously, rose when she saw me, and when she'd heard the contents of the letter I'd taken, sir, I was delighted to see her joy at your arrival. You are accepted into her retinue, along with all your people – even if there were four thousand of you! In the lists, sir, I saw the horses of four knights lying dead or broken-shouldered after fearsome, mighty jousts. The queen desires nothing so much as to see you.'

The knight bade his lion move, and his four maidens set off in pairs, singing more sweetly than the Sirens, and with the lion at their head they

---

[1] '*Orable*': this is the name given by the Saracens to Guillaume d'Orange's wife in the epic *La Prise d'Orange*, but to fit with Kay's overwhelming sarcasm I have chosen to play on the possible root of the name being in '*orer*' – to pray.

arrived at court. Everyone flocked to meet them amid fanfares of trumpets and drums, and they rode through the gate into the lists in perfect array. The ladies in the stand saw the Knight of the Lion and had eyes for no one but him and his lion and his maidens. The knight, sporting armour like wings, rode into the lists ready to joust, lacking nothing.

'By the head of Saint John at Amiens,'[1] said the maid Forteche, 'here's a valiant knight indeed! God save me, I never set eyes on any man who looked more like the count of Artois!'

He'd stopped at the entrance to the tourney-ground and was waiting for an opponent to be sent, thrilled that he'd be with the ladies once he'd jousted (no one would be admitted unless he'd done so – except the duke of Lorraine,[2] who'd been with them since the start, before he'd jousted). The knight stayed waiting at the entrance till the lord of Longueval appeared at the far end of the lists and summoned him at the top of his voice to defend himself. The Knight of the Lion charged as fast as his horse could go.

'Love!' cried Sir Aubert de Longueval.

And may God protect them both from harm, for they were charging fast and close and straight and their lane was rather narrow! They were well aware of that, and as they charged they could hear the ladies praying for them earnestly! The Knight of the Lion charged valiantly indeed, and dealt his opponent such a blow that he smashed his lance to pieces. And good Aubert didn't shirk: he returned a blow that alarmed the lion, awed by the mighty crash!

'God and the holy cross help us!' said the queen. 'Bring us from this day with honour – this is a fearsome joust!'

The four maidens followed the knight on their palfreys – so pleasing and so fair they were that everyone gazed at them with delight – and escorted their protector back to his mark and attended him till he'd run his courses.

'Sir,' said Cardonelle, 'you rescued us from sorrow and woe; and in doing us the great honour of returning us to the court where we were born you have greatly enhanced your standing. I suggest you go now to the queen and take us with you, for henceforth you are of her household.'

'Your advice I shan't refuse!' said the count of Artois. 'Let's go!'

He quickly dismounted and helped the maidens from their palfreys and led them straightway to the queen, who was seated aloft in the stand. He greeted her most courteously and said:

---

[1] The cathedral at Amiens holds the supposed skull of John the Baptist.
[2] Ferry (or Frederick) III, duke of Lorraine 1251–1302. Sarrasin is not happy that the duke has circumvented the requirement that knights should joust before joining the ladies; he is about to comment also (twice) on the duke's lack of largesse at the festival.

'Your knight comes as called, lady, and will gladly do whatever you command. Armed as you see me, I am at your service.'

'A thousand thanks, sir,' she replied, 'for the honour you have done me. Go now and disarm and come and sit with us and watch the jousts. I've much to discuss with you. If you wish to take the maidens with you they'll go and serve you willingly: you've well deserved it. And may those who've caused them grief get *their* deserts!'

'I promise you truly,' said the count, 'they were fairly treated as prisoners and suffered no impropriety. And it's led to a happy outcome for the knight their captor. That's all there is to tell.'

The count was now disarmed. And the queen said: 'Their captor is not to be reproved. He didn't do it malevolently or as an offence to me. Let's forget the matter now, and see what this can be.' [2905]

Away to the right, towards the pavilions, they could see what looked like a chapel in the air, wondrously beautiful and gliding through the air towards the tents. Everyone was trying to work out what it was! It was the duke coming, imprisoned inside! Which duke? Tell me! It was the duke of Lorraine, placed there with the condition that he could in no way be released but by four maidens! He pressed on till he reached the lists, where his prison was broken open by the queen's fair maids. Then he was armed most richly: his caparisons, surcoat and fine mail sleeves[1] were without a doubt worth more than five hundred livres tournois.[2] It would have been a courteous deed and counted much to his credit if he'd proffered some initial gift to the poor.

An opponent was now sent to face him: a fine and most esteemed young knight, bright, well raised and courtly, loyal and endowed with all good qualities. It's only right that you know his name: it was the good Gautier de Fouilloy,[3] and I promise you in all honesty he's even worthier than I've said. Sir Gautier waited till the duke was armed. The day had turned as beautiful as God could ever make. When Sir Gautier saw the duke take up his lance and shield he waited no longer; he took hold of the necessary and thrust in his spurs of steel and charged the duke who was coming wholeheartedly to meet him. Good Gautier gripped his lance, strong and stout, and dealt the duke such a blow that he broke and shattered it. He rode on past and turned again, and smashed his next lance down to his fist. The duke, braced behind his shield, hit the lord of Fouilloy so hard that he almost made him tumble, and Gautier owes God fervent thanks that he didn't topple and lose his seat. With his third lance Gautier struck him on the shield and very nearly pierced

---

[1] '*bracieres*': the mail covering the arms.
[2] 'Tours pounds': the *livre tournois* was the most stable standard currency in thirteenth-century France.
[3] On the Somme, east of Amiens.

it, and both of them smashed utterly the shafts placed in their hands. I must limit what I say about the duke, because he contributed no largesse to the feast and placed himself among the ladies on the first day of jousting. But I think it was a case of forgetfulness, for he is courteous and generous. The counts of Clermont and Artois each gave two hundred pounds to the feast at the very outset, an act of courtesy and honour.

Two renowned young knights now came forward to joust. One was Raoul d'Estrées[1] by name, son of the Marshal of France, God preserve him! And the other was Gautier de Halluin,[2] a good and valiant knight of high standing. They charged full tilt to exchange mighty blows, and delivered them so well that I don't know which to credit more.

Elsewhere two others charged at full speed and played their parts well: Mahieu de Warlincourt[3] gave Mahieu de Vaudricourt[4] a blow in the chest from which he suffered long, a blow witnessed by more than five hundred, and there were many in the lists who thought it had killed him; but hurt though he was, he broke his own lance down to his fist. From far off the queen could see him slumped unconscious in his saddle and she was most alarmed; but it's all part and parcel of jousting.

And now you'd have seen knights jousting in five or six lanes. Jehan de Castenai[5] came mounted on a most handsome destrier – it's a shame he was the only one to have a fine horned saddle. To meet him spurred Sir Guillaume Donsele,[6] and both of them, as I saw myself, broke their second and third lances. [3017]

It was then that a beautiful blonde-haired maiden approached the queen, riding, I remember, a scrawny white nag without a saddle. And this maiden, let me tell you, fair and white-skinned, had a lance propped on her shoulder and was carrying a sword. And a wicked, foul-natured dwarf was riding behind her on another skinny nag, this one piebald, and at every step he was beating her about the shoulders and arms with a many-knotted scourge. Ahead of her rode her lover – it was he who was bringing her in this cruel fashion: he'd turned against her – for no other reason than her admiration of the queen's good knights! The wicked dwarf kept beating and abusing her as she trailed behind the knight, and you could hear the dwarf bawling, to humiliate her all the more:

---

[1] The young son of Raoul II d'Estrées, who had been made Marshal of France in 1270 while accompanying Louis IX on the Eighth Crusade. Estrées is just south of Douai.
[2] A Flemish knight: Halluin is north of Lille.
[3] He jousted earlier: above, pp. 21–2.
[4] Near the coast west of Abbeville.
[5] Unidentifiable.
[6] Unidentifiable.

'On you go, you filthy whore, you foul and dirty good-for-nothing!'

He wouldn't stop his flogging, and she wept and cried and wailed. Everyone who heard her felt dreadful pity and crowded round, while her lover rode before the queen but made no bow or greeting and stayed with helm on head. The maiden, most distressed, had to suffer and endure this cruelty, and her crying grew so intense that the queen looked down from the stand and saw the wicked dwarf – may he burn in Hell – beating and flogging the girl. She asked her what was going on and the girl told her the story.

'Ah, my lady! I'm suffering all this pain and shame because of you! A dozen weeks ago we were at home talking of one thing and another till the subject turned to knights, and my lover said he'd like to know if your knights were as valiant as was reputed far and wide. I said that in the whole wide world none finer could ever be found, and he was so outraged by this that without a moment's pause he put me straightway in the saddle! No damsel was ever so basely treated! Have pity on me, queen, for he's sworn an oath that I'll endure all this till one of your knights has jousted with him. I promise you, the first to challenge him will set me free!'

A knight promptly presented himself to the queen, finely armed and mounted and bearing a shield with a field of red and silver bars and a handsome stripe of vair with five gold shells; he was seated on a sorrel horse, a fine-looking steed indeed. The queen turned to him and asked him to go without delay and face the knight who was treating them with such disdain. He took a lance and told the knight he'd better prepare to defend himself, for he'd joust with him there and then. The knight took up his position, and his sweetheart trailed behind with the dwarf still doing his business, beating and lashing her about the arms and crying:

'On you go, you whore! It'll pain your heart to see Robert de Coupigny[1] topple this knight who's putting himself in danger! He's mad to take on such a valiant knight, and all because of you!'

Without a word of challenge they both thrust in their spurs of steel and set their horses charging. Together they came and exchanged tremendous blows, their lances shattering on their shields. And still the girl had to follow her lover, with the dwarf ever at her back, whipping and flogging every step of the way and yelling:

'You worthless slut, it's not going to turn out as you think, oh no! You'll be in a wretched state tomorrow – you'll go on foot and naked! You're getting no help today from what I can see!'

The knights rode swiftly on and returned to their lines. There was no holding back – both of them gave their mounts free rein once more: the girl's lover charged to meet the knight, Wautier de Hardecourt,[2] and Sir

---

[1] Probably Hersin-Coupigny, north of Arras.

[2] Hardecourt-aux-Bois, just to the north-west of Le Hem.

Wautier galloped down the lists and delivered such a well-aimed blow that he smashed his lance down to his fist; but the girl's lover missed with his, and the girl said, loud enough for her lover to hear:

'I haven't been wrong so far!'

And he knew exactly what she meant. Blazing with rage and frustration, he gripped once more the lance with which he'd missed the blow and said that if he failed to unhorse the knight he would forgive the girl all ill will and seek the queen's pardon. Again he launched into a fearsome charge. Sir Wautier, passionately eager to save the girl, saw him coming and gave his horse free rein and landed a mighty and awesome blow while his opponent, dauntless, tried to strike but missed: he'd aimed his lance too high. And so the girl was freed. She straightway took the sword that had been hanging from her neck and came to the knight who'd rescued her and presented it to him. He responded at once, saying:

'Dear girl, you may go now as you please: either with me or back to your sweetheart. But the dwarf who's given you such a hard time will stay with me: I'm taking him to court.'

So saying he went to disarm, while the one who'd dared to disparage the queen's good knights rode straight to Guinevere and, as soon as she was within his sight, said:

'My lady, I was a boastful fool. I presumed too much: I didn't think I'd ever find a man who could vanquish me – nor have I ever till now! My lady, I crave your mercy: pardon me your wrath and bid your knight return my sweetheart and my dwarf to me.'

'God forbid, sir,' said Kay, 'that you ever have the damsel back to make her ride saddleless and be flogged by your dwarf! But if you give your word and pledge as a true knight that she'll suffer no more after what's happened here, my lady the queen will do as she deems most fitting.'

He gave his promise and it was accepted, and all four – he and the dwarf and the girl and the knight who'd saved her from her suffering – were led from the lists on horseback, hand in hand. The queen and Kay were looking down from the windows of the stand, and Kay said this:

'Damsel, we saw your suffering all too clearly. Many today have witnessed how the one who claimed you were his sweetheart treated you: you may have been his beloved but he treated you like an enemy! But now he has no hold on you, so you're free to make your choice: either to go with him or to stay with my lady here, who'll keep you in most honourable state.'

The damsel, without hesitation or seeking anyone's advice, ran and embraced her lover and, in view of everyone, covered him with kisses. And this is what Kay the seneschal said:

'I like what I'm seeing! The worse you treat women, the more shame and humiliation you make them suffer, the more love they show you and the more you can have your way!'

The knight and the damsel took their leave of the queen, and she called the seneschal aside and told him:

'By God, Sir Kay, it'll soon be time to set the tables. Go and see to it – it's time to send word to the kitchen. We'll just see one or two more jousts and then we'll come to dine.' [3241]

The good knight Mahieu de Hyencourt[1] saw Willaume des Granges[2] coming to face him: he had to joust, and so he did. Bracing himself behind his shield he charged down the best part of the track, and des Granges charged likewise down his chosen line. One dealt a blow and the other paid back in kind; with their other lances, too, they exchanged such fierce and telling blows that they didn't have a shaft left whole. Many of the court said that Sir Mahieu de Hyencourt had excelled.

Two other knights took to a newly marked track and had such fine sport that they won the admiration of all. I assure you, without a word of a lie, you couldn't hope to see a finer joust – so Sir Kay declared. Sir Willaume de Careu[3] and Jehan de Bailleul[4] fixed their sights on one another and let their powerful chargers go, and truly, I tell you straight, they exchanged such blows that the pieces of their shattered lances flew more than forty feet skyward. The heralds were crying after them at the tops of their voices:

'Behold the forest-wasters!'[5]

Bailleul went in so close with his second lance that he smashed it to smithereens, and his opponent, I think, struck back and broke his, too. Both then took another and charged again full tilt without a word of challenge, pounding with their spurs of steel, and landed such blows that everyone thought thunder and lightning bolts were crashing on their heads! Both knights were left so stunned by the blows that they didn't know what had hit them. (The same was true for twenty others I could name!)

Next to joust came Mahieu de Roye, lord of Guerbigny,[6] against Jehan de Soiri,[7] who mounted a fine charge, straight and swift. Sir Mahieu, the moment he had his lance in hand, set off and went and dealt him a blow full in the chest that made him reel. In his next course he struck him high up on the throat, smashing his lance in the process. Nor did Soiri fail to land a blow: he broke his lance right down to his fist. On they rode,

---

[1] See the note about Muis d'Avaine, note 1, p. 31.
[2] An unidentifiable 'outsider'.
[3] Unidentifiable.
[4] This is John Balliol, later to be king of Scotland from 1292 to 1296. See note 1 above, p. 28.
[5] i.e. because trees will have to be felled in numbers to replace all the broken shafts!
[6] Mathieu I, lord of Roye and Guerbigny, south-east of Amiens.
[7] Unidentifiable, and written variously as *Soiri* and *Soisi*.

shields still set, and took two more fir-wood lances, stout and strong, and struck each other on their shields, smashing the shafts to pieces but riding on without losing their seats. It did those two young knights no harm at all: breaking their lances in such fine style earned them a deal of praise.

Next up was a knight who jousted well and with a will: I heard his name given as Jake du Bos.[1] But no discredit was due to his opponent, Sir Jehan de Fay,[2] who didn't miss with any of his three lances: he broke them all.

The queen now came down from the stand and made her way to the castle, while the heralds cried:

'All who wish to eat, come to court! None who comes will leave before he's dined and drunk amid the finest display ever seen at any queen's court. And the drawbridge won't be raised by rope or chain!'

Horns sounded to summon the water. Everyone washed and sat down to dine, and from all sides wine and food were served to every table. You'd have heard no romances or tales being told, only talk about deeds of arms and love. Then there was dancing which lasted almost without a pause till dawn. [3341]

The ladies and knights retired and slept a little. Then they heard mass and went to lace their helms – both wise moves!

Sir Gui de Saint-Pol[3] arrived on a great black destrier to face Gérard, lord of Sorel.[4] The queen was already in the stand and watched their joust most keenly. Sir Gui was first to charge, but Sir Gérard came to meet him fearlessly and with his stout lance dealt him a great blow on his shield. Sir Gui struck him back on the head of his leopard.[5] They reduced their lances to a load of stumps: of the six they bore not one remained whole, as was seen by many. Not that I care – it's not my loss!

Sir Gérard de Boubers[6] now came to joust against a fine, strong knight of great vigour, perfectly cut out for tourneying: his name, I tell you truly, was Jehan de Fignières.[7] Risking body and horse alike they charged full tilt and smashed their lances so awesomely that they earned a deal of praise.

---

[1] Unidentifiable.
[2] Just south of Le Hem.
[3] This is either Guy III, count of Saint-Pol (a county centred on Saint-Pol-sur-Ternoise, west of Arras), who was Robert of Artois's stepfather, or his son Guy IV.
[4] A few miles north-east of Le Hem. Wautier de Sorel, presumably a relation, jousted earlier: above, p. 29.
[5] i.e. the leopard emblazoned on his shield.
[6] Boubers-sur-Canche, west of Arras.
[7] He jousted earlier: above, p. 32.

Next up was Jehan de Barres.[1] Jehan de Couin[2] was ready to face him and charged to meet him; both were clutching stout lances, and they rode three courses without missing a blow.

Then you'd have seen two more knights come forward, ready to joust, and I know that, come what may, whatever might befall them, they'd go for each other unswervingly: Jehan de Bosquel[3] saw Alenard de Seninghem[4] coming, and, choosing the best line for his charge, spurred to meet him. Before they passed, Bosquel struck him on the top of his shield, snapping and breaking his lance; their horses would have paid dearly if they'd collided in the least, for Bosquel was intent on doing his utmost. With his second lance he dealt another mighty, all-out blow, but Alenard, undaunted, came right in and delivered a tremendous strike, committing every ounce of his strength. And with his third Bosquel charged full tilt, so close and straight that a collision was unavoidable. Jehan de Bosquel, God keep him, knew how to use a lance!

On another track two knights now charged, summoning from their steeds all the speed they could. Let me tell you their names: one was Gilles d'Oisy,[5] and the knight facing him was Jehan de la Tournelle.[6] They both dealt blows that smashed their lances into shards, then took two more and broke those likewise. With their third lances they met head on, and it finished with Jehan de la Tournelle having broken all three of his lances, never missing, and Gilles d'Oisy the same.

On a fine, broad track Sir Mikel Coupliau[7] was ready to joust if he could find a knight to face him. Sir Jehan d'Épagny[8] took his lance and charged to meet him, delivering a mighty, weighty blow and breaking his lance and then charging again. Three times he charged, and never missed or fell.

To a track furthest from the stand came Gérard d'Écaillon.[9] His opponent was told this, and the moment he heard he took his lance, handed to him by his nephew, Sollars de Morlaine. The uncle, Pierre de Morlaine,[10] confronted Gérard in splendid style, but Écaillon showed no sign of fearing him, and they charged without more ado, straight and swift and bold.

---

[1] Not possible to identify with certainty.
[2] South-west of Arras.
[3] The scribe uses four different spellings of the name; it may well be Bosquel, south of Amiens.
[4] South of Calais.
[5] North-east of Saint-Quentin.
[6] Villers-Tournelle, south of Amiens.
[7] Lord of Hulluch, north of Lens.
[8] North of Soissons.
[9] East of Douai, a close neighbour of Lallaing.
[10] He jousted earlier, p. 29.

Morlaine attacked with fearsome might, and left the ground strewn with the wreckage and stumps of all three of his lances.

Into the lists now rode the vidame of Picquigny,[1] with the lord of Saint-Mard,[2] Renaut by name, coming to face him. Both were bearing their lances high, boldly and in fine fashion; the vidame landed the first blow, and a daunting blow it was, but Renaut returned its equal to level matters.

'There's nothing to reproach in these two!' said the queen, and she wasn't wrong. 'The vidame's making a fine show, I'd say: his shield is braced quite perfectly, and he's set as firm as a rock, not budging an inch.'

They both came spurring fiercely, with a will, blood spurting from the flanks of the vidame's mount. He struck Sir Renaut close to the throat, so hard that he smashed his lance to pieces. With their third lances they thrust and struck so fearsomely that they soaked their shining hauberks with their bodies' blood. Not that this led to any discord: they were at peace when back in court.

Good Jehan de Harcourt[3] now charged to meet Adam de Cardonnoy.[4] They dealt each other blows that they keenly felt, then rode on past and returned to their marks, reset their shields and helms and thrust in their spurs once more. Then you'd have seen Cardonnoy mount a splendid charge indeed, and he struck Harcourt on the shield so hard that his lance couldn't take it and he shattered the shaft, while Harcourt struck him high on the head where he'd aimed, not wanting to clash lances.[5] You can well imagine the splintering din! And into the breaking of their third lances they put their all! Sir Kay expressed his approbation of their fine display in this joust.

Next to joust was Wautier d'Antoing,[6] against Anseau de Chevreuse.[7] I'm told they both broke all three lances, never missing.

After these two, Carbonnel[8] came forward to face the lord of Olhain.[9] The day was clear and fine, the sun in splendour shining on all the gold and blue and silver of the arms. Sir Kay was watching from the wall to

---

[1] Jehan, lord of Picquigny (north-west of Amiens) was vidame of Amiens. The vidame, derived from the Latin *vicedominus*, was a secular official appointed by a bishop to act as protector and to exercise the bishop's temporal authority.
[2] Near Roye, south of Le Hem.
[3] Later to be Marshal of France; Harcourt is in Normandy, south-west of Rouen.
[4] Near Roye, south of Le Hem.
[5] Literally 'strike the fist-guard'.
[6] Lord of Bellonne, between Arras and Douai.
[7] A knight from the Île de France who was later to become Marshal of Sicily; he was killed fighting the Flemish at the battle of Mons-en-Pévèle in 1304 while carrying the royal battle standard, the *Oriflamme*.
[8] Probably Pierre Carbonnel, from what is now called Villers-Carbonnel, just south of Le Hem.
[9] Jehan d'Olhain. Olhain is west of Lens.

see how each knight fared. Carbonnel sprang from his mark and charged full tilt down the track, and Olhain came to meet him with all the speed he could summon from his mount. Carbonnel hit him on the top of his shield, but his opponent's blow smashed his. They passed at speed and returned without a pause, and Carbonnel – God grant him honour! – broke three lances in no time at all. It was about the middle of the day when Carbonnel left the lists.

Then Gieffroy de Milly[1] jousted with a fine, strong, stout and vigorous knight named Sir Waléran de Luxembourg,[2] but we don't know what happened in their meeting.

Then two more came and I saw them joust well and mightily, and it gives me pleasure to record what I saw and know for sure. Sir Mahieu d'Épagny[3] and Gossuin de Saint-Aubin[4] met and exchanged colossal blows, truly. It's only right to record the good and draw a veil over the bad, and I tell you, those two young knights jousted with might and main quite splendidly, right before the wall close to the ladies, which is where I was.

And now came Dreux de Roye,[5] with Henri de Soiri[6] facing him. I remember well how the queen prayed for them wholeheartedly, for both these knights were very young: she prayed to God to keep them safe. Sir Dreux was on one side towards the castle, and with shield braced fast and boldly in place he spurred towards Henri de Soiri who charged to meet him with all the speed he could summon. They smashed each other's shield and galloped on past. I don't know for sure what happened with their next lances, but Sir Dreux shattered his third lance utterly, earning much admiration from the queen, and the ladies around her hoped that God would grant him honour for he was the son of a worthy knight.

Sir Jehan de Brimeux[7] charged down the lists full tilt to meet Robert de Foucaucourt,[8] who sprang forward to meet him likewise, bearing shield and lance in handsome style. They charged as fast as their horses could go: they both meant business! Robert jousted splendidly, as did the lord of Brimeux.

---

[1] Probably Milly-sur-Thérain just north of Beauvais.
[2] A prominent figure in *The Tournament at Chauvency*, he was the second son of Henry V, count of Luxembourg.
[3] Presumably related to Jehan d'Épagny, above, p. 43.
[4] The son of Gossuin III of Saint-Aubin, a fief dependant on the castellany of Douai. He was the liegeman of Count Robert of Artois, but was later, as Gossuin IV, to side with the count of Flanders against him.
[5] The sixth son of Mahieu de Roye, who jousted earlier, above, p. 41. Roye is just south of Le Hem.
[6] Like Jehan de Soiri (above, p. 41), to whom he is presumably related, this 'outsider' is unidentifiable.
[7] Near the coast, west of Arras.
[8] Presumably related to Pierard de Foucaucourt, above, p. 28.

Just a brief moment after them another entered the lists, Adam de Blémur[1] by name. Enguerran de Boves[2] came to meet him, passionately eager to win honour. Forward he charged, thoroughly fired, helm on head and shield braced as if he and the shield were one and he'd been born so; he looked the part indeed! He let his destrier feel his spurs and they came to meet, I promise you, in so close a clash that Enguerran smashed his lance to pieces; and his opponent didn't miss: he delivered a mighty, ferocious blow – I saw it. Before they'd run their courses they'd earned the admiration of the ladies for breaking their lances in such fine style.

Then up came Manicourt the Younger,[3] who entered the lists with shield round neck and lance in hand, and his opponent, Jehan de Cautens,[4] emerged at the other end to face him. Manicourt wouldn't deign to wait till he was ready! A thousand present can vouch for that, for before Jehan could even set his lance in place, Manicourt was off! But Jehan charged to meet him fearlessly and well. And when the moment came to deliver their blows one of them broke his lance but the other missed: Manicourt aimed too high and struck a foul blow in the eyes – but it could have paid off: it's one of the places a lance might be broken, and I've heard the ploy commended. But Manicourt did break his other lances, and the queen – God grant her honour! – praised him highly for it.

Next up was the Uncle of Friaucourt,[5] confronting Adam Gourlé.[6] They dealt each other mighty blows, for they both were full of vigour and the Uncle was big and strong. He took a stout lance and gave Gourlé such a blow in the teeth that he broke it – yet still, I promise you, Gourlé didn't buckle or shift an inch; rather, he did the business with his lance and dealt the Uncle such a great and wild and weighty blow that he struggled to withstand it. And if you'd seen their third joust it was something to behold! They dealt each other battering blows as if with clubs or crowbars! So furiously did they strike that they and both their horses suffered.

Then Sir Pierre de Hodenc[7] set out down a good, fine track to face Jehan au Bois-Guillaume.[8] Both were ready with shield and helm, and they charged with their first lances and delivered blows that smashed them down to their fists. Sir Pierre de Hodenc earned much praise from this joust: in one quarter I heard it said that he was one of the best. But it's

---

[1] North of Paris.
[2] South-east of Amiens.
[3] i.e. a younger son of the house of Manicourt, near Nesle, south of Le Hem.
[4] An unidentifiable 'outsider'.
[5] Friaucourt is near the coast west of Abbeville. The identity of 'the Uncle' is unclear.
[6] Not possible to identify with certainty.
[7] Near Beauvais.
[8] A Norman knight, from Rouen.

not possible to give due credit to every single one of the one hundred and eighty jousts that took place.

Not that I'm exaggerating in the case of Hoteri.¹ He came to face a knight, I well recall, who cut a brave and strapping figure indeed: in the days of regular tournaments he used to win all the horses! Hoteri saw this Jehan de Gannes² coming, shield braced, and thrust in his spurs straightway, and they dealt each other fierce and terrible blows upon their shields: they performed and jousted splendidly. But I'm not going to carry on about exactly what befell each of them.

The lord of Cayeux³ now faced the lord of Cramaille.⁴ The mail of their hauberks was unbreachable, which was just as well, for Sir Kay ordered a herald to proclaim that the forests were at risk!⁵ The herald roared at once:

'Here come the forest-ravagers! They'll turn the woods to wastes!'

The lord of Cayeux sprang from his mark impressively, and charged to meet his opponent on a superb black destrier. Both knights went full tilt, but bore their lances so high that both of them missed, much to their dismay. With their next charge they did their best to keep a close, straight line, and this time held their lances so firm that the points clashed full on and the shafts shattered down to their fists without either of them striking helm or shield. With their third lances they missed again, and were mortified – their wives were with the queen, watching in the stand. But you can't win them all!⁶ There's many a mishap in tourneying! God keep all our friends from coming unstuck! [3711]

Sir Aubert de Longueval could see that the knights from those parts⁷ were being given a hard time. He swiftly braced a shield and swore by God and all the saints that as long as he was in one piece he'd take on anyone, no matter whom. He set himself at the end of the lists and drew all attention to him. From far off at the other end he saw a knight approaching – a fine, courageous, worthy knight named Wautier d'Antoing.⁸ Sir Aubert rode full tilt to meet him, of that you may be sure, and I promise you they met so fast and close and boldly that their charge was

---

¹ Unidentifiable.
² North-east of Beauvais.
³ Probably Cayeux-sur-Mer on the coast, west of Abbeville, making him the husband of the lady of Cayeux mentioned earlier, p. 6 – hence the remark which follows shortly about his wife being 'with the queen, watching in the stand'.
⁴ South of Soissons.
⁵ See note 5, above, p. 41.
⁶ Literally 'no one plays who doesn't fall' – i.e. you can't compete and never lose.
⁷ '*lour gent*': 'their men' – i.e. knights from the surrounding lands competing against 'outsiders' from further afield.
⁸ He had jousted earlier, above, p. 44.

much acclaimed. Both smashed their lances down to their fists, creating such a shattering din that everyone watching, great and small, thought the castle's timber hall had fallen in! But neither of them lost his seat.

'Ah, sweet mother of God, help us!' said the queen. 'Protect my lord and brother[1] this day, and guard the knight who jousts against him, too – let no harm befall them!'

They rode back smartly to their marks and as soon as they were sorted they set their shields in place once more and charged to strike again – and they were both well pleased with the speed their horses summoned. They dealt each other blows that left one of them rather more shaken than he'd have wished. And with their third lances they met so close that they smashed them both – and felt the points right close to their flesh, for neither of them held back but struck with all his force. Many stopped watching the other jousts to fix their eyes on theirs. They'd met at such close quarters that they both felt the effects: as Sir Aubert passed they crashed together, and the impact sorely hurt both of them. Be sure of this, I promise you: their joust was highly praised. And let me tell you, Sir Aubert de Longueval had dislocated his shoulder, but despite the pain he made no show of it till that night.

'Lady,' Kay said to the queen, 'I'd say your brother had the better of that joust, and I don't think his horse has suffered harm.'

'I tell you, Kay, you'd have been a dead man if you'd said otherwise! Curse the hour you became so ill-natured!' [3777]

Aigre[2] now jousted against Guillaume de Lières.[3] They both aimed high and landed blows that broke their lances, I believe.

Elsewhere Sir Jehan de Chaulnes[4] faced a powerful knight by the name of Guy de Neuville:[5] they spurred their horses to their utmost speed and dealt each other blows that sent chunks of their shattered lances flying skyward.

Good Jehan de Pierremont[6] didn't dally but came forward with a will; and with no mean horse beneath him he went full tilt to meet Raoul d'Estrées[7] who was charging nobly and with firm intent. I'll come straight to the point: Jehan de Pierremont gave him a blow that almost knocked him senseless, but Raoul didn't spare him – he smashed through his shield as if

---

[1] As noted previously, 'Guinevere' is Aubert's sister. She probably refers to him as her 'lord' because she is not yet married.
[2] An unidentifiable knight who jousted earlier, above, p. 28.
[3] West of Béthune.
[4] See above, p. 32.
[5] He appeared earlier, above, p. 23.
[6] South-west of Béthune.
[7] Above, p. 38.

it had been the shell of a snail. Anyone who jousts half-heartedly is mad, and these two landed such whole-hearted blows that I don't know which to credit more.

I saw two others charging now, as fast as their horses could bear them. One of them, I know for sure, meant to do his duty, whatever might befall him: Jehan de Jumel[1] was armed to perfection, wanting nothing, and would, I'm sure, not be leaving his horse without breaking a lance. And he could boast that he was jousting against a fine young knight whose name I shan't omit: it was Guillaume de Heule.[2] Both laid their bodies and their horses on the line, and rightly so. I tell you, Jumel charged unswervingly, and their horses were on the brink of death unless one of them pulled back! Jumel struck him full on, and such a blow it was that he hurt both knight and mount, I do believe. Not that de Heule lacked courage: he dealt Jumel a blow in return that brought blood gushing from his teeth. But Jehan de Jumel never missed: he smashed all his lances to pieces on de Heule.

Then I saw Sir Gui du Plessier,[3] raring to go, mounted on a swift and powerful destrier, lance gripped ready and shield in place; he spurred in fine style down a track some way from the stand, charging to meet Jehan de Long,[4] a knight from over towards Ponthieu. But he found him a pretty tough customer. If you dole stuff out you must expect to be repaid, and when Sir Gui gave him an awesome blow, mighty, heavy and dangerous, Long fully accepted it and thought it only right and proper to return the compliment! Both of them were superbly mounted and charged a second time without delay. Sir Gui, holding nothing back, came at him fast and furiously and hit him so hard that he made his horse stagger and his lance flew into pieces fully six feet in the air. Jehan de Long was anguished, mortified that he'd twice now failed to strike. With his third lance he struck him high up on the top part of his shield, cracking and smashing it; Sir Gui struck higher, with a blow to the throat that almost knocked him senseless, but Long's blow had gone clean through his shield and landed painfully in his ribs.

After them I saw two others charge and they jousted well – I saw it for myself: Sir Enguerran de Rogy[5] and Pierre the Horrible.[6] Their joust added two more lances to the court's tally[7] only, and I'll tell you who broke them

---

[1] Above, p. 29.
[2] In Flanders, near Courtrai.
[3] Lord of what is now Le Plessis-Brion, near Compiègne.
[4] South-east of Abbeville.
[5] South of Amiens.
[6] Pierre de Fampoux, east of Arras, who was later, in 1286, recorded as being a judge in Arras.
[7] Literally 'for the insiders', Rogy being a knight from the 'home' region.

– it was the lord of Rogy. His opponent meanwhile was red with shame, having had so little success. But then again, you can't win them all![1] And on any given day many of those who fail are worthy and valiant men indeed – it's the nature of the game.

Up now came two more knights: on a track that was seeing plenty of action Sir Ernoul de Fosseux[2] came to face Bernard du Plaissier.[3] They both charged with resolve and vigour, with all the speed they could summon, smashing their shields and shattering their lances to earn much applause from the ladies. [3894]

The count of Artois was watching from above with the ladies in the stand, and saw knights, fully armed, coming in great numbers to joust for the outsiders against the knights of the court. Without another word he hurried away and armed and mounted and rode into the lists – and since he was one of the court he stayed at the castle end. He was nobly mounted on a swift and powerful destrier and superbly, impeccably armed. He went and asked the queen's permission to joust again if it pleased her; she gladly gave him leave, but said that if he would forgo it and come and take his ease with her she would be most grateful and it would make her very happy to have him avoid the potential danger. The count said no more: he rode, lance in hand, helmet laced and shield firm-braced against his chest, and charged from the very edge of the lists to face Pierre de Bauffremont,[4] who came to meet him boldly, I'd say. They met each other with lance-blows full in the face. No one should resent my recording deeds that are worthy of note, but malicious, slanderous tongues will never approve; and let me tell you, if you stick around for the next ten years you'll see the count strive constantly to crush the envious – he's determined. Ah, God! When these days shall we see the envious all die a miserable death?

'Soon!' So said the maid Forteche. 'For my lord the count of Artois is so full of largesse and courtesy, of loyalty and integrity, and so devoted to chivalry, that wherever he goes, be it for tournament or war, he'll find companions aplenty; he never tires of doing good deeds and never will. He fulfils his duty admirably. Sarrasin, I pray you as you love me and hold me dear, speak well of all men, and if any – no matter how lowly a knight – does something that's best kept quiet and hidden, record the good and omit the bad. All good, true knights will love and cherish you for it.'

---

[1] The same proverbial phrase is used as previously: '*nus ne jue qui ne kiet*'. See note 6 above, p. 47.
[2] West of Arras.
[3] Le Plessier-Rozainvillers, south-east of Amiens; he is presumably related to Dreux, above, p. 28.
[4] Beaufremont, south-west of Nancy; Pierre was lord of Removille, close by; he appears also in the tournament at Chauvency.

'Look there! That man cuts an impressive figure!' said Gilles de Neuville. 'A fine figure indeed!'

The count set his shield in place once more – he knew what he was about. Bauffremont was heading his way like fury. The count, from the moment he charged, levelled his lance at his teeth. But Bauffremont was burning to do the business and didn't spare the count – he let him have it full on the shield. In all my life I never saw a knight take so great a blow and not move an inch; instead the count returned a tremendous blow that hit home right in the teeth, a blow that earned the praise of many. On they rode, their lances broken. They stunned each other with their third lances; they made them bend and shatter and sent their helmets flying from their heads.

'I pray to God to keep our loved ones from misfortune!' said the queen. [3979]

'Lady,' said Forteche, 'I think the lord of Bazentin's in luck! He should joust with the Landgrave[1] who's coming this way: he deserves to face a worthy knight, truly. Send word to them – see if they're willing.'

'I've no objection,' the queen replied. 'Let's do so.'

She sent all her barons to spread the word that the lord of Raineval[2] and Forteche agreed that those two should joust together. They were both informed of this, and Bazentin returned his thanks to the queen for the honour she had paid him.

'The Landgrave's a great lord indeed,' he said, 'and comes from a country, I've heard men say, that's the birthplace of fine jousters!'

The trumpets sounded two blasts and the lists were cleared, and I tell you truly, the tourney-ground was long and wide. As four blasts rang out they went to find Huart de Bazentin, who was arming in a lovely garden. He came out right before the gate, with shield grandly borne and braced and spurring his horse in handsome style. He launched into a gallop down the lists to test that all was well. The queen, so good and gracious, was seated above; with her was a fair company of ladies and damsels, most pleasing, comely and beautiful, watching from the windows of the stands. Sir Kay the seneschal, injured in his own joust, had set the lists in fine order, and he and others led Sir Huart to his position before the castle gate. The Landgrave now made a dashing ride down the lists and back again. Then the lord of Bazentin gripped his lance and took to the track like the experienced jouster that he was; and as soon as he saw him move, the Landgrave thrust in his spurs of steel and charged. In all truth, the lord of Bazentin rode – as five hundred and twenty clearly witnessed – so fast and straight and true, spurring so magnificently, that it was a joy to behold, and

---

[1] A German prince, never more precisely identified by Sarrasin.
[2] Above, p. 19.

the Landgrave came to meet him in German fashion. The one who bore the fleurs-de-lis[1] was roaring his battle-cry:

'Montauban!'

To see him was a true delight as he charged so straight and swift – and down the very centre of the track, so exactly that no one could have said which half on either side was greater. When the moment came they struck each other on their painted shields, landing colossal, mighty blows. It was a perilous clash, a tough and awesome joust. Both rode back and set their shields in order, then charged once more with all the speed they could summon from their mounts. Some of those watching were aghast: they were holding so straight a line that had it been a narrow track they'd have collided unavoidably. The heralds' roars of 'Landgrave!' and 'Montauban!' were so loud that no one at Le Hem could make himself heard! There was a mighty din indeed. Huart, determined to excel, smashed all three of his lances into countless bits; he bore himself so splendidly that everyone who saw him showered praise. With their third lances they charged like fury, and their shields when their lances struck stood no more chance of surviving than straws in a fire. They dealt each other blows that made them groan, either out loud or under their breath, but no one heard them. But I can tell you this for sure: the bearer of the silver shield[2] would have jousted very differently had it not been for certain people who'd begged him at the outset – I saw this, and know it to be true – to do his utmost not to collide, and he'd said:

'By the faith I owe my beloved, if my opponent avoids it I shall, too: I won't be forced to pull out because of a crash.'

He made this promise and he kept it, having heard that it was the queen's wish, too; so he refrained from colliding, but feared it might be counted against him. Before the ladies they saluted one another and then rode off, while the ladies gave thanks to God on high that neither had been injured. [4099]

Two others took their places on the track they'd left: Sir Henri de Soiri[3] and Jehan de Neuville[4] came forward, long, stout lances in hand, and charged without another word. Lord of no one, Iron-stare,[5] dealt Soiri a blow that dismayed some of those watching. Soiri struck him back – he did what he'd come to do at Le Hem! – but Iron-stare broke his lance so impressively that he earned the ladies' acclaim, the applause being led by

---

[1] Bazentin's shield was blue with silver fleurs-de-lis.
[2] See previous note.
[3] Above, p. 45.
[4] Another of the Neuvilles competing at Le Hem.
[5] '*Ex-de-fer*', literally 'Eyes of Iron', is evidently the sobriquet of Jehan de Neuville, who is 'lord of no one' because he is a landless younger son.

Forteche, whose view that he could do no wrong can be well trusted – let no one say otherwise! He is brave, liberal and loyal, and I've yet to see any of the Neuvilles who compare. Prowess and Largesse bathe ever-present in his heart. By Saint Stephen the Martyr, if I were king of France, he would wear the cross with me to where Christ was crucified.[1] King of France, put your faith in him – if you can engage him in your household: it would be a wise and worthy move!

When Iron-stare had finished jousting, Sir Enguerran de Mametz[2] entered the lists, for sure; Sir Jehan de Douai[3] charged full tilt to meet him, and boldly, swiftly, fiercely aimed to give it him in the teeth. What happened then was witnessed by many: Douai missed his blow, but so did Sir Enguerran, to the consternation of all the folk who'd come from Mametz.[4] In his next charge Enguerran did as well as can be if you fail to break your lance, but earned harsh deprecation from his neighbours. With his third charge he went like fury, and this time smashed his lance down to his fist.

With shield firm-braced, into the lists rode Jehan de Dompierre et Montel[5] to face Tolart du Haitiel,[6] a knight of good standing. They closed with all the speed they could summon from their mounts and broke their lances to much applause. And Jehan de Dompierre acted in most noble-hearted fashion, sending his young opponent a palfrey; such a handsome gesture should not be passed over but reported far and wide.

Then you'd have seen Sir Henri de Soiri come swiftly to face a fine jouster who met him with a mighty blow; Pierre de Montaigu[7] it was, who scored well, I've heard: he well and truly shattered all three of his lances.

And I can testify, for I saw it myself, that Mathieu de Vic[8] rode boldly into the lists to face Bretoul de Houdancourt.[9] They charged full tilt, and Mathieu[10] dealt him a blow to the top of his shield that split and broke it and smashed his lance to pieces. But his opponent didn't miss – he broke his

---

[1] i.e. accompany him on a pilgrimage/crusade to the Holy Land.
[2] Just to the north-west of Le Hem, a close neighbour of Bazentin and Longueval.
[3] It's obvious where he's from, but his identity is uncertain.
[4] Mametz being only a few miles from Le Hem, Enguerran's neighbours are there in numbers.
[5] Dompierre is just a mile or two south of Le Hem; his other fief, Montel, is a little further south, near Chaulnes.
[6] An unidentifiable 'outsider'.
[7] Probably the son of Garin (below, p. 58), lord of Montaigu in Auvergne.
[8] Vic-sur-Aisne, between Soissons and Compiègne.
[9] Not possible to identify with certainty.
[10] An unresolved rhyme reveals an accidental omission here, and it's unclear which of the two knights delivers this blow. The flow of sentences suggests, however, that it's Mathieu.

own lance, too, and then returned [for a second charge, in which Mathieu][1] broke his lance down to his fist. He rode on past, shield firm in place, and drew rein before the gate, where Carbonnel arrived bringing a strong lance, finely wrought; Turel[2] passed it to him and Sir Mathieu took it, and his horse sprang forward the moment it felt his spurs. With this lance he dealt a colossal blow that his opponent properly felt: it nearly knocked him senseless. At this their joust concluded.

Sir Gautier de Fouilloy[3] took to the lists on the side by the gate and charged to meet his opponent, a young knight of good repute named Hue de Halluin.[4] They came together with awesome force and their lances crumbled like bark; their jousts were much praised: they'd not missed a blow and they'd kept their seats. [4207]

On another track, long and broad, came the count of Clermont,[5] shield round neck and helm on head.

'God and all His saints keep you from harm!' said the queen, who couldn't help herself: she cared deeply for both knights and commended them to the Holy Spirit. I find as I read the notes I took, and I've heard it said by others, that no knight in the whole proceedings made as fine a showing as the count. I know for sure that the one who came to face him at the other end was called Sir Erart de Brienne.[6] The count set his horse in motion, then let go the reins and thrust his spurs of steel. The other charged at once, and boldly, but the count struck him so fierce a blow that he made him reel and his lance flew into pieces. They passed at speed. Then the count, shield set firm in place, rode before the queen and saluted and bowed to her; she saluted him in return, and the count found himself rewarded with bows of the head from the whole gathering of ladies, and damsels too, acknowledging him most graciously. He gazed at them all and said:

'God repay your courtesy, ladies! May great honour come your way, and let no misfortune cross your path!'

And he turned about and prepared to charge again, spurring his horse to its utmost speed. His opponent charged at once to meet him, and they exchanged tremendous, fearsome blows, bending and shattering their shafts into so many pieces that the longest measured barely a foot. As the count

---

[1] There is another missing line, in which the subject must have returned to Mathieu.
[2] Presumably an attendant.
[3] He jousted earlier: above, p. 37.
[4] Brother of Gautier, above, p. 38.
[5] The king's brother who appeared above, pp. 26–7.
[6] Impossible to identify with certainty.

rode back the queen turned to him at the windows of the stand and called to him to go and disarm, and he did so. [4260]

Forward now spurred two more knights ready to joust. I don't mind taking the trouble to record their names: one of them, I'm told, was Gaucher d'Autrêches[1] and the other was Jehan de Fignières.[2] They faced each other with big, stout lances, and laying their lives and limbs on the line – their horses', too – they charged like valiant knights indeed. A fine showing it was, and they broke their lances impressively, earning the ladies' admiration.

Without more ado the knight with the chequered shield, heir and lord of Hangest,[3] took to the lists and had great good fortune in his joust against Robert de Wavrin,[4] who mounted a fine charge. Hangest did the business and broke all his lances before he withdrew.

From the other side came a superbly mounted knight from Auvergne. He charged against Robert Burnel,[5] who came to meet him boldly.

And Buridan de Walincourt[6] came to the head of a track, lance in hand, and Nicole des Amoises[7] appeared in the distance and charged to meet him. And it nearly cost him, for Buridan de Walincourt gave him a hard time with all three of his lances, breaking them in his ribs.

Before he'd even removed his helm, two others took to a track on the far side of the lists: Jehan de Pierremont[8] confronting Henri the Bastard.[9] Intent on striking in the teeth with all his force Jehan gave him a blow that almost stunned him, but the Bastard struck back as he passed. With his next lance Jehan de Pierremont aimed good and high and broke it while the Bastard missed. With the third he caught him high on the top of his shield with a force that unseated him, and the Bastard should thank God he came to no harm, for Sir Jehan had been charging at breakneck speed, and the Bastard, unless I'm much mistaken, had been going bravely, too!

---

[1] Between Soissons and Compiègne.
[2] Above, pp. 32 and 42.
[3] See above, p. 22.
[4] Lord of Saint-Venant, north of Béthune. He was later to become Chamberlain of Flanders and governor of Guyenne.
[5] Unidentifiable.
[6] Eldest son of the lord of Walincourt, south-east of Cambrai.
[7] Unidentifiable.
[8] Above, p. 48.
[9] '*Henri li Bascle*' of Meudon, south-west of Paris, a French knight known to have joined Louis IX's crusade.

Aubert de Hangest[1] came in noble style to joust with Gaucher de Châtillon[2] – God keep him from harm and misfortune – who laid himself and his mount on the line as he charged all-out, full tilt. But Sir Aubert wouldn't deign to be daunted. They went for each other in no mean fashion: one gave a blow and the other repaid it in full! I've yet to see a finer joust. And Sir Kay cried out to all within earshot, saying that in this world there are two things at which apprentices are masters![3] I can't report how many lances they broke, as dusk was setting in, but they jousted well – indeed faultlessly: they earned the acclaim of all. [4335]

Everything now was hotting up! They were jousting now on more than six lanes; knights of the court and outsiders were charging so thick and fast that I couldn't record all the names! From the court's side a young knight of good repute came riding fully armed: Jehan de Hargicourt[4] it was, facing Jehan de Lindebeuf.[5] In two jousts in which he engaged that day he broke six lances.[6]

Anyone still keen to joust was busy in the lists! You'd have seen Boisset[7] charge with Wautier de Heule[8] against him, but I don't know which of them came off worse.

Then up came Louis de Beaujeu,[9] and by all God's saints I don't believe anyone jousted better at Le Hem. Forward he rode, spurring a well-built destrier, and charged to meet one of the outsiders, Robert de Wavrin;[10] they exchanged such blows with the heads of their lances that Sir Louis's left hand was broken and ligaments torn. Had it not been for this injury his joust would have been much acclaimed. But he said:

'May Our Lord be praised for whatever He chooses to send me.'

---

[1] Aubert V, lord of Genlis, a fief south of Saint-Quentin.
[2] This is probably Gaucher V (1249–1329), lord of Châtillon-sur-Marne, count of Porcien, later to be Constable of Champagne and then Constable of France from 1302 until his death.
[3] Love and combat. Kay's comment may be specifically meant as praise for Aubert (a local!): Aubert V was only in his mid-teens, but Gaucher, if it is indeed Gaucher V, was nearly 30.
[4] A few miles east of Le Hem.
[5] A Norman knight: Lindebeuf is south-west of Dieppe.
[6] Literally 'three fewer than nine' (Sarrasin needed '*neuf*' to rhyme with '*Lindebeuf*'!). Six is an impressive score, meaning that he broke his lance in every charge, as it's clear throughout that the format is to run three courses per joust.
[7] Above, pp. 22–3.
[8] Presumably related to Guillaume, above, p. 49.
[9] Either Louis de Beaujeu, lord of Montferrand, or his son Louis II.
[10] Above, p. 55.

Then Jehan de Vilers[1] headed straight and swift, thrusting with his spurs of steel to meet Guillaume de Ghistelles.[2] He dealt him a blow that smashed his lance to pieces, and broke and shattered his next lance, too, and with his third he charged all-out.

'God protect so young a knight!' said the ladies lined along the wall. 'He's jousted hard and well, and Ghistelles was a fine opponent.'

Then Dreux de Salives[3] came to joust against Boursaut de Mequelines,[4] who surged forth on a fine destrier. Without a word of challenge they charged, and I well remember how they landed blows on each other's shield that dashed and smashed and shattered them.

Guillaume de Locres[5] came to face Jehan de Soiri,[6] and I saw them exchange mighty, fearsome blows; de Locres came out of it very well, breaking three lances in a row.

Then Boisset[7] promptly took to the lists with Sir Gautier de Halluin[8] facing him. Bright sparks they sent leaping from their iron and steel: it was a fine joust indeed and should not go unrecorded.

After them two young knights met, one named Jehan de Francières:[9] of high repute he is, a fine and brave and valiant knight, and he sprang forward on a destrier to joust against Rogier d'Englume.[10] It was almost time to light torches now, for night was fast approaching. Sir Jehan de Francières spurred his destrier and struck d'Englume so hard that he tottered and lost his seat.

'Ah, sweet Mother of God, help us!' cried his men. 'Save us from dishonour this day!'

Jehan de Francières broke his second and his third lance, too, and the queen and all her entourage judged that he'd jousted splendidly.

With darkness now descending, Pierre de Hodenc[11] spurred his destrier to meet Boissart de Reninge,[12] but it was late and I don't know how they fared.

---

[1] Difficult to identify: there are many place-names beginning 'Villers' in north-east France.
[2] A Flemish knight: Ghistelles ('*Gistele*') is just south of Ostend.
[3] A knight from Burgundy: Salives is just north of Dijon.
[4] Unidentifiable with any certainty; possibly Mechelen, north of Brussels?
[5] Guillaume III of Béthune, lord of Locres in Flanders, south-west of Ypres.
[6] Above, p. 41.
[7] Above, pp. 22–3 and 56.
[8] Above, p. 38.
[9] North-west of Compiègne.
[10] An unidentifiable 'outsider'.
[11] Above, p. 46.
[12] A Flemish knight: Reninge is north of Ypres.

Daulés de Wavignies[1] took on Enguerran de Goeulzin;[2] they gave each other blows that shattered their lances, both together, and of their three lances, I believe, they hadn't one left whole.

Night was falling quickly, so everyone went at it as fast as they could! The lord of Moreuil,[3] shield-straps firmly braced, charged on a magnificent destrier to meet Simon de Lalaing,[4] and no one should feel disdain about jousting with that young knight. Simon de Lalaing let his mount go; he was handsomely armed and cut a fine figure, bearing his lance and shield in splendid style, and they both performed so well that I don't know whom to credit more. I heard all three of their courses highly praised, and so resounding were their clashes that it sounded as if the stand had been demolished!

Bridous de Baillet[5] went galloping down the lists to meet Robert d'Englos,[6] and struck him high up on the helm to bring horse and knight together crashing in a heap.

Then you'd have seen jousts start everywhere, right across the lists. My lord the count of Clermont, most noble and courtly, and my lord the count of Artois now came to the queen, who was still seated above in the stand, so immersed in watching the jousts that at first she was unaware; then she saw them kneeling before her, and they said:

'Lady, we've come to escort you hence, if you've no objection.'

She rose and greeted them and said: 'I'm at your command, good sirs: it's time to go to court.'

Kay the seneschal hurried off and had so many torches lit that it seemed as if the castle and the tourney-ground alike were all ablaze. You'd have seen people following the queen from all directions. But I tell you truly, even after the queen had gone there were more than twenty jousts that carried on – I can't record them all! But in the torchlight I saw Garin de Montaigu[7] come to joust, and had he jousted with a sharpened head he'd have wounded Robert Burnel[8] with the blow he struck him but, thanks be to God, he came to no harm. [4489]

Meanwhile the queen had left the stand and gone to her chambers to make ready; she was quickly back and the trumpet summoned the water for the washing of hands. The queen didn't require a grand paved

---

[1] North-east of Beauvais.
[2] South of Douai.
[3] This appears in the MS as the unidentifiable 'Mareuil'; I suspect this is Bernard de Moreuil, introduced above (pp. 29–30) as 'the lord of Moreuil'.
[4] '*Monart de Laleng*': see above, p. 23.
[5] Unidentifiable.
[6] Just west of Lille.
[7] Lord of Montaigu in Auvergne, probably the father of Pierre, above, p. 53.
[8] Above, p. 55.

hall for dining: she went and sat where she saw the greatest gathering of knights. Then the food was served to the tables.

The queen revelled in the company she had, but then, much to everyone's puzzlement, became quite lost in thought. Some began to whisper about this but no one dared to speak to her. Absorbed she was for at least the time it would take to walk a league, and all the while, in one of her hands, she was holding a sharp little knife. But in this reverie she was laughing and showing every sign of happiness, much to the relief and cheer of all those watching, who thought that since she was laughing there couldn't be much wrong. Then the count of Clermont and my lord of Artois kindly and politely said:

'Lady, you've eaten little...' [4519]

[At this point the final folio of the manuscript has been torn from top to bottom so that only odd words and fragments of words survive of two of the three columns. So little remains that it is impossible to reconstruct the missing passage, but a tentative suggestion, based on a handful of significant words, is that key elements were: The queen wishes they could see yet more jousting; Sir Kay replies that she could return to the stand for there are still knights jousting in pairs in the torchlight; they rise from the tables and dancing begins; next morning, after everyone has slept, a prize is given to the knight who has jousted best.]

[4600] ... Sarrasin in this little book has recorded the jousts he witnessed, awesome jousts indeed, and set down the adventures you've heard – the splendid adventures of the knights and maidens and the good and renowned Knight of the Lion, and all that happened there. The queen who was present at Le Hem commissioned Sarrasin to write it, and told him that if he made a good job of it she would have her people pay him handsomely – he'd have no cause to complain!

'Don't you worry,' said the lord of Bazentin. 'You can count on me, by Saint Martin,[1] if she calls on me to contribute!'

'That's good enough for me, sir! I shan't let you down: I'm confident I'll have it for you, all done and dusted,[2] before the year is out!'

Here ends the Romance of Le Hem, and Sarrasin says that if he's come up trumps with it, a large part of the credit should go to God.

Explicit the Romance of Le Hem.

---

[1] The patron saint of, among other things, beggars!
[2] Literally 'crust and crumb'.

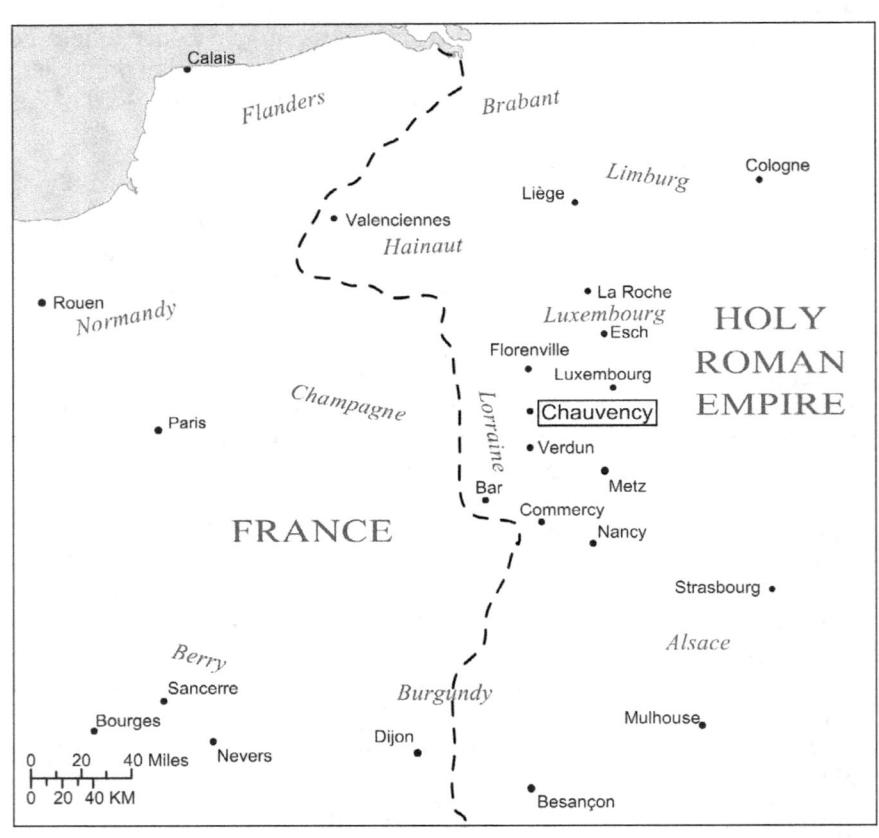

Chauvency: The Surrounding Lands

Jacques Bretel

The Tournament at Chauvency

Love is a fine beginning: God grant that the ending and conclusion prove as happy as the outset and the start! Say 'Amen to that – God grant that it be so!' The matter of my poem is love and arms and joy, and good and fair and noble people with glad, exuberant hearts and spirits, renowned in many lands far and wide; so worthy is my matter that I must approach it with a clear, unsullied mind. So bear with me and don't worry: I'll do my best to ensure that neither today nor tonight nor at any time will I say anything to displease you! God forbid! And may He guide me to bring this work to fine fruition for you, that word may go round among the good that Jacques Bretel has done a grand job!

Twelve hundred and eighty-five years after the birth of the Virgin's son, who knows and sees all worthy deeds, on the holy feast of the birth of the Virgin, mother of the almighty king (and I'm not guessing the date but know it exactly), eight days after the end of August,[1] I began to compose my book. It was at Salm in Alsace, in the castle of noble Count Henry;[2] and may God protect him from shame and grant him long life, for he surpasses all others in courtesy and largesse, sincerity and gentility: he is the embodiment of true nobility, and it gives me joy to recall his virtues and qualities, for I love worthy lords with all my heart. [42]

On the feast day of Our Lady who can save both body and soul, when the watch had sounded the dawn, I rose just as the sun came up and went out to enjoy the wood and seek inspiration, composing some little couplets about love. So beguiling was the scenery that I became quite lost in thought and fell silent. In the middle of my pondering I saw a knight approaching, holding in his hand the stump of a great, broken lance. I knew

---

[1] The Feast of the Birth of the Virgin is indeed 8 September.
[2] Henry IV, count of Salm. The castle of Salm is near La Broque, a few miles west of Strasbourg.

him by his distinctive manner and speech: his name is Conrad Warnier.[1] He recognised me the moment he saw me, and began to babble and make mincemeat of French, saying in a mangled version of our tongue:

'I bid you most well and heartily come, Mister Jacquemet!'

'God save you, sir knight!' said I. 'I commend you to Him!'

Then he said in his Teutonic brogue: 'By Mary the Saint, where do you mean to be going? Let us speak a word or four! Tell me what news you have. What has become of knights? Where will all the worthy be?'

'I don't exactly know, sir. But I can tell you this: anyone who goes to Chauvency[2] at the feast of Saint Remy[3] will find plenty of men to test his prowess in jousting and a mêlée. And before it's over there'll be a deal of dancing and merry-making, too! Ladies and girls will be attending to see how seekers of love's joys perform! So don't delay! Come and see the great festival!'

Nodding his head in high excitement he replied: 'I'll be able to well communicate, so perfect my French being! Bring I shall knights from Alsace, each with his stout lance in fist! All the jousters will be outwiped! I mean it, by God!'

'I don't doubt it, sir!' I said; then I added: 'I'll pay all your expenses myself, no matter how much, if they don't find worthy opponents!'

'God be your help, on that I shall uptake you! Now tell me who the lords will be, and the ladies fair and the maidens fair, and I'll tell the news to the king and his knights. They'll all there come!' [106]

'Gladly, sir,' said I. 'The first I'll name is the worthy count of Chiny and the noble countess, too.[4] They're of the highest rank, generous, courteous and gracious indeed. You couldn't ask for a more illustrious start!'

'God's body, Jacquet, spot-on you are! A fine start to be sure! A valiant knight and countess, twice as wise and courtly as you say.'

'True enough: you won't find any to surpass the count. That's proved by his love of worthy men; as for the unworthy, he detests their company so much that he wishes them all in Beauvais![5] He's most astute and cultured.'

'Well said, Jacquet, by God.'

---

[1] Konrad Wernher, a German nobleman of the prominent Hastatt family. Ruins of his castle remain at Pflixbourg, south-west of Strasbourg.
[2] Chauvency-le-Château in north-eastern France, to the west of Luxembourg.
[3] 1 October.
[4] Louis V de Looz (c. 1235–99), count of Chiny since 1268, and his wife Jeanne de Bar, the aunt of Henry VI (Henry the Lion), count of Luxembourg, who will be one of the main competitors at Chauvency.
[5] i.e. he won't tolerate their presence; there's probably no slight intended to Beauvais in particular – it's simply that it rhymes with 'mauvais'!

'Truly, sir, I've spoken from the heart. And the noble countess of la Roche and Luxembourg[1] will be there – I know no finer lady anywhere, in every respect: I love her as dearly as God, and rightly so. And in her company she'll have one steeped in all good qualities: Margot, who emanates courtesy – nothing else exists within two yards of her! And she's of a joyous, singing spirit. With her will be her sister Yolant, fair in face and heart alike, ever inclined to kindness – I know of no lovelier being. These two are the daughters of Blondel of Luxembourg,[2] who in my view was so good and valiant that none could match him in prowess – so if you're following my drift you'll see they're the sisters of the count who in prowess so resembles him.[3] So then, Conrad Warnier, what do you say?'

'By Our Lady of Paradise, your words cheer my ears! At this event who else will be?'

'Agnes, the damsel of Commercy, most fair to behold, and Mahaut d'Apremont, too:[4] both fine examples of courtesy and true grace.'

'God save me, your speaking is on the spot! Mahaut is a good damsel and Agnes de Commercy's a beauty: if I could have my wish, my wife would be just so!'

'Right enough, by God! You'd be well off there! And if you're keen to hear, let me tell you more about who'll be at the festival, and which ladies. My lady of Apremont will be there – and anyone hoping to find a fairer or finer lady, more fitting to grace a feast and celebrations, will be mad and disappointed! And there'll be a most honoured lady from the castle of Florenville[5] in the Ardennes, with a lovely gem, her daughter Agnes, radiant and fair of face and quite angelic. I urge you and all others to head straight for Chauvency, and bring men fit enough to withstand the mighty blows that'll be meted out!'

'By Saint Mary, Jacquet, say no more! I'll bring all the goodest knights and jousters in Alsace and the Rhineland! You've fine, great knights around here, valiant, brave and strong and lively: for such a business perfect!'

'And let me tell you, if you want to see feasting and dancing at its most joyous and refined, be at the castle on the Sunday. The Monday will be a different matter: all day long you'll see tumult in front of the stands! Lances shattered, horses killed, and the men well and truly sorted from the

---

[1] Béatrice d'Avesnes (1240–1321), wife of Count Henry VI. 'La Roche' is La Roche-en-Ardenne in Luxembourg.
[2] Henry V of Luxembourg, who had died in 1281.
[3] i.e. his son Henry VI, the present count, husband of the countess of Luxembourg.
[4] Agnes was probably the third daughter of Simon III, lord of Commercy (west of Nancy); Mahaut d'Apremont (just north of Commercy) became her sister-in-law when she married Agnes's brother Jean, who was to be lord of Commercy from 1305 to 1341.
[5] West of Luxembourg.

boys! The jousting will last all day. The stakes will be raised even higher on the Tuesday! Then on the Wednesday there'll be a delightful feast and in the evening they'll discuss the next day's mêlée:[1] if possible all will be arranged without contention,[2] but if not the golden thread will be stretched out and defended boldly, wholeheartedly, by the host's side.[3] Anyone short of courage had better stay well clear! I reckon there'll be a good few wishing they were safe at home and sparing themselves a battering! So, then: what do you think, Conrad Warnier?'

'God's body, it's all good news! What luck for me, Sir Jacquet, that I met you in the wood! All this talk of feastery and ladies: to my ears it is music!'

'God forgive me, sir, I haven't done it justice, not by half!'

'Holy Mary, I've never heard the like, not in these parts or anywhere! What honour and joy there'll be for the one declared the winner!'

'By Saint Quentin, go back to your house at Hastatt and get ready to come! You'll not regret it!'

'Come I shall, Jacquet, by Saint Nicholas! And I'll bring my son with me!'

'God see you safely there and back, fit and in joyous spirits!'

And with that we went our separate ways. [244]

I returned to Salm, where food was ready and the tables set. Worthy Count Henry was seated before the gorgeous spread. My table was set beside his, and his gracious servants escorted me to my seat. As soon as he saw me, the count asked me where I'd been, having risen so early. I promptly told him of my meeting and exchange with Conrad Warnier, complete with his wonky French and misuse of words: the good count laughed a lot!

Once we'd finished eating I took my leave of the noble count, but I promise you, by Saint Germain,[4] I didn't leave empty-handed: he saw me thoroughly refitted with a tunic, surcoat and green gown, and gloves and a hat lined with finest squirrel fur. He gave me a splendid send-off, escorted by one of his servants.

I left Salm behind, and Metz and that whole region, passed to the left of Briey[5] and spent a most happy, agreeable night at Auviller.[6] I carried on

---

[1] '*tornoi*': a tournament proper, a mêlée between two teams of knights rather than a series of individual jousts.
[2] '*Il iert fais par acort*': i.e. the arrangements and conditions will be agreed in advance.
[3] This is a puzzle, as no further reference is made to this golden thread. The host's side ('*ceus dedens*' – 'the insiders') will be the knights from the surrounding lands, the home side, confronting the 'outsiders' from further afield.
[4] Renowned for generous alms-giving.
[5] North-west of Metz.
[6] Probably Malavillers, north of Briey.

thus till I reached Chauvency on the Sunday of the feast.[1] There was quite a rumpus and to-do in the surrounding farms and houses, as a good few didn't know where to stay and it was high time to find lodging. [282]

As soon as I entered the town I ran into Bruiant[2] the herald. He showed me all around the castle; no doorman barred my way – they all bade me welcome – and hand in hand Bruiant ushered me into the feast. I said to him:

'Bruiant my friend, take it from me: no one should join the dancing unless he's a knight or one of appropriate station: it's frowned upon for a man of lowly birth. Let's sit down beside this pillar.'

Bruiant took off his emblazoned tabard and spread it on the floor beneath the pillar; I sat down and he beside me. Knowing he was well informed about arms and chivalry and knew all the knights, I began to ask him who each of them was, and from what land. He answered:

'I know a good many of them. Over there is the count of Luxembourg,[3] a most worthy knight and full of honour, and next to him his brother Waléran,[4] a brave knight and fine companion, noble, courteous and generous indeed.'

'And who's that, Bruiant, that handsome figure on the right, walking past the ladies?'

'That, Jacquet, is Perart de Grilly;[5] he doesn't fall short on looks or on goodness, I promise you: he's endowed with every virtue. And over there is the lord of Esch,[6] the most courteous, straight and noble ever born, and wise and cultured, too. And there is Philip the Fleming,[7] with Florent of Hainaut[8] beside him; next to them is Gautier de Hondschoote;[9] those others are all Hainauters. And over there is Conrad Warnier, who babbles that splendid brogue of his, half-French and half-German! Around him are knights from Alsace: there's Conon de Bergheim,[10] and Emich and Friedrich von

---

[1] i.e. the feast of Saint Remy (above, p. 62). It has taken Bretel a full three weeks to go no great distance, so he has presumably stopped many times en route to invite lords and knights to the tournament.

[2] It is obviously impossible to be sure, but 'Bruiant' may be a soubriquet rather than a real name: 'noisy, clamorous' is fairly apt for a herald.

[3] Henry VI: see above, p. 63.

[4] Waléran I, lord of Ligny, later to be killed with Count Henry at the battle of Worringen in 1288. He had participated also at Le Hem (above, p. 45).

[5] '*Perars de Grilli*': probably Grilly, north of Geneva.

[6] '*le signor d'Aixe*': this is Joffroy d'Esch (-sur-Sûre, in north-west Luxembourg), an important figure at the Luxembourg court.

[7] The fifth son of Count Guy of Flanders; he was about 22 at the time of the tournament.

[8] The son of Jean I, count of Hainaut, he was later to become prince of Achaea and Morea through his marriage to Isabelle de Villehardouin.

[9] South-east of Dunkirk.

[10] '*Cuenes de Barquehain*'. Bergheim is south-west of Strasbourg.

Leiningen,[1] and Rogiers de Miriessai,[2] too. And over there beside the ladies, the knight who just went past is Waléran de Fauquemont,[3] with the lord of Apremont[4] beside him; with them is Renaut de Trie,[5] tall and stout and handsome. And there is Henri de Briey[6] with his brother Ourri; and over there are Beckart de Maizey[7] and André and Wichart d'Amance.[8] That one is Roufous de Nueffville,[9] a knight free of guile and wonderfully brave – but very short of cash! Over there is the count of Chiny,[10] a knight endowed with all qualities; and there is Gerart de Looz, his brother, and by the faith I owe my father he's a fine man indeed. Those behind them are Burgundians: that one's Étienne d'Oiselay,[11] that's Simon de Moncler,[12] and those are the two brothers of Saint-Remy and the lord of Faucogney.[13] Next to them is Hugues de Negréz,[14] with Miles de Ronchamp[15] at his side. Yonder are Guiart de Nuefveille and Nicolas de Cumières.[16] On the right is the count of Sancerre[17] and on the left is Jehan de Prie.[18] Over there is Eustache de Conflans,[19] and

---

[1] '*Admes de Lunenge et Ferci*'. Leiningen is in the Palatinate, south of Koblenz.
[2] Unidentifiable.
[3] Fauquemont (the French form of Valkenburg) is in Limburg, east of Maastricht. Waléran III de Fauquemont was 31 at the time of the tournament, and a renowned warrior.
[4] Joffroi d'Apremont, the husband of the lady of Apremont mentioned above (p. 63).
[5] Near Gisors in the French Vexin; Renaut was later to be Marshal of France.
[6] North-west of Metz.
[7] '*Bekart de Marzei*'. This is probably Hugues Beckart, lord of Maizey in Lorraine, a close neighbour of Apremont.
[8] In Lorraine, north-east of Nancy.
[9] Joffroi le Roux de Neuville (-sur-Ornain, in Lorraine, another near neighbour of Apremont).
[10] Louis de Looz: see above, p. 62.
[11] North of Besançon.
[12] Probably Moncley, a close neighbour of Oiselay.
[13] Aymon de Faucogney, from a powerful Burgundian family; Faucogney is west of Mulhouse. The brothers of Saint-Remy were his vassals, Saint-Remy being a few miles to the west of Faucogney.
[14] Impossible to identify with certainty.
[15] Another of Faucogney's vassals: Ronchamp is west of Mulhouse, not far from Faucogney.
[16] Bruiant is no longer naming Burgundians. Guiart is unidentifiable, but the surname suggests he is a relative of Joffroi le Roux de Neuville; Nicolas's name appears as '*Colart de Cuminieres*': Cumières is in Lorraine, near Verdun, which would make him a not-too-distant neighbour of Guiart if he is indeed a relative of Joffroi le Roux.
[17] Étienne II, count of Sancerre (in Berry, north-east of Bourges).
[18] Lord of Busançois, from Berry like the count of Sancerre.
[19] '*Hue de Confilont*'. Conflans was Constable of Champagne.

there Pierre de Bauffremont,[1] and the one by the wall is Jehan de Rosières.[2] Those knights yonder are from over the sea: they're English, and splendid fellows – brave knights, wise and true; they've come to see this great event.'

'As God's my witness, Bruiant,' said I, 'I don't think you'll ever have seen one better organised – or participants more fearless! That's plain to see: everyone's in the highest spirits, determined to give it their all – I can't see anyone holding back.'

While the dancing went on I stayed sitting by the pillar with Bruiant the herald till it was gone midnight and everyone was weary from the singing and merry-making. Then another herald, named Martin I believe, stood on high and called to the whole gathering:

'My lords, I summon you all to the fields in the morning! So leave your singing now – the ladies are weary.'

With that they all retired their separate ways to chambers and to solars, while squires ran down to the cellars and returned with wine and fruit and napkins, and a variety of nuts both large and small. Then as soon as this serving of fruit was done all took their leave and went to their beds. [402]

That happy Monday morning, the first day of the week, the day after the feast of Saint Remy, the knights made ready. As soon as God had lent them light the servants were off preparing the weapons and boys and pages set to work with saddling and harnessing, creating a din that was wondrous to hear. Soon you'd have seen many a fine destrier – piebald, chestnut, white, black, dapple-grey and iron-grey – leaping forth beneath those knights, all of them with their hearts set on having the first joust. It was now the third hour of the day[3] and mass had been sung in the castle, and many a lady had gone to the stands to watch those eager to put their bodies on the line to defend their honour, paying their full dues to Prowess, who says to Her son Courage:

'Go boldly, dear son, and do all that must be done in Honour's name; none should show fear; love honour and dread shame if you wish to be counted among the worthy; otherwise your standing will not be great.'

That's how Prowess lures the young knight till he's learnt the craft that can lead him on the upward path to glory.

Into the stands, set close to the gardens, the noble count had gone with the countess of Luxembourg and many other worthy ladies too numerous to record. Then I looked and saw heralds coming from the castle of Chauvency all yelling like mad, with pairs of trumpeters blasting fanfares,

---

[1] He had participated at Le Hem – see above, pp. 50–1.
[2] Related by marriage to the Bauffremont family, this is Jehan de Rosières-aux-Salines, a few miles south-east of Nancy.
[3] Terce, the third canonical hour: in modern terms around nine in the morning.

leading the knights in such a ravishing display of arms that I've never seen anything so wonderful in all my life.

At the very front I saw a knight sporting a shield of red with five gold rings; he was utterly determined to have the first joust, come what may and whatever the cost, and was seeking another to take him on. Then I heard the heralds crying 'Chardogne!' and 'Vanne!',[1] and serving-lads and pages bawling, horses whinnying, drums pounding: there was no point trying to talk – the thunderous tumult was too great! The knight now set his helm on head and rode forth into the field, where his lance, short and stout and green, was placed in his hand. The knight preparing to face him was from Hainaut. The heralds were bawling, some in French and some in German, and I called out 'Bazentin!', being sure that that was who it was.[2]

A herald said: 'Who taught you your heraldry – the Devil?'

'Shut your mouth, you leper! It's Bazentin, God damn you!'

'You're full of rubbish!'

He wanted to clobber me for calling him a leper! He'd have given me a smack in the mouth – I'd no kinsmen to protect me! – but I shifted fast into the throng!

Then I saw to right and left these two knights of fearsome bearing; both were astride great destriers and planted upright in their stirrups, fixed fast as stakes. And let me tell you, Ferri was such a proud, overbearing figure that he fancied the king might tend his geese! He thrust in his spurs and his horse leapt forward, devouring the ground. With shield braced against his chest, helmeted head bowed low and lance levelled, there wasn't a hint of cowardice but a heap of courage, and he came galloping so bold and fierce that I thought the earth was quaking. His adversary charged straight from his starting-line, head down, helmet laced, shield firm braced and lance in hand; into his horse he thrust his sharpened spurs, and down the long and narrow track he came like a lightning bolt. The ladies were packing the stands for a better view. Like thunder came Ferri, lord of Chardogne, and Bazentin roared at the top of his voice; but the crowd was as hushed as if they'd been hearing the mass. As the knights charged together and dealt their blows they smashed their lances right down to their fists and collided, they and their horses alike; they flew from their saddles, heads, bellies and bowels reeling. They'd clashed with a noise like a thunder crash, so awesome that even the bravest trembled.[3] But no one wasted time on words: they all rushed to their aid, and a great crowd gathered to see them helped to their feet; but the knights lying there at the centre of the carnage, overcome by pain, were oblivious to it all. [536]

---

[1] These are the cries of Ferri, lord of Chardogne (in Lorraine, just north of Bar-le-Duc), the knight with the shield described.

[2] i.e. Huart de Bazentin, one of the protagonists in *The Romance of Le Hem*.

[3] The Oxford MS adds 'and broke into a sweat with alarm'.

At the foot of the stands you could hear the heralds bawling at the damsels, girls and ladies, going mental at them, saying:

'God's shame on you, women! It's for you these knights make their eyes reel and fly from their brains! The joy of your precious love is dearly bought! May you all suffer dismally! Look, cruel women! Those who risk their bodies and souls for you are lying there in such a state that neither head nor foot is stirring. Ah! Do you feel no pity? It's for your love, women, that they lay their bodies on the line. And that's not all they risk: after their bodies they stake their lands when this sport turns to war. Their toil and suffering never cease: they strive all day and lie awake all night in agonies of desire! Sighs and cares take their toll on the body. A blight upon your own health, women, if you show no pity for these knights suffering for your sake! With promises and favourable looks you could console these tormented men who wade through mire and wallow in blows, but you offer them so poor a deal that their suffering's worse than death or madness!'

That's how heralds always rant and rave at ladies – and they're convinced it's with good reason.

The knights had now come round and were in fair shape. There was a bigger crowd than words can say, as everyone ran to see the alarming fall-out from the joust, which had been so fierce that anyone with sense would deem it mad. But Ferri had come off lightly: he'd been trampled by the horses but had suffered no more than a broken arm. I tell you, if I ever imagine I'd something to gain by trying my hand at the business, I'll need my head tested! If Ferri came out of it all with credit, good luck to him – I'd rather him than me! [594]

Once this joust was over everyone thronged together to see the next. Close beside me a noble knight was arming, intent on winning honour; he was brave and bold and spirited, and superbly arrayed, worthy to be seen in the grandest company. I saw him on his great destrier, raring to deliver a mighty blow. Heralds then began to cry:

'Faucogney's not holding back! Here he is, ready for action!'

Elsewhere on the field were the knights from Alsace, and a striking sight they were, ready to test themselves and prove their worth. First to spur smartly forward was the lord of Bergheim;[1] Faucogney charged straight to meet him, eager to strike well – heart and strength and will were all combined. They met at speed and each dealt a blow to the other's throat. Their well-forged lance-heads dashed off each other's helm and barbiere,[2] and the force of the blows rocked them on to their horses' cruppers; but they

---

[1] Both Bergheim and Faucogney were introduced above, pp. 65–6.
[2] A metal plate with breathing holes attached to the front of the helmet, protecting the lower part of the face.

threw themselves back on their horses' necks as they rode back to their lines. They could barely hold themselves upright: they were stunned, their heads reeling, close to collapse. The heralds were yelling:

'Faucogney has it!'

'The lord of Bergheim!'

Each proclaimed his separate judgement. Among themselves the ladies were saying that the jousts were fine and splendid – and indeed, it's all very fine for them, no matter what the cost and pain to others! [638]

Shortly after this excitement another tough and fearsome joust prepared, both parties bent on winning honour and acclaim. On one side was a knight who didn't loiter by the stands: there was no finer figure of a knight from Cologne to Limoges; and with helmet laced to ventail[1] and red shield with three silver rings slung from his neck and sitting handsomely at his left, and stout lance gripped in his right hand, he was planted, solid as a tree, on a horse which galloped swifter than words can say. Heralds were crying as one:

'Vianne! Noble knight! Vianne! Miles de Til![2] Behold him, ready to show his worth, yearning only to excel!'

Then I saw a knight come forth to face him, and I never saw one more superbly armed. His golden apparel, unsullied by the slightest spot of grime, was blazoned with bands of red and three silver shells: none more handsome have I ever seen. This knight made ready: with lance in hand and shield braced he took his place at the starting-line. Then a herald with a twisted foot, who's wrecked the life and reputation of many a man to acquire his wealth, started shrieking at the top of his voice:

'Sierck! Sierck! Noble Ferci! He vunce struck Haldon fife times viz his lance-blows on his head!'[3]

So he screamed like a beast in his mangled tongue. And Sotin[4] mocked him in his inimitable way, saying:

'Shut your mouth, you wretch! You're not fit to talk of chivalry. You should worry about a comb to sort out your hair – it's like the scalp on a skull in a charnel-house!'

Coquasse[5] flew into a rage at this; he sprang at him, aiming a blow with his iron-clad rod, but his twisted foot failed him; Sotin would have

---

[1] The section of mail protecting cheeks and chin.
[2] 'Vianne!' is the cry of Miles (or Milet), lord of Til-Châtel, north of Dijon.
[3] This is Ferci or Ferri de Sierck (Sierck-les-Bains), south-east of Luxembourg; Bretel is mocking the herald's heavy Alsatian accent.
[4] Perhaps the soubriquet of someone well known to Bretel and his audience, or perhaps he's implying a generic type by the name (rather like '*Pikart*' for a random Picard, below, p. 89); '*Sotin*' suggests 'a bit of a pisshead; a nutter'.
[5] This was probably not the obnoxious herald's real name but an expression of contempt, implying 'an absolute joke' (as well as having a first syllable sug-

pummelled him to a pulp, but at that very moment the two jousters surged into action. I can describe this joust exactly for I saw them both charge, gripping their lances, speeding down the track, and as they met they struck one another as if bent on utter destruction! You'd have heard the lances shiver with a deafening smash, and chunks and splinters flew towards the clouds. Their helms were dashed off, exposing their faces, and those who knew them could see – unless they'd lost their wits – that they were Miles and Ferci. The heralds started yelling and the ladies were ecstatic, all declaring Miles a splendid jouster – and they were right, I assure you, for he did as much that day as others did all week, earning himself the acclaim of all: in twenty-eight courses he broke sixteen lances, a valiant effort indeed! [724]

And now I'll tell you of the fourth joust, which I'm convinced was one of the most awesome. If you weren't there, let me tell you: the clash was so fierce that I saw sparks fly from rochet[1] and helm; and I can tell you who the knights were and why all who saw them had reason to praise them. God bless me, I should indeed do my best to record the achievements of the good – credit always where credit's due – and such record isn't lost on the ears of worthy listeners but enjoyed and celebrated. So it's only right to speak well of the good: it benefits them greatly – and less worthy men sometimes take note and, sooner or later, change their ways and better themselves. So, God save me, let me tell you what I know about these two: the first to come forward was so handsome to behold – in every respect and from every side: front and back and head and face! – that none cut a finer figure all day. And his horse was no slouch: he sat astride a mighty Spanish charger. And what of his arms? He bore a shield of gold with a black cross, and on the cross were five silver shells. This knight from Burgundy bore himself most graciously; with helm on head and lance in hand he braced his shield and rode at an elegant pace before the ladies. The heralds proclaimed him:

'Grilly![2] Knight of noble stock whose renown should spread from Ireland to Rome! Worthy Grilly! Grilly the valiant! Grilly!'

Then another knight came forward, and very young he was: in the Ardennes and in Limburg he's known as Conon.[3] He was thoroughly the master of his horse, guiding him exactly at will at a prancing pace; feet fast in his stirrups, balanced and poised and as straight as a rod, he was tall and strapping as a Frisian, in body the image of a Palatine count but

---

gesting a brainless bird with an abrasive voice – hardly ideal in a herald).
[1] An attachment to the head of a lance, designed specifically for jousting as opposed to war.
[2] Perart de Grilly, introduced above, p. 65.
[3] '*Cuenes*'. This is Conon d'Ouren, north of Luxembourg.

with the head of a Saracen, his hair black and frizzy. There was a joyous commotion while he took up arms: you'd have heard ladies and maidens laughing, making merry, singing new songs, while trumpets blared and drums pounded; flutes and pipes were hard at work, and serving-lads and pages yelled and bawled. The jousters delayed no longer: horses leapt and lambels[1] fluttered, while heralds wrangled on about proceedings. Conon was charging, lance levelled, roaring from inside his helm: 'Ouren!' Perart de Grilly didn't hold back, and down the track they galloped, spurring like true jousters. Right in the middle of the lists they met, exchanging such fearsome, mighty blows that their horses staggered, their eyes were full of stars, and their lances shivered with a shattering noise. Their intense commitment earned them great acclaim that day. The heralds were off again, gassing on, each saying in support of his man:

'He's a born tourneyer!'

'He gives every bit as good as he gets!'

'He's a fine and handsome knight!'

'He strives for honour tirelessly!'

'The ladies should have their eyes on him: he's courteous, charming, honest, a splendid wielder of a sword, and young and bright and brave and rich, and never mean or stingy!'

Such were the claims they made for these knights from Germany and Burgundy. And as the knights returned to the ends of the lists there were plenty of friends and lords and kinsmen to acknowledge them, too. The ladies in the stands were pointing out the knights to one another and saying:

'Look at him, sisters! That knight knows his business! How well he looks with his shield and shining helm! Did you see how he bore his lance as he charged, and with what ease? Do you see with what skill he handles his steed? He looks the part indeed!'

'He should be a brave performer, right enough,' said another. 'He has the wherewithal for sure!'

Such were the private words of those who were driving the knights to compete on the field where the valiant win honour. [846]

Now came the fifth joust, which wouldn't have been to a coward's taste: it was a dauntingly fierce affair! No man of unworthy stock would meddle in such a business, not even for a bushel of gold – not even if he were given Paris! But a man born of a long and worthy line, with heart willing to do a hundred times more than body can endure, he will engage in such a joust – and I can see him now, God guide him! All the heralds were howling and bawling at the tops of their voices:

'Briey! Briey!'[2]

---

[1] Pendants attached to harnesses.
[2] Henri de Briey, introduced above, p. 66.

He bore a shield of gold with no other device but three red pales.[1] All the ladies blessed him with the sign of the cross and commended him to the king of kings. The sister of the count of Bar,[2] a lady of high worth indeed, said:

'May sweet King Jesus, seated above and seeing all from afar, watch over you, Henri de Briey, for you are a most noble knight. Among all those held in high esteem I deem you the highest!'

As she said this Briey rode past. Then the noble count of Chiny, Louis de Looz, who deserves all praise and honour for staging the tournament – he's generous, courteous and open-handed, and all the knights involved found him a fine lord and companion, earning him the esteem of all – the noble count, I say, son of a good father, endowed and imbued with all honour, stood beside his knight Briey and instructed him in how he should proceed, concluding most courteously with:

'Go! And Saint George be your guide!'

The moment Briey's charger felt his spurs it leapt forward. Then I looked toward the far end of the lists, turning my eyes at the perfect moment to see a knight appear sporting arms of gold with a red saltire, emblazoned above with a gold rowel[3] to distinguish him from his father. Heralds began to cry once more:

'Hastatt! Young Conradin!'[4]

Hastatt means 'high city' in the German tongue, and Conradin was astride a great destrier. His father Conrad Warnier told him:

'Forth go, dear son: the knight behold who jousts with you! By the body of my lord the king and by Cologne's Saint Peter, if you don't make a good showing you don't come home! I chase you out with a bludgeon! Out you stay for a month!'

Thus in his usual mangled French he harangued his son! Conradin planted his lance beneath his arm and thrust in his spurs; his mount sprang forward and into a charge. The track was firm, not powdery, as there'd been a little rain. The knights were wholly committed to their joust: it looked as if they'd plough straight through each other! Cries went up on every side:

'Ah, Saint George, help here! Help!'

Saint George was invoked and I think he was there – had he not been, the clash would have been calamitous! They were both intent on mighty

---

[1] Vertical stripes.
[2] Jeanne, countess of Chiny: see above, p. 62.
[3] '*moleste*': in heraldry the 'mullet' (French 'molette') is a kind of star in the shape of a spur-rowel.
[4] Conrad Warnier (of the Hastatt family) had said he would bring his son with him (above, p. 64): this is the son, Conradin.

strikes, and delivered such fearsome blows that their lances were wrecked – and so were their horses, crumbling together in a heap.

'They're dead! They're dead!' cried everyone. 'Lord God, what a disaster!' [941]

Everyone pressed forward to see, while I stood back. The knights still weren't on their feet again, but people returning, much to my relief, were saying:

'If it please God, they'll be all right.'

Then a herald, rather more courteous than the one before, came before the ladies; his eyes were full of tears, but through them he said:

'Look, ladies; see what these knights inflict upon themselves: for your sake they risk their lives and lands – they're in danger of death! It's all your fault, so help me God – all for the sake of winning your love! You should come down and with your smooth, white, delicate hands stroke their brows and temples, wipe them with the fringes of your mantles and so soothe them! Their hauberks are soaked and their faces stained with sweat! And all for your love, ladies! To whom else can I appeal but you, the object of their devotion! You should at least relieve their suffering and help them recover – those knights who truly, sincerely love you – with looks of gentle favour. It would inspire them to even greater valour: the brightest clerk ever made by God couldn't edify a knight in sixty years as a lady could in a fortnight! Love is such a mighty force that none can refuse His urgings; all obey Love's commands, as you can plainly see in these two lying on the ground, who hold Love in such adoration and esteem, and are so intent on winning honour, that they yearn for nothing else. And why is Love preeminent? Because Love is the driving force of courage and prowess, of courtesy and largesse; and all knights who aspire to improve themselves need courage, courtesy, true love and an unsullied life. When Love takes a man in His alluring way, He fires his heart with desire to excel in all worthy deeds. No one can rue being stricken by Love; and if any man finds himself suffering woe, if Love then smiles upon him he'll find one blessing makes up for a hundred pains! Such is Love's reward!'

So said the herald. A most charming, gracious lady was listening – God send me good fortune, it was my lady of Apremont. The herald looked up when he'd finished his speech, and the lady called him as soon as she could, saying:

'Come here – I've a question for you.' This king of arms, Maignien, went straight to her, and she asked him: 'Who are these two knights whose joust has cost them so dear? They've brought themselves to the brink of death unless God sends swift remedy.'

'That's Henri de Briey, my lady.'

'I know him well, Maignien,' the lady said. 'What of the other, who jousted with him? Tell me – him I don't know.'

'He's from Alsace, lady – a youth, the son of a worthy man.'

'What's the father's name?'

'Conrad Warnier, lady: that's his rightful name, and his son's called Conradin.'

'A worthy man he is indeed,' said that knowledgeable lady, 'and I've heard of his adventures. Three or four times I've heard it said that when he went a few years back to fight with the king of Germany against the king of Bohemia, he was among the most outstanding.'[1]

'He's truly brave and valiant, and the son takes after the father.'

'Then he's a credit to the mother!' said the lady, laughing. Such were the words that passed between the good lady and the herald.

Then the great mounted crowd that had gathered round the knights began to part, and I went to see that martyr to arms who had suffered much and exposed his body to torture like the crucified Christ. But the herald concluded that, if he'd chosen to embark on the career of arms, he'd have to accept it or give it up! [1056]

I leaned against a post and listened to an admirable minstrel talking. I heard him referred to as Henri – from Looz, they said – and he wasn't speaking Breton but a fine and elegant French, and his words were eloquent, polished and apt – not one ill-chosen or wide of the mark – as he boldly declared:

'He's a worthy and passionate man indeed who puts himself through such suffering. A heart that can make such a sacrifice truly cherishes honour and dreads shame. When a knight strives to excel with every ounce of bone and flesh and blood, and once he has his helm on head would never shirk or show the slightest fear of death or wound, imprisonment or ruin, that knight loves, trusts, respects and fears God truly: his heart is set on nothing else. I'd apply that to the one who bears the gold shield with the three red pales. And now he's lying there! Let's go, sirs, and see these two martyrs! No matter which has come off lighter – Conradin or Henri – he'll still be half-senseless from the blow he took! I tell you, anyone who fancies trying his hand at this is welcome to it – I'm sticking to the job I've got!' [1092]

Such a fine time I was having that it's nothing but a pleasure to record and recount. I now saw an amazingly handsome knight come forward, a gold shield with a red cross braced firm against his chest. God had chosen to make him big and tall and broad, with a noble heart and an open, honest face: he looked a valiant knight indeed. His powerful, sprightly mount leapt proudly forward, and the rich adornments with which he was decked all over streamed in the wind.

---

[1] In August 1278 Rudolf I of Germany had defeated and killed a rival for the Imperial crown, Ottokar of Bohemia, at the battle on the Marchfeld.

'Prigny!' cried the heralds. 'Robinet de Watronville![1] He brings no discredit to the profession of arms, only honour!'

At that very moment I saw another knight emerge from a crowd of Limburgers – and formidable they looked indeed. Out of this crowd came this daunting figure, riding swift as the wind. Robinet, jousting for the hosts,[2] was ready to defend, and now you'd have seen shields riven, lances smashed and helmets dashed – you can't imagine how splendidly these two charged. Heralds were squawking like a flock of crows – hungry for trinkets, not carrion.[3] Not even Herod,[4] the embodiment of greed, was a hundredth part as grasping as a herald out to grab what he can. But I'll say no more – it's better to speak of the good than of that lot: would to God there were just two heralds in all the world who knew enough to do the job for the whole pack of them (not that they'd ever see eye to eye; I'm not saying that heralds' wrangling would stop if there weren't so many of them – a complete novice herald is as loud and forward as one who's been established for ten or twenty years). But enough: let me tell you about the joust that was under way. Both knights were charging, lances levelled, and as they passed they exchanged such blows that they made their lances shatter, their helmets split and their brains boil.

'These knights are bound for success,' said the ladies watching, 'when they thrust their lances so thrillingly!'

'Are they, by God?' said a sneering snake of a herald. 'If it impresses you so much they're daft not to go on and break their necks.' [1158]

As the afternoon wore on[5] and the sun began to sink, I saw knights approaching – three, I think – coming faster than falcons. The heralds didn't stay quiet long: the moment they saw them they rushed yelping from the stands, though some stayed behind. Those who went met them with such riotous joy that I came down from the stand and went to see. I recognised them immediately: leading them was the count of Blâmont, advocate of Vic;[6] I also knew all the company taking their gear to their

---

[1] Robert de Watronville, just east of Verdun. The cry 'Prigny!' announces him as a knight of Lorraine: it's the duke of Lorraine's battle-cry.

[2] '*cex dedens*': he was an 'insider', representing Lorraine against knights from further afield.

[3] Heralds could profit handsomely from snapping up arms and harness scattered during a joust.

[4] '*Hanris*'. This may be a curious reference to someone called Henry who was well known to Bretel's audience, but seems more likely to be a scribal misreading of a better-known exemplar of avarice. Herod might be a candidate, but I suggest this with no great certainty.

[5] Literally 'after the ninth [canonical] hour': in modern terms after about 3 p.m.

[6] Henri de Blâmont, a cadet branch of the house of Salm; he was cousin of the count of Luxembourg and of Count Henry of Salm (above, p. 64). An advocate

lodgings, while the knights came riding to take a look at proceedings. One herald stopped and said (it was rather over-the-top):

'By God, ladies, these new arrivals will make all the difference: they'll truly grace this festival of arms!'

'The festival of jousting's under way, the mêlée comes soon,' said my lady de la Roche.[1] 'Tell me, herald, do they mean to joust?'

'So help me God, lady,' he replied, 'not today, but tomorrow. And I can promise you that all day long you'll see a thousand whole-hearted contests! But look: unless I'm much mistaken one of them's already armed and advancing ready with helm on head and lance in hand.'

I went right close to the herald and craned my neck to hear, and the noble, gracious countess asked him:

'Herald, by the faith you owe me, who is this knight?'

'Raoul de Baissi,[2] lady, a fine knight, courteous and brave.'

'By God, herald, he looks it, that's for sure!'

And up the knight rode, helm on head, bright with enamel, and bearing a fine red shield with a white band.[3] The herald, I can tell you, yelled: 'Baissi!' And at the other end of the lists another knight, fully armed, came forth; he was mounted on a great destrier, and he certainly looked keen to impress the ladies, judging by his bearing and the massive lance he held. From opposite ends of the lists they charged; no horn or trumpet sounded: it was as quiet as in church. They went about their business boldly, fully, and I still remember vividly how they dealt blows that would have been heard from the hilltops or inside the castle! You could hear the heralds Bruiant, Garnier and Wauterel crying loud and clear:

'Baissi! Valiant knight!'

Other heralds, those from Germany, were yelling the cry of the other knight in their own tongue.

But I can't tell you any more than that: I don't know every detail – I can't record every action and give the name of every knight. In fact it's only right that I don't! The old hands, who've lived and borne their shields longer and performed more deeds of arms, they're the ones I should be telling of, and they offer material aplenty; the younger knights, if they do as they should, will achieve enough in time to be talked of likewise, to their credit and advantage. [1246]

('*voéz*') was a lay lord exercising civil jurisdiction in the domain of a monastery or church, and was expected to protect the church with arms in the event of attack; Vic is now part of Nancy.

[1] The countess of la Roche and Luxembourg (above, p. 63).
[2] Hard to identify with certainty: possibly Boissy in Champagne, south-west of Reims.
[3] '*face de travers*': a horizontal stripe.

The sun had now completed its turn and was hidden behind the hills and the keep; the great gathering, in countless numbers, was now in shadow. Down from the stand and into the castle went the noble countess of fair Chiny; so did the other countess, of Luxembourg, whose goodness and character improve, instruct and uplift all who share her company: she loves, fears, respects and trusts in God and is unfailingly committed to doing right. Such are her ways; and with her she has two companions who hunger and thirst to treat all people with honour, and who conduct themselves with great nobility, striving ever to improve: to be quite clear about who they are, they're the sisters of the valiant Lion.[1] Both seek ardently to do good, and such is their nature that they're loved by all; of each of them it's commonly said: 'God made her – and her he cursed', referring to some other in a crowd. That's the view of all. And as they came down from the stand where the noise and bustle were greatest, these two sisters, such fair and charming damsels, began to sing:

> *'Shame, shame on anyone who ever repents of love!'*

To which a band of Hainauters replied: 'Quite right, by God! Anyone who's come to learn love's ways and then repents of having loved should be decried and flogged, denounced as a wicked, craven coward!'

Then Florent of Hainaut began this bright, delightful song:

> *'I've an invisible wound right by my heart;*
> *And God! None can draw the arrowhead from me!'*

In this charming company was my lady of Apremont, of whom I've heard it said by many that no lady of so young an age was ever so good and wise, and her goodness was matched by her abounding beauty. Her sweet nature and open heart are ever plain. To her right she was holding the fingertip of her sister-in-law, her husband's sister, the courtly Mahaut d'Apremont – God send her all possible honour; and her left arm she'd given to Agnes de Commercy, who's neither base nor plain but young, noble, gracious, and so eager to sing that she sang out loud:

> *'If you wish to take the path of alluring charm – follow my steps!'*

All the Burgundians, a fine band of young knights they were, joined in the refrain. This fair company made merry and laughed and revelled together in delightful fashion, without a hint of rowdiness or impropriety. In joyous but decorous order they entered Chauvency. I never saw a festival conducted less immodestly, more courteously and properly – though it was

---

[1] Henry VI, 'the Lion', count of Luxembourg (a red lion was his blazon). He had five sisters; which of them are referred to here is uncertain.

not without its cruelties in the end: I can't help but rue them, but I don't want to talk about that now.

In tents as well as halls, and in leafy lodges as big as the grandest market stalls, trestles and tables were set up. The common folk were packed along the brattices, towers and battlements, but I remember not a sign of discontent or rumpus. Then I looked and saw a host of ladies in rich attire, and gallant knights mixed among them, and counts and countesses, sitting together here and there and side by side on handsome couches.

I'll say no more about the feasting, save that the food and service were all that could be desired – and they ate little but sang a lot! And as soon as they'd eaten they were on their feet and the tables and trestles were down and cleared: it was time for trumpets and flutes and drums and pipes! My lady of Chiny was the first to start the singing, being the leading light, the banner of this glorious feast, its rallying point; and everyone heartily joined her in singing:

> '*Fortune frown on anyone who doesn't join the dance!*'

What a pleasing, lovely sight it was to see the ladies and knights step forward, hand in hand; no one resisted or refused – everyone joined the joyous dance. I can still hear Simon de Moncler singing:

> '*Do you know the cause of my mortal pain?*'

And after that worthy knight had sung, Étienne d'Oiselay sang with Agnes de Commercy:

> '*With hands clasped, sweet lady, I pray you have mercy.*'

In such joyous entertainment they spent a great part of the night, everyone striving more and more to win the prize for singing; so intense indeed was their merriment that they pleased God and His saints. And how could they have failed to please Him? For by the Virgin, never in my life have I seen any people in such blissful, high, elated spirits.

When at last it was time to retire, they embraced and asked and granted each other leave. They undertook to joust the following day, then departed hand in hand and took to their beds till morning. Tomorrow you'll see lances shattered, horses charging – and horses killed. [1384]

On Tuesday, at the very break of day when the watch sounded the horn, everyone woke in their various lodgings, and on all sides out came harness, arms and horses, and the place began to fill with splendid knights.

All were keen to have the first joust, but most determined of them all to have that honour was a fearsome, daunting figure of a knight with a face covered in slashes. Anyone slight or light of build would have been foolish to offend him: he had a massive belly and backside – he was bigger round the middle than he was around the shoulders! – and was planted rock-solid in his stirrups. Forward he rode, mighty and assured, and I never saw a horse so fat and less troubled by its rider. In his hand he clutched his lance – short, fat, strong and stout – and round his neck and firmly braced hung a gold shield with a black cross.[1] The heralds didn't hang around: they started yelling 'Prigny! Prigny!', the cry of the great duke Ferry[2] whose land borders three realms. I went with Bruiant to watch the joust, and saw the knight sat in his saddle, fat as a baggage-sack, and then pounding with his spurs like fury. An English knight – I don't know who – charged to meet him instantly. Thundering noise and tumult followed! They came at each other, heads down, bold and straight and swift. The crowds watching this mighty charge were enough to make an army. Anyone seeing them braced in their stirrups would have said they were masters of their mounts indeed; and no one could accuse them of holding back – they were flying like deer across a heath. And they didn't exchange any pleasantries! They met one another with almighty blows, smashing shields, ripping off burlets,[3] splintering lances and rocking each other back in their saddles. They rode on past without wound or bruise, but reeling from the force of those blows. The heralds were at it instantly: each of them grabbed a trumpet and started blasting. A curse on the lot of them: always on the take, giving not a thing, and full of lies and pomposity. [1448]

I watched the proceedings with delight; and as I looked on I saw a body of knights approaching in fine array: to say that this great company looked superb is an understatement. And there was one in particular who came to the fore: tall and strong and upright, his armour so becoming him that he looked as if he'd been born and raised in it. Like a winged angel he was; his arms were red with gold chevrons; he was mightily admired by the ladies that day! A herald plastered with coats of arms was prancing behind him crying:

'Vaus! Vaus, for Beckart!'[4]

His horse sprang forward, hooves churning the ground, and from the other side a French knight came roaring, so superbly armed and so clearly skilled that he was a wonder to behold. Jehan Porrés[5] was his name; I can't recall his shield exactly, but I believe his arms were ink-black bla-

---

[1] Although this knight is never named by Bretel, Delbouille in his edition identifies him from his arms as Renier de Creuë, in Lorraine to the north of Commercy and Apremont.
[2] Ferry (Frederick) III, duke of Lorraine, who had appeared at Le Hem (above, pp. 36, 37–8).
[3] Rolls of padded cloth on saddles.
[4] 'Vaus' is the cry of Beckart de Maizey (in Lorraine, a close neighbour of Creuë); he was introduced above, p. 66.
[5] Unidentifiable.

zoned with three bars-gemels[1] of fine gold, and very handsome they were. Thus accoutred he came surging from his line, and Beckart charged full tilt to meet him. It was almost more than their mounts could bear, and they clashed with a force that smashed their lances to shards. It sounded as if two barrels had collided! But with the utmost aplomb they rode on past unmoved, still fast in their saddles! The heralds started crying:

'Vaus! Beckart the forest-waster![2] What a dealer of blows! He knows how to behave: he wields his weapons in the field and holds his tongue indoors! There are doers and there are talkers, and braggarts just debase themselves.' [1496]

The day was fair with a shining sun, but it didn't trouble the jousters as it was coming from the side. I turned to look in the direction of Montmédy and its fine castle,[3] and as I did so I saw a great company of knights riding over the hilltop with a train of packhorses and servants. They were in three parties, one in front of another, and those nearest, at the head, came crying 'Montjoie!' I was thrilled to hear it, and asked a herald named Wauterel:

'Hey, Wautier! Who's that?'

'Truly,' he replied, 'he's the worthiest knight in all Germany! There's no other to compare. It's Waléran de Fauquemont,[4] whom Nature and his good heart summon to be courteous, noble and upright. If any kingdom had two such knights the whole land would benefit.'

I watched him come down and ride before the stands, charmingly singing as he did so:

> '*I've brought joy with me here!*'

On he rode past the ladies, superbly armed astride his destrier. Then he made his way to his starting-line and waited for a moment till a knight of Lorraine came forward amid loud cries from the heralds of:

'Here we have Jehan de Mirouat!'[5]

And they went to join the youth who was bravely advancing to compete. There was no turning back now! Both knights shook their reins and their horses charged like lightning bolts, surging over the dust and sand. The knights had lances levelled as they raced towards each other, and as they met they both struck home and the lances flew into pieces. The ladies had plenty to say! The noble countess of Luxembourg declared

---

[1] '*gemelles*': pairs of stripes.
[2] The same epithet is used in *The Romance of Le Hem*, above, p. 41.
[3] Just three miles east of Chauvency, the castle of Montmédy was built in the 1220s by the count of Chiny.
[4] See above, p. 66. 'Montjoie' is his battle-cry, Montjoie being another of his fiefs.
[5] Unidentifiable.

82   *Jacques Bretel*

that both knights had fulfilled their promise. There was much acclaim for Waléran, and much praise too for Mirouat from all the ladies and damsels in the stands.

'Truly,' the girls were saying, 'what a fine and worthy knight he is who bears the silver shield with the red lion with the forked tail![1] I saw him last evening, I remember well: you couldn't wish for a finer knight. He's been engaged in war non-stop for a good two years, in his own land and elsewhere.'

Both knights were duly praised. And the heralds grabbed their usual rewards (though in God's name they don't deserve them): they were quickly out in the lists slinging cruppers and collars around their necks.[2] [1568]

The day was fine, the weather fair. Pennons, banners and pendants[3] fluttered in the wind, horses neighed and whinnied and stamped and kicked and galloped, sending stones flying around the lists, enough to dash rochets from lance-heads.[4] Before the ladies in the stands rode Joffroi,[5] that valiant and worthy man's son, fully armed astride a swift and powerful horse. His arms were red, his shield blazoned with a silver cross. Heralds were yelling like crazy:

'Apremont! Son of that noble lord![6] Expect him to prove a good knight indeed: his father was good in every way, as were his grandfather and great-uncle – all of them fine knights their whole lives long. If Joffroi is valiant, so he should be: all his forebears were!' And the herald who'd said this sprang forward then, crying: 'Lord God be with Apremont!'

Just then a young, impressive knight rode past in spirited fashion, catching the eye of everyone with his bright, appealing manner. Heralds pranced along at his right hand, crying:

'Sancerre![7] Valiant Sancerre! The fine and worthy youth Sancerre!'

Once the joust was agreed there was nothing else for it: without a moment's pause or another word they both rode from their marks, helms on heads, lances gripped, and charged towards each other like fury. They were fine knights and came out of it well: of ten or twenty jousts it was the most admired. Between their helms and their shields adorned with orfrey[8] they

---

[1] i.e. Waléran.
[2] See note 3 above, p. 76. This is an attempt to reconstruct a sentence interrupted by an accidental omission in the MSS: an unresolved rhyme indicates at least one missing line.
[3] Lambels, as above, p. 72.
[4] See note 1 above, p. 71.
[5] Joffroi d'Apremont, introduced above, p. 66.
[6] Joffroi's father was Gobert III d'Apremont, evidently a figure much admired in Lorraine.
[7] Étienne II, count of Sancerre, introduced above, p. 66.
[8] Bands of fine embroidery, usually incorporating gold.

aimed their thrusts, striking with such force that their lances shattered into shards; both knights were unseated and sent flying, arms and shields flung wide, stirrups lost, burlets sundered, helmets smashed. [1621]

These blows were greeted with huge acclaim. All were watching with rapt attention. And the heralds of arms were sounding off, ever keen to proclaim success and condemn failure; and one of them, a bald fellow, Champenois by name, said:

'By God, I've good news for you ladies, maids: those were the blows of valiant knights for sure! You should summon them here and comfort them with gifts of your veils and lace and embroidered stuff and promises of sweet kisses and amorous trysts! Knights who earn praise and recognition you should take to your hearts and greet with joy and celebration. But worthless failures should be whipped and flogged – if they won't change their ways they can all get lost!

'But ladies, if a youth appears who's struggling to succeed but has potential, I pray you in God's name give him good direction; don't be harsh or hard on him but encourage him with kind words, saying: "Dear friend, this is what to do if you want a place in our hearts!"

'You'll see him do it at once! For the chidings of ladies to lovers are a sweet delight: when eyes and heart are smitten by the sight of a lovely face, the lover will do anything the sweet lady says! And if two hearts come together and the love is mutual, you mustn't show it too soon! You should couch your feelings in exhortations to courtesy and valour, to fire him to love with a true, pure heart: thus you'll make a courtly knight of the callow youth. Ladies, it will be an honourable and worthy deed to turn the reluctant into proper knights – if you don't it'll be a grave failing and the fault will be yours! Just by responding kindly you can make the craven bold – just by saying "I love you, dear" you can make a rough fellow right chivalrous! It's a lady's part to speak fine words: there's much to be gained from her schooling.

'Honour and disgrace are dependent on God and on you, ladies. So in God's name do the right and honest thing in this respect, for no one wants to see worthless cowards! Even the bad hate a worthless knight! As for the good, they despise every last one of them – worthless knights are admired by none. So take this admonition of mine to heart, ladies – it's well meant. If you do, it'll be to your honour and their benefit – all, of every degree, know that.' [1690]

After the excitement of these formidable jousts there was another, and you've never heard of finer, better-struck blows than those delivered now. A knight who's made himself tough enough to deal them is clearly never self-satisfied! And it's only right that true worth reveals itself – it always does: a refined and truly worthy heart is reflected outwardly. Nobility may come from lineage, high station from inheritance, but refinement – true worth – is dependent on a good heart. And a good heart rightly manifests all three: nobility, high station and refinement; for any two without the third are worthless: how little high station would be worth if not attended by nobility, and nobility would be of no value without refinement! It's my firm belief that a refined, truly worthy heart is seen outwardly in a properly worthy man – as defined by the philosophers who speak of three key qualities: wisdom, loyalty and courtesy. A man can and should be endowed with these three qualities, and display them in his deeds: then his heart can be called truly worthy.

But I digress! I must return to the joust, which involved two knights both resolved and ready to suffer in their bid for honour and enhancement. Let me tell you about the first: he was the very image of Lancelot. But that's enough praise for now! I'll leave it at that and move gracefully on! He rode past the ladies most elegantly, bearing red arms superbly blazoned with two salmon wrought in silver. Heralds – German and French alike – went rushing, blasting their instruments and crying:

'Blâmont! Blâmont!' and 'Balquenbert!'[1]

On they went in their usual way, singing out in the shade of the banners, passing before the ladies and flocking together at the end of the lists. There they made ready his helm and lance. The ladies were marvelling at his handsome figure and bearing; they said God should have given him a kingdom: it would have been well bestowed on one endowed with such wisdom, honour, largesse, loyalty and prowess. Hearing the ladies talking thus, I leaned against a pillar to listen to what they said. They were discussing at length the great qualities of the knights, as variously bestowed on them by God. It was a joy and delight to hear; but my attention was drawn to a most striking figure of a knight: I clearly recall that his shield and apparel were blue, emblazoned with an indented[2] cross of gold. Heralds were bawling:

'Gevigni![3] Son of a worthy father whose valour is renowned on both sides of the sea! Gevigni! Behold him here, this gracious, noble knight! All should plainly envy him: Count Renaut of Boulogne[4] never cut a more splendid figure, and his prowess has passed down to his heirs: this one doesn't disappoint! He's been the object of many a prayer from the ladies watching here!'

---

[1] 'Balquenbert' being the cry of the count of Blâmont, introduced above, p. 76.
[2] i.e. the edges of the cross are not straight but notched.
[3] It is impossible to identify with any certainty this unnamed knight, whose cry is 'Gevigni!' and who is evidently descended from the count of Boulogne.
[4] The renowned lord Renaut de Dammartin, count of Boulogne (and Dammartin and Aumale) in the late twelfth and early thirteenth centuries.

Thereupon these knights so full of valour delayed no longer; both set off at a gallop down the lists, bearing their fine, nail-studded shields, spurring to the speed of a merlin after its prey. I can't tell you what a splendid sight it was as they charged towards each other, and they exchanged such blows with their stout and rough-edged lances that they smashed them down to their fists, tore loose their saddles and ruptured armour and split and sundered shields.

'What a brilliant clash!' the ladies said; whereupon a herald, one with all the charm of a watch-dog, butted in with:

'God help you, ladies, I'm glad you approve and it gives you such pleasure – they may find it's all worthwhile! A curse on the head of any knights who look to strike such blows: their folly's plain when you choose not to show them favour!' [1810]

It was late in the afternoon before I moved from my place, for I had an excellent position, sitting on the fourth step of the stand, and I loved having such a full and perfect view. To my right – and how it made my heart rejoice – I saw seated in the stands Solace and Joy, along with, I promise you, Beauty, Modesty and Sweet Welcome, sights to ravish a noble heart! Meanwhile, below, earnest Courage was making bodies shake with passionate desire to give and take blows mightier than Power alone can manage. Once Courage penetrates the heart and the body shakes and trembles, Strength is born and grows apace, along with Will; the heart swells, desire intensifies, and Prowess (which governs all) is set alight. It leads to many a deep, deep sigh, fearing it's more than the body can yet endure: the heart is filled with such desire that the flesh shakes under the burden. But when the valiant knight then goes to it and does as he has vowed, he finds his flesh has unforeseen protection. For when the heart overtakes the mind and follows the body's craving, heat rises to a furious pitch and the body can boldly achieve all that the heart desires. And so it proved with these two. For while Pleasure was revelling up in the stands, Courage was riding below as I've said: I saw it as plain as day.

Then I glanced to one side and was startled to see a company approaching across the fields; I didn't know who they were but from their voices they sounded German, and as they came they were calling the feared cry 'Limburg!' for which two brothers are renowned:[1] God has given them rich shares of courage, prowess, courtesy and largesse, and having endowed them with these four qualities, He wants to support them and see them achieve yet greater heights. They're young, prosperous, valiant, and many will benefit and many suffer if they fulfil their huge potential. One of these two came riding up; the shield hung from his neck had silver

---

[1] As will become clear, this is the battle-cry of Henry of Luxembourg and his brother Waléran de Ligny.

and blue barrulets and a gold chief and was emblazoned with a red lion rampant.[1] He rode right through the throng, head down, face hidden in his helm, and shield braced as tight as the wings of a swooping falcon. I saw him go to the far end of the lists, with pages and heralds following him, bawling an endless torrent of cries:

'Limburg! Son of worthy Blondel, lord of Luxembourg![2] Behold this valiant knight of Limburg! Limburg! Limburg! Holy Mary be at his side and protect him and enhance his honour, for we've a fine lord here indeed!'

Those at the other end of the lists were crying: 'Amance! Wichart![3] Amance! Amance we say, two hundred times! Amance – the courteous knight Wichart, admirable, flawless!'

He was indeed a delight to behold: as sparklingly clean and fresh as if he'd just come out of a box! Anyone with an unjaundiced eye would have seen a strong, robust knight, full of vigour, perfectly poised astride his mount. It would do us no harm to have plenty like him! In head and shoulders, in chest and limbs, he was a fine figure indeed, and had heart enough to accomplish all. This Wichart set off, and Waléran spurred his great destrier – no lame creature: it went like a greyhound! They came at each other across the dust faster than arrows or crossbow bolts. The fearsome blows of their mighty lances sent helmets, barbieres and burlets flying and tore through hauberks; the knights rocked like scales under the force of the blows and the horses beneath them shuddered with the shock: the impact was a lot to bear. You'll never see a joust so fierce without a knight being unhorsed. In threes and fours the heralds were bawling, some of them 'Limburg!' and others 'Amance!' One lady spoke out declaring she'd given her love to Waléran of Luxembourg, while another proclaimed she'd given her heart and undivided love and everything she possessed to the noble knight Wichart!

'Well let's hope you mean it!' said a herald who heard them. 'They've paid in full, so complete the transaction! Love and a rapturous welcome await them! Since you're so enamoured, no wonder they break their necks!' [1938]

It was a glorious festival, full of life: so many charming ladies, sweet, courtly, gracious, so many appealing maidens, so many young and valiant knights I saw filling the fields that day. The weather was fair and temperate and the setting broad and beautiful. Right beside the field was the castle, from which the knights came and thronged around the stands where

---

[1] These are the arms of Waléran de Ligny. Barrulets are narrow horizontal bars; the chief is a broad horizontal stripe, usually covering about the top third of the shield.
[2] Henry V of Luxembourg, as noted above, p. 63.
[3] Wichart d'Amance was introduced above, p. 66.

the ladies were ensconced. I watched them exchanging pledges to joust; before the day was done there'd be many a fine blow struck: between terce[1] and noon good knights would need to prove their prowess and win honour if they were to win the ladies! The heralds were crying:

'Let's be having you! Come, my lords, it'll be getting dark! If you've rochets get them fitted: those knights yonder have fixed theirs ready on their great, stout lances. They're out to challenge for the ladies, so let's see you compete! Where are our amorous knights who want to win delicious kisses with their prowess? This is no time for shirking!'

While all this racket was going on, out from Chauvency and into the field rode a knight as dazzling as snow. I knew him by his arms: silver emblazoned with a red cross, with a lambel to distinguish him from his father.[2] A herald sprang forward yelling like crazy:

'Neuville! Joffroi de Neuville![3] Bold and fearless, strong and tough and fierce in attack and defence alike! He's truly courtly, upright and honest, generous and great-hearted – but in grave need of money![4] It's a great shame, and does nothing for a lord's honour.'

So this herald blathered on. Meanwhile at the other end of the lists Florent of Hainaut was leading forward by the reins a knight of his country, a companion of his household, a fine knight, bright and courtly, bearing arms of Douai; I'll describe what I saw: a green shield with an ermine chief[5] and a red indented border. It was Baudouin d'Auberchicourt.[6] A herald headed his way, hopping and skipping and crying 'Douai! Douai, valiant knight!' And at that cry the horses leapt forward, the knights thrusting their sharp, pricking spurs; they aimed their stout lances at the very top of each other's shield, and their rochets struck home with such force that the shafts of their lances shattered. Damsels and ladies prayed to God to guard them from danger when they were capable of dealing such awesome blows. The knights rode on past and heralds came flocking in twos and threes crying:[7]

---

[1] The third canonical hour, in modern terms about nine in the morning.
[2] In heraldry a lambel (usually 'label' in English) is a horizontal band with three or more tabs hanging down, the distinction of the eldest son in his father's lifetime; the word probably reflects the resemblance to the pendants hung from harnesses (see above, p. 72).
[3] This is 'Roufous de Nueffville' (Joffroi le Roux de Neuville) introduced above, p. 66.
[4] This point was made earlier, above, p. 66.
[5] Ermine being silver-white with black markings representing the animal's fur.
[6] Just east of Douai; Baudouin was one of a long-eminent family, castellans of Douai.
[7] The Oxford MS adds: 'howling and bawling with all their might'.

'Neuville! Rufus! Gallant, valiant knight![1] He's clearly the brother of Espaulart,[2] God have mercy on him: in him there was so much goodness and God-given grace that he would have achieved great honour if he'd lived, but it pleased Our Lord to take him now.'

These sentiments were heard by all, and there were fulsome tributes voiced for the knight and prayers for him from the ladies in the stands. [2030]

Once the hottest part of the day was past, all went into full swing and the watching crowd was roaring with excitement. A knight in superb array, young and agile and mightily strong, emerged from the castle and came riding to the far end of the lists. His arms were vairy of gold and red with a smart blue baton.[3]

'Bauffremont!'[4] his supporters cried, and they all went pouring, prancing past the stands singing:

'You're not in a sprightly mood – unlike me!'

They stopped with him at the end of the lists. Fierce as a bristling lion he looked, with shield round neck, braced fast to his chest – he wouldn't be shifted from his stirrups that day! Then forward down the track he surged. From the other end a knight came charging – I don't know who he was and never gave it any thought, but I can assure you of this: when he came to use his spurs he went about it boldly! And he knew how to set his shield – the bottom planted low and the top thrust forward. He aimed straight for his opponent's teeth – but when Bauffremont received the blow it was like a stick of bread hitting a solid wall, as he set his vairy shield with the blue baton right before his teeth. Rochets were smashed and dashed from their shafts, lances shattered to smithereens, and the almighty crash could be heard from miles away.

'By God!' one herald said. 'Is there any way of selling blows like that? Damn me, if they were put on sale the merchants would make a packet! And if you were the seller of such merchandise, you'd want to be paid cash down! Better to be safe than sorry! No question of credit – you'd want payment up front from the lucky buyer!'

That's how that herald rattled on, but another replied: 'You can't buy blows like that, dear man! By the faith I owe my father's soul, they're the product of hearts fired by Courage, and of the strength of powerful arms.

---

[1] The Oxford MS adds: 'Bless the men who strike such fine blows!'
[2] Joffroi's brother, deceased.
[3] Vairy ('*vairié*') is the heraldic term for a pattern of alternating colours representing 'vair', the fur of the squirrel; the baton is a thin diagonal band.
[4] This is Pierre de Bauffremont, who had participated at Le Hem (pp. 50–1) and was introduced above, p. 67.

Money won't do you any good – what you need are heart and will. And I see the knight with the vairy shield's still full of both! He's jousted with opponents up the lists and down again – and with a third and then a fourth! And he knows how to fight indeed!'

To this a Picard bloke spoke out, saying: 'Yeah, 'e should be well chuffed! If 'e don't find no one to topple 'im, they'll all keep comin' an' 'e'll take 'em all on! Blimey, 'e's a tough'un all right – like a bloomin' guard dog! Blimey, is 'e 'avin' a laugh? Is 'e gonna beat the lot, all by 'isself?'[1]

'You're bloomin' right – lazy he ain't!' said a leading minstrel.[2] 'No, he yearns to win honour – that's plain to see from his daring display.'

Everyone was showering praise on him. I heard and noted it all, but I've kept my description of his jousting short to give time for fuller accounts, for I've plenty more to deal with yet. [2110]

Just a moment later I saw four banners emerge from Chauvency in glorious fashion. Ahead of them, crying 'Rosières!', thronged pages, servants and heralds, and armed knights, bold and valiant, riding in fine formation bearing the lozenged shield.[3] And at the head of them all I saw a knight eager to enhance his honour and prowess. He came, singing, to the end of the lists, and all those with him sang as one, most joyously and beautifully:

'Here's the talk of the town – and the dearest, fairest company!'

I couldn't take my eyes off them – the sight of him and his companions was a sheer delight. If you think I'm overstating this, I'm sorry! But it seems to me that if one sees a noble knight bent on delivering mighty blows one can't overdo praise – the truth should be told! When his heart is willing and he lays his body on the line, wholeheartedly ready to attack and defend, he should be given joyous recognition. (On the other hand, if his heart fails him, it's very wrong to reproach him.) When the heart finds the will to act worthily and suppress its weakness, resentful men will give no credit – they can't bear to see good come to the fore! That's why I'll never stop saying what my heart bids me say, honestly and ungrudgingly. There's nothing wrong in celebrating courage – and it can be uplifting and

---

[1] This Cockney rendition is an attempted equivalent of Bretel's mockery of a thick Picard accent. In his edition, Delbouille assumes 'Pikart' to be the soubriquet of a Picard herald, and takes the first word of his speech, '*Hachet*', to be a knight's name. The first assumption is plausible (but the second is not – '*Hachet*' is Bretel's rendering of a Picard saying '*Assez*'); but rightly or wrongly I take 'Pikart' to be any old Picard, a spectator rather than necessarily a herald.

[2] In the minstrel's first line Bretel has him mimic the Picard before returning to 'standard' speech.

[3] The arms (blue and gold lozenges) of Jehan de Rosières, introduced above, p. 67.

inspiring – so I hope I'll gain approval for doing so: courteous words deserve courtesy in return! That'll encourage me to continue speaking well of the good and keeping kindly quiet about the bad.

So hear now what I have to say about Jehan de Rosières. I watched him as he came and saw what a splendid sight he was, with helmet laced upon his head and his strong shield firmly braced. And splendid too was his adversary. Both were staking their heart, their all, their everything, on mounting a grand charge and performing well. With all the speed they could summon from their mounts they came to meet, landing blows in each other's face: even the less stunned of them thought the sky was full of stars! A thousand shards of their shattered shafts flew skyward, while the knights and destriers swept on past like lightning. At each end of the lists the fanfares rang amid the shields and banners of Bauffremont and Rosières.[1] [2182]

It was a glorious day, graced by very fine lance-blows and horses taken to the limit, by songs sung soft and sung out loud, by gallant and gracious words of love and its various delights, mixed with sweet and pleasing looks – some given in private, furtively, if mischief was involved!

The lists were long but narrow, and I could see a throng of men and horses right at the foot of the stands. To one end I saw riding a skilled, impressive knight;[2] his arms were diagonal stripes of gold and red with a striking blue lambel and roundels.[3] At the other end was a valiant knight driven by Prowess; as he sent his destrier leaping, turning, the ladies had their eyes on him and plenty to say on the subject.

'God!' they said. 'Who's this one? What a fine and handsome figure of a man, perfect in every respect! How good all his equipment looks: helmet, ventail, shield and lance! And look how his charger gallops and leaps beneath him. I'd say he really means business! You couldn't wish for a finer knight – bless the woman who bore him! I don't think there's another knight here to match him.'

'Tell me, lady,' said a herald. 'Which one are you on about now?'

'I mean, my man, the one with the gold arms with the bend compony blue and silver bordered in red.[4] He's given a home in his heart to Courage, who knows how to distinguish the worthy from the rest!'

---

[1] Bretel has not made clear who Rosières's adversary was, but this last phrase suggests that it was Bauffremont, still taking on all comers.
[2] The Oxford MS adds: 'God keep him from harm'.
[3] '*besantéz*': having roundels in its border representing gold coins (bezants).
[4] A bend in heraldry is a diagonal stripe; compony means that the stripe is composed of a row of squares of alternating colours, in this case blue and silver. The bend here has two red 'batons', thin red borders defining each edge of the stripe.

'Lady,' I said, 'that's Renaut de Trie,[1] who's given his son the title Billebaut.[2] One thing's for sure: he loves war and combat! He's the worthiest, finest knight I know among the French.'[3]

While I was still in mid-speech, before I'd finished, both knights started moving, lances aloft; then they charged full tilt and collided, body, shield and breast together, with a force that seemed as full of contempt as it was of courage. But when the body has strength combined with surging pride and resolve, it's bound to result in ruthless blows. And such were theirs that it looked as if they'd smashed each other to pieces. But I heard the knight with the bend compony roar 'Boulogne!' Those who use their youth to such effect are truly blessed. And a herald was crying over and over:

'Looz! Looz! Looz! Gerart,[4] who blazes and burns with courage, valour and daring – and then, as soon as his helmet's off, bathes in courtesy, loyalty, largesse, fortune and gentility! That's how he is in the field and then in the house!'

Hearing this he struck me as being well schooled! I felt in my heart that I'd never in my life heard a herald speak more agreeably! I went and stood beside him and saw that he was elderly, grey-haired; I asked him where he was from.

'I was born in Hainaut, the home of fine knights! They call me Malparlier.[5] What's your name?'

'Jacques Bretel.'

'Knights, heralds, minstrels all speak well of you – as do I! I've been wanting to meet you.'

I sat straight down beside him and he declared his warm friendship. In return I promised him my wholehearted service. Then we spoke at length about love and arms and honour, and who were the finest lords – we could think of many, far and wide. After voicing his wise choices, he swore that in the whole kingdom of France and all Germany he knew of none so endowed with all refinements as the lord of the Flemings, the count of Flanders[6] – God grant him a place in Paradise! He considered him the finest, most courteous, most utterly to be trusted in all the lands from Wissant to Brindisi.

---

[1] Introduced above, p. 66.
[2] '*Bellibaus*': this refers to Plessis-Billebaut, one of the fiefs inherited by Renaut.
[3] i.e. from the French royal domain: see note 4, above, p. 5.
[4] Gerart de Looz is the count of Chiny's brother, introduced above, p. 66. His cry is 'Boulogne' because he is descended from Renaut de Dammartin, count of Boulogne.
[5] Curiously (in view of Bretel's view of him), the name appears to mean 'slanderer'; it may, however, suggest rather that he had a status akin to an allowed fool – that he could, if he chose, say 'improper' things with impunity.
[6] This is Guy I, count of Flanders 1251–1305.

'But Malparlier,' I said, 'God save me, this is a mighty gathering: there are countless worthy men here!'

'By God and the Virgin!' he replied. 'You think I don't mean it? Condemn me to torment this very day if I don't deem the count of Flanders worthier than any man could wish!'

When I heard this I was delighted by his words and seized him by the hand: I would never tire of his company and charming character.

We went off then to our left into a garden beside a meadow, and spoke at length of Flemings and of Hainauters, of Brabanters and Picards and how well they'd jousted. But we hadn't been there long before the sun began to sink and the jousts drew to a close.

So that's what happened that Tuesday – and there was even more than I've described. Then down from the stands came the ladies who inspire all this pomp and turmoil in the world!

That was the second day. [2322]

The evening was sweet and pleasant. Ladies and maidens went merrily over the fields and the young knights followed after them. Each was soon escorting a partner, and happy were those who found one filled with love and able to voice it with a fair response: it's a glorious joy when a lady's heart knows how to respond agreeably! Walking on thus, hand in hand, they spoke of their yearnings for love and its delights – and all most properly, without any unseemly words or behaviour. I can confidently declare it was exactly as I say. Then each of the girls and ladies mounted palfreys or carts, and it's hard to describe the high, euphoric spirits of the knights: any courteous soul who'd witnessed the scene would have thought it a joy to behold. On every side they were singing songs, many together loud and clear:

'Stand back! Make way! A merry company's passing through!'

So singing they entered the castle, revelling and rejoicing to such a degree that they were cured of all their cares. By Saint Nicholas I swear I saw a band of ten of them who'd have given the whole of Germany for less – and it would have been a fine and fair exchange, worth every penny! It's not to be wondered at if I describe all this vivacity: a time entirely free of woes, of ill will or anger or deceitfulness or wrong of any kind.

The tables now were set and the companies of knights and ladies took their seats. All was prepared in the cellars and the kitchens, and the servants went about their business most courteously, without any fuss or bother.

With each course songs of love were sung – love, which assuages all troubles, leads gentle hearts to live in happiness and hard ones to shrivel and die. Squires eagerly sang the responses when rounds were sung, and every word and act was full of joy and celebration. Minstrels were busy on tabor and fiddle,[1] while others entertained the ladies with fair words.

Meanwhile knights were discussing how to proceed with the hastiludes, and how this festival which had begun so well might be brought to fruition; they all declared that on the Thursday they must take part in a mêlée without fail. You should have seen how the heralds leapt at this, and the serving lads and varlets roared and brayed! The squires went rushing off to the knights' lodgings to prepare their helms and hauberks, to see their shields were properly strapped, to furbish swords and daggers, to see their streamers and favours were crisp and smart, to shoe the horses and make clubs! All went about it with a will.

The same was true in the castle hall, where all were intent on singing and dancing in wondrous style; candles were ablaze in every corner, and the middle was filled with dancing to the fiddle, knights opposite damsels and ladies opposite knights.

Meanwhile in a score of places there was talk of love – most courteous and refined: some were saying how love-stricken they were by the sight of the beloved, others how hot and ablaze they were with longing and desire. But one there'd be who couldn't confess to the pain that pierced his heart or force a word of it from his mouth: he lives on in agony, his heart ever straining to reveal his desire but unable to part his lips to voice it – instead he gazes wide-eyed, his mind quite lost! And how can he do otherwise once Love has bidden him love, and he sees before him the very image, the banner of love, white as frozen snow and blazoned with the clearest red, casting upon him such promising looks that with fair words and sweet laughter she entirely steals his heart? The heart would have to be dead indeed if it failed to respond to that! God forbid that any well-bred man holds back from loving – but I hope no worthless rogue ever has the option! I'd sooner be dead than live in a loveless world – or see a rogue enjoying love! I'd rather he were out in the deepest sea – without a boat or so much as a plank! [2437]

That's what was going on privately in chambers and in bowers, while elsewhere ladies and maidens were gathered together to dance. What cause could I have to reproach or chide? I felt nothing but delight at seeing their joy. As they danced I heard a lady singing: gracious and pleasing she was, neither thin nor plump but young and vivacious and elegant and sweet, and she was holding by the finger Renaut de Trie, who was no less handsome than she was fair. He needed little prompting to start gaily singing – and his face showed no trace of trouble or care:

> '*Ah, most sweet Jehannette, you've stolen my heart!*'

---

[1] '*Vielle*': the medieval forerunner of the violin.

And Jehanne d'Avillers[1] turned her eyes on him: she wasn't shy or timid but as I've just described. I watched as she extended an arm and then turned away and prepared to sing most happily and started at once:

> '*I've never loved before –*
> *Ah God! what happy chance, I've now begun!*'

And I thought to myself: 'I'd say you're very well matched!' Everyone sang in response to the lady – and upon my soul, they should all have been in love with her! For in her I know no flaw – and anyone doubting the truth of that could discover it with ease: if he's courteous and well bred he'll soon recognise her nature.

Next to sing was a girl who's endowed with so much beauty, wit and virtue that I know of none surpassing her; Aëlis de Louppy[2] it was, who sang with feeling:

> '*Shining blonde I am, and ah, alas, I have no lover!*'

My response was: 'It's a pity indeed when so fair a face and body is without love! It grieves me sorely! She's so gracious and courtly and well deserving to be loved, appealing so to everyone in her song!'

Jehan d'Oiselay[3] was escorting her, holding her most courteously, and in reply to her he sang, loud and clear for all to hear, this song:

> '*Love me, blonde-haired maiden, love me –*
> *I shall love only you!*'

He hadn't completely finished his song before an esteemed young lady of noble line, fair of face and comely of body, beautiful in all respects and good withal, sang in turn most prettily:

> '*God, grant my sweetheart triumph in arms and joy in love!*'

A worthy, valiant knight, blazing with courage, Fastré de Ligne[4] from Hainaut, laughed and said:

'I wish you good fortune! Such a charming damsel deserves a sweetheart of distinction!'

Then he asked me to tell him who she was, of what line and country.

---

[1] Daughter of Thierry d'Amelle, lord of Avillers (north-west of Metz).
[2] Daughter of Gérard, lord of Louppy (Louppy-le-Château, in Lorraine near Bar-le-Duc).
[3] Brother of Étienne, above, pp. 66 and 79; Jehan was lord of Flagey, north-east of Besançon.
[4] One of a prominent Hainauter family, Fastré was later to succeed his brother as Marshal of Hainaut.

'Sir,' I said, 'she's of the Florange family, daughter of the good and worthy lord who achieved much honour in this world, and her name is Hable de Boinville.[1] Festivity becomes her wonderfully, I'd say, and judging by what I've seen of her, her manner's entirely genuine.'

At this point Joffroi d'Apremont began to sing:

'I've devoted all my heart to loving truly.'

Then Aëlys de la Neuve-Vile,[2] who'd thrown herself heart and soul into breathless revelling, sang in rapturous fashion for all to hear:

'Oh the happiness I feel! Oh the joy!'

So delightful was this gathering that my happiness doubled – I hadn't a care in the world! It was nearly midnight before the festivities ended and people departed; and before then the merriment redoubled and was brought to a fitting height. [2532]

As everyone sat down in the hall there appeared from a chamber a charming maiden of elegant figure, sweet and wondrously pleasing, wearing a sleeveless gown of red scarlet[3] adorned with tiny bells. Squires were clustered together, gazing at her with delight and asking each other who she was and what was known of her.

'Her name is Agnes de Florenville,'[4] said those who knew her.

Then, with all the knights and ladies seated, Perrine d'Esch[5] played beautifully on the fiddle. She'd donned a costume, too; and before her now sprang a boy with his clothes hitched up: he was playing the part of a simple shepherd, the very image of one of those grotesques carved on the end of a citole![6] Then he heartily, merrily struck up a tune while the maiden danced around him like a shepherd girl for her shepherd swain! The shepherd was quite beside himself with joy! He had his gloves tied swinging from his back and his hood twisted up in the shape of a raffish bicorn! He danced and pranced and jumped and whooped, and then, laughing, begged

---

[1] Florange is in Lorraine north of Metz; Hable was the wife of Jacques de Boinville (Boinville-en-Woëvre, to the west of Metz, near Verdun) and mother of Jehannette de Boinville who is about to appear below, p. 96.
[2] She may well be related to the Neuville knights, but it is not possible to identify her with certainty.
[3] To be precise she is described as wearing no sleeved undergarment; 'red scarlet' is not a tautology: scarlet was a quality fabric (of silk or wool) rather than the colour.
[4] Introduced above, p. 63.
[5] *'Perrinne d'Aixe'*. Impossible to identify with certainty, but presumably related to the prominent figure Joffroy d'Esch (likewise written as 'Aixe') above, p. 65.
[6] A stringed instrument related to the lute.

for her hand in marriage[1] and beat at the ground with his fists. But that was the least of it! When he started feeling her buttocks, breast and nipple he felt like a king! He strutted away so stiff with pride that he might have been walking on air. He hadn't a thought for her: he was lost in his own bliss! Back he came and kissed her twice while she wasn't looking; everyone laughed and said the kissing was more appropriate! I asked a servant who the chap was who was enjoying himself so with his mischievous act. He fell about laughing, and said:

'What? Don't you know?'

'No, by God! No, in Love's name! No, by my life, not at all! And I really want to! So tell me, dear fellow, whose son is he? Who's his father?'

'You can be sure of this much, Jacques: he's a daughter, not a son!'

'You're kidding me!'

'No, I'm not, I promise you! I shan't keep you in the dark: it's Jehannette de Boinville. I tell you, by Saint Gilles, she's worth her weight in silver[2] entertaining everyone like this – her foolery's got them riveted!'

'All the while she made me think she was a young chap taking liberties!'

Just then squires came in bringing a fruit course of pears and nuts, with white napkins and bottles of Beaune wine. When all was finished they rose from their seats and parted; the ladies took to their beds in the happiest of spirits, while in the hall the knights, of whom there were many of great worth, gathered beside a pillar. [2613]

At this meeting they discussed tourneying and its great rewards – dependent of course on generous giving, without which the profession of arms isn't worth a penny. You must all know that largesse is one of the defining marks of true worthiness; the second is courtesy; and the third is to be much encouraged – and what might that be? Integrity. Any man endowed with these three qualities along with prowess deserves to be truly honoured – and would be, if lords were as straight and decent as they used to be. But these days each is in thrall to unworthy mentors, to false counsellors[3] in whom they trust, causing their honour to fracture and wane. But I'll hold my tongue and say no more: I'd better keep my head down, for my tendency to tell the truth upsets some people.

It was Joffroy d'Esch who began the discussion, saying: 'It behoves you, sirs, and would be very fine to stage a mêlée on Thursday. There are Flemings and Hainauters who've come here to compete, and there are

---

[1] Literally 'threw the apple', a reference to the Ancient Greek custom of throwing an apple at someone as a proposal of marriage.

[2] This is a free translation of a phrase which evidently baffled the scribes of the extant MSS: they give the equally meaningless renderings '*a or ci malcon d'argent*' and '*ait or si mal com d'argent*'.

[3] '*un mahommet*', implying less than reliable counsel.

plenty of ladies eager to see a mêlée. They'd be very upset – and you'd be shamed! – if it failed to happen.'

Louis de Looz, the count of Chiny, spoke after him: 'We'd be disgraced, sirs, if we failed to stage a mêlée.'

Forward then came Henri de Blâmont Maucervel,[1] saying: 'Sirs, our festivity and revels here and all we've done so far have been splendid and all that we could wish, but the ladies have never seen a mêlée before and long to. And so they shall, I say! It'll be to our honour – and they'll realise what their sweethearts do for them!'

'You won't see me object!' said Joffroi d'Apremont. And with that they rose and parted, the staging of a mêlée all agreed. They summoned the kings of arms Grehei, Fildor, Maignien and Huvelle to organise matters. Louis de Looz said:

'Maignien, you must go at once to Montmédy; tell them that the companions here at Chauvency send them greetings, and inform them of the mêlée. Go and return before noon. We'll talk to them tomorrow – there's no need for letters and seals.'[2]

Maignien set off at once and rode swift and straight to Montmédy. There he found Hainauters and men from Limburg and the Rhineland, along with the high-born, fierce-hearted Lion of Luxembourg[3] and his brother Waléran, who's worthy of being emperor for his largesse and courtesy. Also in the company were Florent of Hainaut, splendidly prepared to tourney, and Waléran de Montjoie[4] – God send him honour and joy, a knight whose admirable character should please and satisfy all. Present, too, was Philip of Flanders,[5] who should certainly not be counted among the least but among the finest and the greatest: he strives ever to excel, being son of the worthiest man I know in Christendom. Maignien went up to the castle and promptly delivered his message, saying:

'My lords, the companions at Chauvency wish you all to know that the day after tomorrow a mêlée is on offer! The plan is to have no festivities tomorrow, nor is any man to go and joust: there'll be no jousting. It's better to suspend it than have something happen that puts the tournament at risk: someone might be wounded to the detriment of the mêlée. I prefer to see the clash of swords, maces, clubs, fighting, men sprawled on their bellies, whinnying, yelling, chasing, fleeing, horses' nostrils steaming, snorting, knights exerting every muscle, than attend on individual jousting! So tell me your minds: the details will be discussed tomorrow.'

---

[1] The count of Blâmont, introduced above, p. 76.
[2] As noted above (p. 81), Montmédy is only three miles from Chauvency.
[3] Henry VI ('the Lion'), count of Luxembourg.
[4] Waléran de Fauquemont: see note 3 above, p. 66.
[5] Son of Count Guy of Flanders, introduced above, p. 65.

The count of Luxembourg replied: 'Maignien, we'll go there tomorrow and see the company at Chauvency. I suggest we take arbiters[1] to arrange the sides and organise matters so that when the time comes to join in combat there'll be no need for words beyond exhortation! No need to be discussing niceties: straight down to business – deploy, take stock and charge! Smash into the opposing lines, straight into their midst, and give and take mighty blows! Every man should do his duty in the sight of the ladies and maidens for whom we strive for honour, triumphantly or otherwise. When the ladies take their places in the stands to see the knights meet in combat, let's hope all goes splendidly. One thing's for sure: there'll be some who'll note where their sweethearts are likely to be seated! And every man should be roused and fired and strive his utmost to be pleasing in the eyes of his beloved!'

'My lord count,' said Maignien, 'I know a fair few who'll be willing and able to suffer pain and toil when you come to blows. I shall go now: I have your answer, and commend you to God.'

And up he leapt, and the count said: 'God keep you, Maignien!'

So Maignien left Montmédy and rode back to Chauvency where he gave the knights his news.

'Sirs,' he said, 'I shan't beat about the bush: I've news about the tourney and it's all good, so help me God!'

'Excellent!' said Gerart de Looz. 'In that case I say we should announce in the morning that no one's to take to the field tomorrow.'

'With respect, sir, it would be better to do so tonight: make sure the ruling's hard and fast.'

So they told a herald what had been agreed and bade him clamber on a table and proclaim loud and clear: 'Hear what the knights of the feast have declared: there can be no jousting tomorrow. Anyone venturing into the field and arming to joust will forfeit his horse!'

Then he stepped down and everyone cried: 'Well said!'

There was a great stir and bustle then, as all mounted and made their way to their lodgings, for day was drawing near and it was time to take to their beds. [2792]

Early on Wednesday morning, as soon as mass was sung, all the knights left Montmédy and rode straight to Chauvency to discuss arrangements for the tournament. Into the festival ground they rode, to find a great throng of ladies and knights. Some of them stopped and others rode on as each found his counterpart; and then, after genial greetings, they came together to discuss matters.

I heard a lot of their deliberations, though not all; but I'll tell you what I know if it please you. The knights were gathered in the hall, all standing,

---

[1] '*diseurs*': men appointed by both sides to organise and judge proceedings.

and there was much joking and laughter. The first to speak was Count Henry of Luxembourg who, laughing, said:

'What a formidable assembly we have before us, sirs: such a bright and spirited gathering of men esteemed in love and arms! And any man who loves and has a fair sweetheart is bound to triumph! What are we to do, who have no beloved backing us? We'll just have to work like fury! But go on, take the lot: there's nothing else for it – we're going to get battered! We must be mad, performing before these ladies here! It'll cost me every penny – you'll empty my saddle and take my all! But all the same we'll agree to it: we'll have a mêlée tomorrow morning – and some will come out of it better off, in money and in horses!'

There was much amusement at this. Then Maucervel looked up and swore to his brother Thomas and his father Ferri de Blâmont[1] that he'd well and truly turn the joke around.

'I don't know,' he said, 'who the losers will be, my lord and cousin of Luxembourg: the field will be full of mighty men. You have the Hainauters, the Brabanters, the Rhinelanders, the men of Flanders and Hesbaye,[2] and we have the knights of Burgundy, Lorraine and Champagne: there's not a scrap of difference between us!'

'True,' said Florent of Hainaut, 'but you've forgotten something: you have the ladies backing you! When you all have the love of your charming blonde beauties, who will survive against your swords? Anyone on the end of your weapons will be a dead man, soaked in sweat and blood! Entertained by your maces, amused by your clubs – what fun! And so much more so seen through a battered helm! The enjoyment will all be yours in the thick of the fray. And I'm only too pleased, by the Lord I am – I wish you triumph: you're my dear and splendid neighbour!'

'By God, dear cousin,' said the count of Chiny, 'you've outdone us on the jesting front, so go ahead and laugh at our expense. I know you'll be deadly serious when we come to blows. But the joke will finally be on you.'

'If you say so, sir,' Florent replied. 'But there's no need to be cross with me: your breeding should enable you to stay cool. As for the joke ending up on me, that'll be down to your mighty valour.'

'I can see the way things are going,' said the count. 'I'm going to have to pay for this sudden warm regard – God keep my dear horse Morel: I hope you'll be a good master to him!'

Everyone laughed at this, and when Joffroi d'Apremont heard it he came forward, beaming with delight, and said to the count of Chiny, in the hearing of all: 'Leave Sir Florent be now! We'll never find a tougher

---

[1] He makes his vow to them but they are not actually present: Ferri was long dead and Thomas, later to be bishop of Verdun, was in holy orders.
[2] The region centred on the city of Liège.

customer – if we fall into his hands he'll do us few favours! But if it please God the outcome won't be as he imagines. You can talk all you like but the business must be done out in the field, and I've no idea who'll get the better of the deal.'

Joffroy d'Esch had been listening to this, propped upon one elbow, and was amused by what he'd heard. 'If it please you, sirs,' he said, 'it's time to change tack. Let's appoint arbiters to organise the tournament fairly.'

Both parties agreed to this, and the meeting now broke up. The Chauvency party[1] without any ado appointed Sir Renier de Creuë[2] to assume the role, while the Hainauters straightway chose Baudouin d'Auberchicourt, a good and much-respected knight. These two pledged to do their duty faithfully and well and went off together to discuss matters.

They organised the two sides for the contest in such a way that Conrad Warnier and those under his banner would go and support the Chauvency party.[3] The battalions would be impressive indeed, formed of fine and well-armed men. The Limburgers and Rhinelanders were to face the knights from France[4] and Berry and the others from more distant parts: it would be an excellent contest. The knights from Champagne and Burgundy[5] would confront those from Hainaut and Hesbaye and all who'd come with them: that's how they'd compete.

With the order of the tournament now decided, you'd have seen heralds dashing from lodging to fine lodging, the fastest of them at the forefront crying:

'Raise your banners in the wind! Display your helms and shields and armour, your caparisons and harness and those favours from your sweethearts! You'll be tourneying tomorrow – all is arranged and pledged!'

In no time the castle was a busy hive responding to this cry: every tent and bower and battlement was covered with a vast display of arms; and coffers, caskets and trunks were opened and out came a wondrous array of fabrics, white and red and violet, richly embroidered with finest gold. There was such excitement through the streets at the prospect of the mêlée, and the whole castle was ablaze with the dazzle of arms. [2949]

The day drew to a close and night approached amid great celebration. All were merrily conversing – the most experienced talking the most – and engaged in various games. There was singing and dancing, and true lovers imploring love; and others had organised the role-playing game of

---

[1] '*cil dedens*': 'the insiders', the 'home team'.
[2] See above, p. 80.
[3] Literally 'those of the feast': again, they might be termed 'the home team'.
[4] i.e. the French royal domain, as noted above, p. 5.
[5] And, as will become clear, Lorraine, though Bretel surprisingly doesn't include them here.

King and Queen, in which one plays the king who mustn't lie.[1]

Others meanwhile were talking of Love, the inspirer of all true lovers. I began to listen in! I'd like to tell you a little about a lady and a knight, cultured, courtly and eloquent, and of the words that passed between them; but you won't know who they were – if I'm to put my talents to proper use it would be wrong to compromise them! But so fair was their speech, and so charming the effect of their pleas and responses, that I'm sure you won't mind if I entertain you with them now. Listen, then, in gracious spirit! On a couch richly draped in silk of yellow and green, the lady leaned on her right elbow while the knight sat before her – not too close, a little back, in modest and genteel manner – and sweetly, softly said:

'Most gentle lady, I have frankly given you my heart and body, nor has there been any conflict within me: when my heart said yes it was at true desire's bidding, so Love is rightfully ensconced in me – Love was the instigator! Love it is that has left me with a weight and a shadow on my heart! I pray you now, let the object of my love have pity on my desire, which will not cease. But in God's name, sweet and gracious lady, don't think I'm pressing for your love in this appeal: my only prayer is that you grant me permission to do to the utmost what you wish. If you choose and can find it in you to grant me more, I will heartily accept!

'But, in the name of Love, bear with me if I complain of my sickness to you, who are my remedy; if I am not the right one to bid for your love, and have made my heart your prisoner, bound fast, I shall at least have the comfort of living in hope – ever the spur and inspiration of true lovers – and my suffering will be the less. I want you to know I love you more than anyone alive, with a love that grows and intensifies with every passing day, forcing me – I cannot help myself – to love you with all my heart. And this at least is my recompense: that you are the source and inspiration of whatever honour I accrue; for if my body performs deeds of any worth, it's for love of you that it labours. And I pray you in all confidence from the depths of my heart that it may be with your approval that it does so: then my joy will be doubled and the pain I suffer will be less. Come what may, I cannot renounce this love of mine.'

And with that he gave a deep sigh. Then the lady, who'd been gazing at him fixedly all the while he spoke, replied most sweetly, saying:

'Oh, my dear, why have you kept this hidden from me, never spoken and revealed? How welcome it would have been, and for so long! I would

---

[1] The game of King and Queen (which is played in Adam de la Halle's *Jeu de Robin et de Marion*, written just a year or two before *The Tournament at Chauvency*) involves the choosing and crowning of a 'king' who asks his 'court' questions about love by way of getting them to reveal the objects of their affections; in return they can question the king, who has to answer truthfully. That the questions might be a touch indelicate is suggested by the ban placed on the game in the Statutes of the Synod of Worcester in 1240.

have made you lord of my love and my all, to inspire you to deeds of honour; for I know you to be so good that you would never abuse your beloved in word or action. You would never take advantage: your love is good and true, so all that is mine is yours. So take strength and be valiant: it will give me joy and you great profit! This favour I ask: you have hidden your love till now, so strive to make up for lost time – I pray and command you! And in joining in love I would have us feel able to issue prayers and commands to one another – I to you and you to me, as a faithful lover to his faithful beloved, wishing their love to be entirely without rancour or dishonour.'

With that their conversation ceased, as confections and fruit were served. Then the lady courteously said to me:

'Come and be seated, Jacques! I want to hear your news – the best and fairest told! I'm sure it'll be a delight to hear.'

So I went and sat down, close enough to see and observe the ladies and damsels immersed in joyous talk of love and arms, and of the mêlée they were eagerly awaiting. [3072]

On Thursday at the crack of dawn they began to prepare the horses, arms and harness. The time for the mêlée was fast approaching! The ladies rose early, and the priest in his Latin sang the mass with great dignity, and I saw many knights and ladies praying devoutly to Christ for mercy.

By the time the service had been sung the sun had risen high: it was past terce – almost midday! Then heralds rode to Montmédy and returned with knights, pages, servants, squires; and minstrels and messengers and all kinds of other folk went back and forth, crying out with news of progress. And the ladies of Chauvency were making merry: joyously, gracefully dancing so elegant a dance that from here to Constantinople and from there to Compostela I don't believe one lovelier was ever seen. They were dancing hand in hand, each taking a partner as they came, but not another man: round and round in a circle they danced while the knights round about gazed with delight – and talked, too, saying to each other: how white that one is, how blooming that other; how pleasing she is, and how gracious she; how gaily that one dances! So they spoke of all of them, and then of each in turn. And my lady of Luxembourg – may God give her good day! – began heartily singing:

'*In such delightful company we should be merry indeed!*'

Just then there appeared a herald with a horse's crupper wrapped round him. Into the hall he came crying: 'Lace up! Lace up!'[1]

---

[1] i.e. 'Don armour and helmets.'

At this the dancing ceased and another herald cried: 'Lace up, my lords: it's high time! The days are short now: it'll soon be dark! The valiant will be disappointed!'

You should have seen the commotion in the hall: everyone went rushing as one – it was hard to get out of the door! Knights, young and strong, hurried through the town in all directions and went to their lodgings and armed. Then out of the town they rode, their horses neighing and whinnying, and clarions, trumpets, horns and drums making such a din that it was a struggle to hear a living soul! The sun was shining, lighting up the gold and blue on the gleaming arms – which had gone from their display along the walls: now the knights were decked with them. Every door and gate was open, and out the knights rode into the fields amid songs and chants and trumpets and horns, so many that they were beyond all counting. [3148]

The sun was already sinking low, declining towards evening. Now everyone was drawn up in the field. I turned my eyes towards the castle and saw Louis de Looz ride forth in glorious array, mounted on a berry-black destrier, almost at a gallop: he wasn't going to be late, for sure! He was fully armed in fiery red, emblazoned with two golden perch and little crosses, very handsome; and he had a splendid company of knights and followers ready to engage and fight and to give and receive fine blows. Alongside, a little further off, I saw Maucervel,[1] fierce as a leopard, bearing the red shield with two silver salmon; astride his great, sturdy destrier, he and his mount alike were superbly clad and caparisoned: his armour was magnificent, and he and his companions were a fine sight as they rode. Between and ahead of these two battalions came the countess of Luxembourg, riding in most noble style and in a spirit of irrepressible joy, a delight to behold. And fair Margot, her sister, began to sing this clear, sweet song, exuberantly:

'This is how one should go to meet one's love!'

Inside the walls of Chauvency there was wild excitement and revelry; boys and roguish youths and common folk were yelling and bawling, the streets all packed, every gate flung open. Into the fields rode the knights with squires and servants before and behind. So many banners you'd have seen, so many lances and splendid shields: I've never seen such a glorious sight in all my life. Lances and swords paraded forth, and helms and shields, and sleeves and pennons, and destriers caparisoned in rich-dyed silk. [3204]

---

[1] The count of Blâmont, as above, pp. 97, 99.

Following this first company, so fierce and proud, Joffroy d'Esch came riding on a great piebald charger. With a tight rein, very steadily, past the gardens he rode and into the fields with his company. He was a fine and handsome sight indeed, elegantly decked in arms as impressive as one could wish, featuring barrulets[1] of red and silver, the same on his head as on his garments, on the handsome crest upon his helm, on his gown and shield, his tunic and trailing sleeves and fringes and on his mount's caparison. In appearance and manner alike he cut a striking figure. Beside him, at his right hand, just a lance-length or less away, knights were riding hand in hand, unhurried, in the highest spirits. At their head was Joffroi d'Apremont, superbly arrayed astride a great, impressive charger, every inch a noble figure, with no coarse fabric on head or body but covered from top to toe in wondrously rich, fine silk – crimson samite it was, emblazoned with a silver cross; he looked like an angel just arrived from heaven to attend the tournament. Two by two they rode between him and the lord of Esch. They'd have readily answered any demand.

Along with this joyous, splendid company, all the way between the meadows and the gardens, riding side-saddle or on carts, came ladies in gorgeous apparel, full of love and gaiety, some following their husbands, some escorting their sweethearts. The fair Agnes de Commercy sang out loud:

'God! whom can I tell that I have a new love?'

And that fine, accomplished knight, ever valiant and bold – called by those who knew him Perart de Grilly – whispered in reply:

'God save me, he's a happy man who hears that of himself! For you are most gracious, sweet, courtly and amorous, courteous and kind in word and deed. The man you deigned to love and once call your sweetheart would be blessed by Love!'

In joyous spirits they accompanied the knights on their way to seek honour and praise on that holy ground where God does right by the worthy. There's no point in the worthless venturing there: they can all get lost! A worthless knight couldn't cope with what's done there, with all the effort and pain endured as the good strive to overcome each other. For when two worthy knights join in combat, then the price of prowess is fixed in glorious blows – and the knight who's paid a high price for prowess wants to sell it back just as dearly! Those who dare to face this test are brave indeed, for if both are strong and mighty then pride intensifies, one party attacking boldly and the other full of courage in reply, going head to head in valour, in victory or defeat. And if the hearts of men involved in this are fired and ablaze with joy, elation, courage, hon-

---

[1] See note 1 above, p. 86.

our and worth, it's not to be wondered at! For there's no company for a man that compares with that of a lady or a damsel – God has bestowed none sweeter! [3300]

After this splendid company, all eager for honour and immersed in joyful talk, out from the castle of Chauvency with the utmost pomp came Gerart de Looz astride a black horse. Renaut de Trie had a sorrel steed, strong and powerful, between his thighs; a fine knight he was, gentle and courteous and generous and brave; he carried neither shield nor buckler, but in his hand was a sword of no great length but notably broad-bladed. He was set in his saddle as if he'd been born and was fixed there; and he struck up the song:

> '*Alas! How shall I live? Love won't let me carry on!*'

They joyously processed to the tourney field, and I don't think any company ever made such a splendid sight. The Chauvency company now gathered by the stands, all of them, both mounted and on foot, creating such a tumultuous din that the hills and valleys resounded. And the ladies seated above were singing high and joyfully to cheer and inspire the amorous:

> '*No coward will ever have a fair sweetheart –
> The brave will take them all!*'

The last had now arrived, and they drew up close to the stands, dividing into three battalions. So many mail hoods you'd have seen, so many pointed helms, mighty chargers and knights all raring to go. [3334]

As the sun went down behind the hills and faded on the woods, word reached Montmédy that the insiders[1] were now mounted and awaiting them by the stands. As soon as the Limburgers heard the news they hurried to arm; they did so without delay and swiftly mounted and rode forth in good order, at a steady pace: no man tried to barge ahead or overtake his companions by so much as half a foot. There wasn't a lance or spear to be seen, but swords and maces, daggers, bludgeons, clubs,[2] iron caps and shining helms. It's altogether a joyous business – but sadly for the world it sometimes all goes wrong; lords are always under pressure, led astray by the surreptitious influence of charlatans – don't ask me who they are.

On they rode across the plain, pressing on between the fields and the hills till they were looking down on Chauvency. As they crested the hill

---

[1] '*cil dedens*': the company at Chauvency – the 'home team'.
[2] '*belles ferrees*', which I take to be a rendering of '*balles ferrees*' and refer to a club like the 'morning star' with a spiked ball, or perhaps to a ball-and-chain flail.

they drew rein and halted, and saw the battalions below them and the row of stands where the ladies were ensconced. There they sat for quite a while, their battalions arrayed with banners unfurled and helmets ready for the mighty blows that are exchanged in the cause of love. Hauberks rent and split asunder, horses killed, mail hoods cloven: that's the way that kisses are earned, and courtly liaisons, and fond looks, and sweet words issuing from lips to touch the tender heart, intoxicating true lovers with the delights of dulcet speech.

At the very front of the battalion, amid a crowd on foot and a great array of horns and drums, the count of Luxembourg sat in splendour with his company: bold in deeds as well as looks, his face ablaze with fierce intent, afire with courage, he was a dauntless, forbidding figure. Any man out to win his horse he treated with disdain: he'd repay him with his sword – he knew how to deal fine blows without a hint of boast or bluster; a truly worthy warrior has no need or time for talking. [3400]

To the left, towards the woods, between four green and leafy thickets dotted across the ground, was the noble Waléran de Fauquemont, fierce as a leopard, raring for combat, Prowess having filled his body with will to overflowing – and when will is beyond the body's control there's going to be big trouble! But I can't express all I'd like to, so I'll keep quiet. Beside this noble knight was Conrad Warnier, armed and mounted, ready for action, valiant and bold, fierce as a wild beast, and he was saying in his Teutonic bastard tongue:

'By Saint Leonard's bones, are we going to idle ze whole day here? Let's break into ze stand, and win ourselves a lady! If I had a proper good woman in ze stand down zere, I'd give up my horse for sure!'

There were hoots of laughter at this from all who heard. To one side of this company, with all his men assembled, was the worthy Waléran de Luxembourg,[1] a passionate aspirer to dignity and honour. Armed like a true warrior, finely mounted and elegantly clad, with superb mail leggings on his straight, fine legs and double-ply hauberk of finest mail on his strong and handsome body – long arms he had, a stout chest, and broad shoulders fit to handle the mightiest blows – he was a hearty, generous, genial companion who scorned all baseness.

On the slopes of the valley, with banner aloft, was Florent of Hainaut, son of Count Jehan d'Avesnes,[2] so well renowned for prowess, valour, prudence and acuity. God grant him good fortune and protect him from mischance! He'd made a fine show outside Valenciennes where he won the field against French and Flemings: you know the truth of that

---

[1] Waléran de Ligny, the count of Luxembourg's brother; see above, pp. 65, 85–6.
[2] John I, count of Hainaut.

well enough.[1] Florent was astride his horse, surrounded by a company well worthy of record, whose prowess should be boldly, clearly affirmed: among them I saw Sandroi de Haussy,[2] Baudouin d'Auberchicourt, Le Blond[3] and Simon de Lalaing; on his other side was Fastré de Ligne, and I also saw Philip,[4] son of good Count Guy of Flanders, whom I heartily pray God may send joy. [3470]

The two sides now could see each other, and the Limburgers set forth and rode towards the enemy, raising their banners to the wind. Heralds started crying:
'On with your helms without delay!'
Then you'd have seen helmets laced, caparisons unfurled, horses whinnying and stomping and the common folk taking fright, rushing and tumbling, and serving-boys and pages clearing the field while battle-cries were roared aloud. You can't imagine what a splendid sight it was! [3485]

I went to the stands and sat with the ladies to discuss and identify who was who, which of them was especially worthy, and who was from foreign parts and who was one of ours. I was in the right place to hear all this and was happy to learn from what they said; for these ladies, who know what makes a good knight, and who purge and improve the less worthy through their gentle guidance and charming company, spoke passionately and with honest decency, extolling the virtues of the good and keeping quiet about the bad.

On the plain before the stands the tourney-ground was a glorious sight, filled with noble knights and squires and servants. The ladies now were watching from their seats, eagerly waiting to see the mêlée: battle would be joined less than a crossbow's range away. Everyone was ready to ride, and Maucervel[5] charged forward. The crowd around him made way and into the field he rode, thrusting his sharp spurs to send his destrier leaping forward. Ablaze with courage, he gave the horse free rein and charged ahead of his battalion as far as a man could hurl a cry. With whetted, shining sword in hand he plunged headlong into the foe and drove the press apart; from inside his helm he cried and bawled 'Blâmont! Blâmont!' and

---

[1] A reference to action in the long-standing feud in Flanders and Hainaut between the houses of Avesnes and Dampierre.
[2] South of Valenciennes.
[3] The MSS variously give 'Le Blanc' and 'Le Blonc'. If, as seems probable, this is the same knight as 'Li Blons' who appears with Haussy below (p. 113) crying 'Montigny', the likelihood is that he is Robert de Montigny who took part at Le Hem (above, p. 27), as he was a close neighbour of Simon de Lalaing, another participant at Le Hem (see above, pp. 23, 58).
[4] 'Philip the Fleming', above, p. 65.
[5] Henri de Blâmont, as above, pp. 97, 99, 103.

struck and smote; he was grabbed and seized and hauled and barged, but he was dauntless and defended well and assailed them even better. But from all sides he was attacked with clubs and maces – he was taking a mighty hammering! All were yelling: 'Pull him down!' He clung as tight as he could to his horse's neck, trying to recover his strength and breath, while squires dragged and heaved, desperate to win his horse; but he hung on, resisting with the utmost valour, till supporters came in numbers from their positions by the stands. Ahead of them all, riding faster than a flying arrow, came Raoul de Baissi,[1] as perfectly handsome a figure as any painted on a wall; and Jehan de Rosières wasn't slow to follow: he caught up with him and together they rode to rescue Maucervel.

Everyone now was flocking to the fray and joining in combat, clashing swords; lips and faces were slashed and helmets smashed, maces shattered, stirrups snapped and reins sundered, while horses and knights alike were steaming – and frothing inside their helms – with all the effort, heat and pain.

While the battalions were locked in this exhausting combat, it was so intense and so confused that I swear I've no idea who lost or won. But a lady pointed out to me that Maucervel had charged into the Flemings and the Hainauters and Brabanters and Rhinelanders; he was being hacked and battered, but resisted as solid as a tower and, rightly or wrongly, clung on to his horse till the Flemings, in anguish, cried:

'We'll never pull this devil to the ground! I think he's locked to his saddle! He's tougher than iron or steel! Nothing's going to shift him from that horse!'

And with that they were gone, driven off by a mighty band. [3582]

The noise and the tumult were immense. Those most embroiled were weary from the giving and receiving of great blows. From before the stands Joffroi d'Apremont now came charging – God save me, only a fool would have stood in his way! He seemed to be flying far ahead of the banners; and beside him were Nicolas de Cumières,[2] Beckart de Maizey[3] and the valiant Perart de Removille.[4] Joffroi cried 'Apremont!' and Perart cried 'Bauffremont!'; Beckart cried 'Vaus!' and Nicolas 'Beaurain!' In

---

[1] Mentioned above, p. 77.
[2] See above, p. 66.
[3] See above, p. 66.
[4] This is Pierre de Bauffremont (above, pp. 67, 88) – hence his battle-cry in the next line – who was lord of Removille (see note 4 in *The Romance of Le Hem*, above, p. 50).

their path they met the castellan of Bergues[1] with Boulet de Fléchin[2] and a great mass of Flemings: I'd gladly give their names but I can't name them all – I'd never be done! Joffroi cried out to them:

'Tourney!'

The castellan tourneyed all right: he turneyed straight to face him! And his mind was turneyed[3] to one thing for sure: he wasn't going to lose his horse! Planted fast in his stirrups he raised his sword aloft and brought it down ferociously on Joffroi's helm, so fierce a blow that he was stunned. But Joffroi repaid him in full, attacking back in sterling fashion: from behind him, over his horse's rump, he swept his sword with all his force, smashing his helm as he struck him full in the teeth; and riding past he grabbed hold of his nasal.[4] Beside him Boulet de Fléchin took on Perart de Removille, and Beckart de Maizey joined in. A mighty, awesome, chaotic mêlée ensued. You should have seen Joffroi wrestling with the castellan, arm to arm, chest to chest! Both were young, and determined to unhorse each other. Squires came flocking to rescue their lords, and you'd have seen boys rushing and darting between the horses, snatching up broken swords and daggers and ruptured stirrups and lengths of shattered spear and club, and ribbed gauntlets and bits of armour from thigh and arm, and steel gloves and spurs and horses' collars, and stuffing them in bags and the skirts of their tunics. The fighting was bitter and furious.

Then a skinny, wizened herald who called himself Baptisiéz started holding forth; he certainly had a way with words, coming out with a stream of stuff so flash and fluent that it sounded as if he had it scripted:

'Holy Mary!' he said. 'Wonders I behold, my ladies! Come down! Come down! What the devil are you doing up there, penned there in your seats? Come, break up these mêlées where the knights are so embroiled: see how they strike and smite! Ladies, it's for your sake and for honour that they labour so, striving to win ownership of love and its delights! All of them have been raised and nurtured by Prowess and by Courage! See with what fierce passion each assails his adversary! Ferocious as guard-dogs they all are, filled with pride and fury!'

'Would you kindly tell me, friend,' one lady said, 'who are those two wrestling there, arms locked?'

'Lady,' he replied, 'I do believe that's Joffroi d'Apremont.'

'And who, Baptisiéz, tell me, is the one grappling with him so?'

---

[1] Bergues-Saint-Winoc, near Dunkirk.
[2] Simon ('Boulet' being a nickname, perhaps suggesting a rotund and heavy figure) de Fléchin, south of Calais and Dunkirk.
[3] This odd repetition is an attempt to reflect, at least in part, Bretel's multiple play here on the words '*tornez*' – meaning both 'tourney (fight)' and 'turn' – and '*atorner*' and '*retorner*'.
[4] i.e. the part of the helmet protecting the nose.

'I'll tell you that forthwith, my lady: that is the castellan of Bergues.'

'By God, Baptisiéz, they're valiant and tough and bold, and they'll have their due reward. They must be in love indeed! And no one should blame a lady for being inclined to share the company of such men and to show them favour: damn those who malign them, the malicious, envious slanderers of all who strive to live a virtuous and worthy life. So help me God, if they could see those two now, and the others so embroiled, they wouldn't dare say an offensive word or upset them in the least!' [3696]

While the lady was speaking her mind about arms and love to the attentive herald, I saw the noble count of Luxembourg, marquis of Arlon,[1] not far from us, come charging past like lightning, and bellowing like thunder from inside his helm: 'Limburg! Limburg!'

The knights of Berry and France[2] were spread broadly across the field, and from all sides they came rushing like wild boars to the attack. Heralds started squawking:

'Where are the valiant knights, raring to defend and attack alike, fired by love? Ah God! Who will win the prize this blessèd day? A lucky day will have dawned indeed for the knight who excels in arms! Dear Lord God, who will venture down the glorious path of prowess? Look – there's one! I think it's Renaut de Trie. See how he has mastery of his mount – and he's charging now full tilt, bent on breaking necks and conquering all! God keep him from harm long enough to perform some feat of prowess!'

The ladies prayed for Renaut likewise, and for the others, too, and declared that honour and the joys of love were rightly due to the man who dared engage in this mighty test and put his body on the line – for every ounce of flesh and bone and sinew must be committed to the task.

Thereupon the battalions clashed with a force that made the earth tremble. The noble count of Luxembourg had a huge company: I don't know how many were under his banner, but he was surrounded by fine knights, to the front, to the rear and on either side of him. Then Renaut de Trie on caparisoned steed came galloping, shield firm-braced and arm aloft, and brandishing his sword he carved into the fray. He was a valiant knight to behold indeed, strong and mighty, filled with confidence, fearless, dauntless, resolute, as roaring his battle-cry 'Boulogne!' he boldly plunged into the mêlée.

'This way, Renaut!' cried the noble count. 'You'll have to come through here!'

You should have seen the heaving press, with youths and boys bawling and yelling amid all manner of feats of arms. And then, when the

---

[1] One of the count's titles: Arlon, now in Belgium, is just north-west of Luxembourg.
[2] See note 4, above, p. 5.

two fine warriors saw each other, they made ready to defend themselves and exchanged tremendous blows on arms and heads and necks, making their helmets ring out loud as they smashed and stove them; they joined so close that they were pounding each other's nasal with their pommels. When their blows were done they wrestled, seizing each other round the helm and pulling and heaving with such force that they almost dragged each other down; but once they'd broken free they struck out again with their blades of steel, delivering massive blows to their hardy helms. On all sides the mêlée seethed as knights clashed with shuddering force; faces were slashed, reins sundered; they fled and chased each other through the throng; horses were seized and horses were lost, some were grabbed and some let go, some fought on and some gave in. One thing's for sure: those keen to fight but poorly mounted were not best placed! But anyone who'd seen the Lion of Luxembourg would have roundly declared:

'There's an awesome knight indeed! Tough and proud and pitiless!'

Not that Renaut de Trie was cowed; and they didn't stand on ceremony as they battered one another with well-aimed blows, assailing each other ferociously.

Then Perart de Grilly and the count of Sancerre came thundering up and cut a swathe through the press wide enough to turn a cart in! The fighting was close to the palisade, and a boy sprang forward and from it pulled a big, hefty, pointed stake and thrust it into Perart's hands. He was ready to defend himself now, for sure, when instead of a sword he had a whacking stake of sharpened oak! Gripping this in his hands he roared:

'Let's hear it for Perart de Grilli! He's playing the part of Rainouart!'[1]

Right in his path he found good Waléran de Montjoie[2] with Waléran de Ligny.[3] He and Sancerre counted themselves cursed failures if they didn't win the horses of these two! Perart was a forbidding sight, hacked and slashed and beaten and battered, and he and the count of Sancerre launched into battle once more, assailing the two Walérans. But they were up against it, for the Limburgers were there in force: the fearsome, dauntless Lion of Luxembourg joined his brother Waléran and, crying 'Limburg!', the three worthy knights[4] charged Perart and Sancerre, and their followers came from all sides, bent on seizing them. Not that they had it all their own way, for Perart and Sancerre defended valiantly. But they were being attacked from all directions and Perart was stormed with blows; he was dragged and hauled this way and that, everyone bent on winning his horse. From

---

[1] A club-wielding giant of Herculean strength in *La Chanson de Guillaume d'Orange*.
[2] Fauquemont: see above, p. 97.
[3] Also referred to as Waléran de Luxembourg; he is the count of Luxembourg's brother: see above, pp. 45, 106.
[4] i.e. the Count ('the Lion') of Luxembourg and the two Walérans.

near and far you could hear the cries: 'Grilly!' 'Boulogne!' 'Passe-avant!' 'Limburg!' 'Montjoie, for Waléran!' and 'Sancerre, for the count!' What a mighty fray it was: utter turmoil, as they wrestled and struggled in all directions, up and down and high and low. [3844]

In the road before the stands they were pitching each other into the mire, plastering faces and chests with filth. Horses were trampling on arms and legs and ribs to bridge the mess, while heralds went round bellowing and knights strove to get clear of the heaving throng. And all were crying at the tops of their voices:

'This is the way to find the brave! This is the way to prove yourself! These are proper warriors! They've earned indulgence – they're true saints and martyrs! They should rightly have a share in the rewards that Honour and Loyalty bestow on their devotees. What true commitment they display in their mighty mounted battle! See there, ladies, the great count of Sancerre: is he mired in shame? No: he exudes true lordship! What a noble contest this is indeed, competing for honour and praise, for prestige and land. I know of no finer path to winning honour than this. It's a great thing when the courtly aspire to prowess; but prowess alone is a specious shadow unless combined with other virtues.'

So said the heralds as they heaped praise on various knights, while the ladies high up in the stands watched the feats of valour and the fine blows being dealt. And how thrilled they were, those watching (men and women alike), to see the blows delivered and received; they ran an endless commentary, pronouncing on their rashness or their well-judged aim. I frequently reminded them that the finest, those most devoted to arms and honour, often endured great suffering and pain.

'And you should honour them highly,' I said, 'and through your love and kindness give them the heart to perform fine deeds: it will be much to your own credit. If love is the root of their endeavour,[1] you are the driving force, and through your entreaties and commands you can enhance and aid your sweethearts greatly: a lover is fired with joy when he competes at his lady's bidding.'

These and other points I made to them; for every woman of good character from here to Nevers[2] should properly love by rights. [3904]

---

[1] '*S'amours en est commancemens*': literally 'If love is the beginning of it all'; my thanks to Elizabeth Eva Leach for her note that this interestingly echoes the poem's opening line '*Amors est biaus commancemans*' ('Love is a fine beginning').

[2] The place-name may be chosen simply because it completes a rhyme, but possibly also because Nevers is at the farthest corner of the 'home' region, on the border with the lands of the 'outsiders' in Berry and the Île de France.

Just as I was in full flow, into the fray came Henri de Briey and his brother, along with Guiart de Nuefvile, Jehan de Rosières, Nicolas de Cumières,[1] Aubert d'Ornes[2] and Renier de Creuë. They cut a swathe unstoppably through the ranks, and then, turning and looking towards the stands, they saw Flemings and Hainauters with Baudouin d'Auberchicourt at their head and Gautier de Hondschoote just behind him; both of them came charging, burning to excel. After them came Sandroi de Haussy, Le Blond crying 'Montigny!', along with Cymar de Lalaing,[3] who's an adept in the matter of love, eloquent in entreaty and response. The two companies clashed so fearsomely that no thunderclap could match the din! You should have seen Henri de Briey take on Le Blond of Montigny: they attacked and defended for all they were worth, each determined to sell his horse dearly before he lost it. Then Guiart de Nuefvile charged, taking Aubert d'Ornes with him; they were roaring 'Vianne!', while Sandroi replied with 'Haussy!', Cymar with 'Lalaing!' and Baudouin with 'Douai!'; Nicolas cried 'Beaurain!', Renier 'Prigny!' and Jehan 'Rosières!'

The mêlées were intense; with night drawing in, in the deepening dusk, the tournament was at its height. The clashes took place right before the stands, and it was only right that the ladies and damsels should witness them: it was for them that their lovers were suffering.

There were three or four mêlées raging fiercely. Beside an old wall backing on to the garden a troop of Flemings and Hainauters had gathered. Florent of Hainaut and Philip of Flanders thrust in their spurs and charged fearlessly into the battalion led by the noble count of Chiny and the lord of Esch. Bending low they attacked in fury, with such force that they sent them reeling back. A mighty combat followed now, in which all displayed their prowess. Philip of Flanders surged forward with the utmost spirit, crying 'Flanders!' and then 'Arras! The count's son's city![4] Arras!' He engaged with the count of Chiny, and sword-blows fell as thick as hail as they attacked and defended. So many feats of arms were performed there near the stands before the ladies, with horses won and lost and felled, cut down and crippled.

'Chiny!' roared the count, and the Flemings fell on him with such fury that he of the red arms blazoned with the golden perch[5] took a dreadful battering. André d'Amance arrived in the nick of time, or Morel[6] would surely have been lost – as indeed he was, but André recovered him, valiantly risking his all: the throng of Flemings had taken that swift and spirited steed, but up came brave André crying:

---

[1] For these three, see above, pp. 66–7.
[2] North of Verdun.
[3] '*Simars de Lalain*'.
[4] As noted above, p. 97, Philip is the son of Count Guy of Flanders.
[5] As described above, p. 103.
[6] The count's horse: see above, p. 99.

'Amance! Fie! How dare you! Take him, would you? God help me, it'll never happen – even if you were four times as many, you wouldn't have him if you fought for the next three days!'[1]

So saying, he swept his arm aloft and belaboured them with a massive club, raining blows till he'd freed Morel from the lot of them! And so Morel was recovered, a feat demanding courage and suffering alike.

Now you'd have seen Hainauters venture into the heart of the mêlée and perform all manner of feats of arms. Florent of Hainaut was at their head, making a beeline for the thickest press, apparently untroubled by the storming combat. He wielded his searing blade to such effect that he sapped a good deal of his enemies' resolve; the blows he dealt and received were forbidding. And a herald, old and grey and balding, was following the fray and yelled for Florent:

'Hainaut! This knight isn't playing safe! He's laying his body right on the line! Strong and fierce and brave and bold his enemies have found him! And his friends have found him courteous and wise, generous and loyal, renowned for good deeds and daring ventures! And so he should be, given the fortune of his birth: Jehan d'Avesnes[2] was his father, and it's only right that his goodness and valour appear in his heir. Anyone in France would be told the same, I know, if the teller had any truth in him!'

On the fighting raged, intense, and many from both sides were unhorsed: on their faces, sides and backs they lay on the sward, covered with cloaks and tabards, while the others carried on trading blows – from far away you could hear the clash of club and mace on helm and shield. [4038]

And in the thickest press, amid a deafening welter of fervent deeds of arms, the lord of Esch was planted like a tower astride his mount. The vanquished and the failing were taking refuge behind him in numbers, and he was a rock for them, valiant warrior that he was, impossible to shift from his position amid the throng, and anyone he assailed stood little chance! A herald was crying with all his might:

'Esch, our father! Esch, bestower of the finest gifts, open-handed, unstinting, never grasping – the haven of minstrels, their hospital! The true sanctuary, ready to receive all the good! Deserving of renown indeed, when in field and town alike he's found to be valiant, brave of heart and guileless, deeply wise, clean-living and the best of company!'

'Baptisiéz, my friend,' I said to this herald, 'by the faith you owe your father, are you sure about all that?'

'May I be dishonoured and abused,' he said, 'if I've overstated it! A blight on the body of any man – may he be rendered helpless! – who wishes the lord of Esch any ill!'

---

[1] Literally 'there'd be time for rescuers to come from three days' ride away'.
[2] The count of Hainaut, as noted above, p. 106.

So saying he took a seat beside me; and I tell you, everyone was laughing about his adoring words on his lord's behalf – though there were many who endorsed them.

Just then some half a dozen knights came riding across the field. I rose from my seat to get a better view, and was thrilled to see who they were, now coming at a gallop: the first was Gerart de Looz, the next Simon de Moncler, the third Étienne d'Oiselay;[1] Joffroi de Neuville was with them, but it was getting too dark to identify the rest – or those who rode to meet and attack them. A host of feats of arms now followed, and there were victors and there were losers, amid mighty cries of 'Looz!' 'Chiny!' 'Esch!' 'Apremont!' 'Passe-avant!' 'Boulogne!' 'Blâmont!' 'Limburg!' 'Hainaut!' 'Montjoie!' 'Arras!' 'Hastatt!' (Conrad Warnier was there!)

Five hundred or more came charging in from all sides, from all directions. But night now intervened. Darkness was causing serious trouble – they could hardly see who each other was! And so it was that they parted. The mêlées petered out and the tourney-ground began to clear; the fighting came to an end. On all sides they retired and the tournament was over. Back to their lodgings they made their way, weary and worn, for they'd battled long, and those so inclined had performed a great many deeds of arms. [4114]

The night was warm, serene. The ladies came down from the stands in joyous mood, and servants set about lighting brands and great torches; then they mounted carts and, happily singing, they made their way alongside a garden, while the knights escorted them on horseback, high in spirits but battered, cut and bruised, covered in wounds on body and face as is the way after combat. All the knights were merrily singing a sweet and pleasant song:

'I hold my sweetheart by the hand – step forward any I offend!'

Those who'd been victorious left the field without a hint of sadness, full of joy and exuberance; the losers and the wounded set off in pairs, two to a nag, to seek comfort back in Chauvency.

The ladies stepped from their carts to find the chambers, halls and bowers ablaze with light. Meanwhile the knights in their various companies returned to their lodgings and took off their mail and helmets and donned gowns before making their way to court, some of them hand in hand. Trestles had been set up in tents and bowers where the knights donned surcoats;[2] a host of smart and able squires attended them and did so splendidly. Then they left the bowers accompanied by musicians and blazing

---

[1] All three were introduced above, p. 66.
[2] Surcoats specifically provided to be worn while eating.

116   *Jacques Bretel*

torches, and went to find the ladies and girls where they were lodged in chambers, solars, pavilions. Servants brought word that the food was prepared and they all set off; those who had a sweetheart led her by the hand, and those who didn't were no doubt full of looks and hopeful imaginings! They went and took their seats at the tables, mingling here and there. There was food and wine aplenty – all had whatever they asked for.

Once the tables had been cleared away, the companies gathered to dance and make merry, while away in a chamber the injured knights were entertained with a *chanson de geste*. When the dancing was over the fitter ones went to see how the wounded were getting on, taking the ladies with them and some of the minstrels. They all took seats around the chamber, and five or six servants appeared bringing Rhenish wine and wine from Auxerre. [4180]

After the wine they gathered together to see who knew how to play the Nun, the Hermit or the Pilgrim, the Provençal, the Rascal, Berengier or the Garland,[1] or some other game to amuse and cheer those suffering from wounds and injuries. It emerged that my lady of Luxembourg[2] knew how to play the Garland, whereupon four knights came forward and earnestly begged her:

'Dear noble lady, the very crown of courtesy and grace, all these knights pray you, in the name of love and God and kindness, be so good as to play the Garland, and choose who you wish to be your partner.'

That gracious lady, laughing, replied: 'My heart's delight is to do whatever you wish – I wouldn't dream of refusing.'

They helped her to her feet at once and led her, arm in arm, into the circle cleared in the middle of the room so that everyone could see her; then they left her and sat down. That lady, tall, elegant, and heartily eager for mirth and fun, took a step forward, head high but eyes lowered, and sweetly sang:

   '*There's no lady more playful than I!*'

Then she took two more steps forward, and to meet her came a minstrel, a fiddle player, as modest and meek as a maiden, who duly played his part by asking her how she came to be wandering alone, without any com-

---

[1]   '*le beguignaige, l'ermite, le pelerignaige, le provencel, le robardel, Berengier ou le chapelet*': the exact nature of these games is unknown, except for '*le chapelet*' ('the Garland') thanks to the enactment of it which follows, but judging by the coming description of this, they may well have all been role-playing games involving the characters listed – the Béguine nun (to be precise not exactly a nun, but a woman living a life of chastity and piety without taking permanent vows), the hermit, etc.

[2]   Béatrice d'Avesnes, the count's wife: see above, p. 63.

panion or sweetheart, in such fine and elegant attire, and playing with her garland. He sweetly sang, for all to hear:

> *'Gentle lady, speak to us!*
> *What does your loveliness crave?'*
>
> *'Sir, what need have you to ask?*
> *I'd say you must be rather dim,*
> *Seeing as I've made this garland gay*
> *Down there in yonder wood!'*

Having sung her reply, she took two more steps and spun round on the third, raised her garland aloft and turned it in her hands, looking at it from time to time before placing it on her head; a moment later she raised it again, all this with delicious playfulness. The one before her then sang this:

> *'Sweet lady, do you long for a husband?'*
>
> *'No! If I didn't have a good one, how wretched I would be!*
> *I prefer my flowery garland to a bad marriage!'*
>
> *'Dear gentle lady, the kind of man you're asking for is found!'*
>
> *'Then bring him to me, sir, down in the meadow!*
> *I'm going – you'll find me sitting by the river.'*

With hands by her sides she turned about, and arranging her clothes and primping her hair most fetchingly she lightly ran and sometimes danced as if lost in loving reverie, playing with her garland in all manner of ways. The minstrel meanwhile, in his plain attire, was casting his eyes round the audience to pick out the lover he'd promised the lady! As he scanned the crowd he saw André d'Amance and made a beeline for him!

'If it please you, sir,' he said, 'I'd like to introduce you to a fine lady! You'll serve my turn perfectly!'

The knight blushingly replied: 'I'm not the one you want! There are thousands fitter for the part!'

'I'm looking no further, sir! I could do a lot worse!'

And he grabbed him by his gown and pulled him toward the lady, who was turning her garland this way and that and singing in heartfelt, playful fashion:

> *'God, he's taking so long! When will he come?*
> *This waiting's going to kill me!'*

When she'd finished singing, the minstrel led before her, tugging somewhat at his sleeve, that valiant, wise, honest, charming and courtly knight, and sang to her for all to hear:

> *'Lady, here's the knight!*
> *For prowess I know of no equal!*
> *Take him, lady, I give him to you:*
> *You'll never find one better!'*

That gracious lady took the knight by the hand and led him off, singing joyously:

> *'I've won God's grace – just what I craved!'*

This game won delighted applause from all! Then servants came down the stairs bringing confections, napkins, wine and other delicacies. [4300]

The ladies and knights now sat down, taking their places around the chambers. And after the wine they relaxed and conversed for a while. Henri de Briey, who was sitting with a girl, called to me and said:

'Jacquet, by the faith you owe that Arbois[1] wine you're quaffing, come and give us some verses about arms, along with love and its charms and its power and strength! And these knights who've been battling to earn love's rewards deserve indulgence after your sermon!'

At Henri's urging I began to recite, and everyone lent an ear. The chamber was quiet and still, and I, only too glad to speak of the blessings Love has bestowed on us, smiled and began:

'May all those devoted to serving Love, and who honour Love, be granted this day the strength and will to have and to retain love's joys and a truly loving heart. God grant that they be ever resolute in their commitment to Love, that a song may finally be sung of their love with joyous words and sweet melody! Bless all who say "Amen" to that! My discourse will be brief. A pithy speech hits home; a long one is wearisome. A brief speech enters by the ear and is ushered to the heart; a long one stops halfway! May Love make me worthy now to speak on His behalf in wise and well-schooled fashion, for the benefit of true lovers – and grant that they follow His biddings. And may you, sirs, good men that you are, open your eyes, raise your heads and look me in the face and pay heed to words of wisdom here whose theme is sweet and pleasant.

'When Love makes of two hearts one it is a precious gift, and the obligations that come with it are to be admired – many of them come from God, and indeed are godly, as I shall briefly show: for hearts that love faithfully would never commit a disloyal act for all the wealth of a kingdom; rather, they strive always to do good, to be courteous and kind; they shun all vices; they seek the joys which come with honour, and honour accrues to them indeed. But to anyone who behaves otherwise, I say Love has no part in him or in anything he does: Love strikes him

---

[1] In the heart of the Jura wine region.

from His register! Love is a noble pursuit, and I say to you that a knight who loves truly, honestly, lives a far happier life than one who loves unfaithfully. But that's not right: an unfaithful lover doesn't love at all! His heart itself is faithless. A true heart will never be bent on fulfilling unworthy desires which harm both body and soul.

'A knight should love in true and proper fashion: the gracious benefits and enhancements that follow are beyond all calculation. A knight should be buoyant and true in heart, clean and trim in body, modest and straight in thought and bearing, and hold his word dear.

'And a good lady should be open-hearted, and receive the true lover's pleas in gracious fashion and give him a happy response; in so doing she will double his strength and prowess and courage and his sharpness and resolve. I shall prove this by example: when Aeneas came to Carthage he found Dido and her court; he stayed with her and she gave him gracious welcome; he sought her love, most courteously granted, whereupon Aeneas strove so hard that he overcame all obstacles and righted every wrong. A great many good deeds derive from love: Queen Guinevere's words inspired many a knight to be worthy and valiant, brave and bold – Lancelot you'll have heard of and Tristan you'll know, and Palamedes the Saracen, and she did much to benefit Kaherdin with a jewel she gave him along with her fair words.[1] In this world boundless blessings come to us thanks to ladies! They are the inspiration, here and everywhere, for all fine deeds and honours. Bless the man who loves and honours ladies in return!

'I entreat all the young to learn the sweet and noble art of love in youth and practise it till old age, till Death takes them! Then they'll go straight to their rightful place in the company of the god of love – but only if they love without deception, otherwise I take it back! I could tell you of a host of boons that come from Venus, who to Paris, Priam's son, made the gift of Helen, the cause of such great suffering for the Trojans. And if you've transgressed against Love and His commands, either in word or deed,

---

[1] Palamedes and Kaherdin feature prominently in the Prose *Tristan*, Palamedes as a rival for Iseult's hand and Kaherdin as Tristan's brother in arms. But this passage is confusing and almost certainly corrupt. The reference to the jewel is strange: it may refer to the golden buckle given at a key moment by Kaherdin to Iseult along with Tristan's ring, but if so, there is no suggestion that Kaherdin had received it from Guinevere. It's likewise unclear how Guinevere was responsible for firing the hearts of Tristan and Palamedes. It's more than possible that scribal errors have shifted the subject fully on to Guinevere and away from Love, in which case the passage could be reconstructed, albeit speculatively, to read something like: 'A great many good deeds derive from love: Queen Guinevere's words inspired many a knight to be worthy and valiant, brave and bold – Lancelot you'll have heard of; and you'll know how love drove Tristan, and Palamedes the Saracen; and how much good was done by Kaherdin with a jewel he gave Iseult [significantly, one MS does appear to read 'he gave her'] along with loving words from Tristan.'

promise to make amends; and by way of penance, abstain from boastful or offensive speech.

'And now if anyone will kindly sing a song he'll be well deserving of pardon! Bless whoever will start!'

At that Sir Simon de Lalaing stood up with a lady in each hand. He took two steps forward, and on the third he sang in heartfelt fashion, with great delight:

'God grant love to those who best uphold it!'

And all those worthy knights and ladies joined in.

After two or three or four more songs they parted, the knights retiring to their lodgings. It was high time for bed, for they'd been up a long while and were very tired and weary from their exertions in the tourney.

I left them and went back to join the ladies, very keen to hear what they had to say about those who suffer the bitter-sweet pains of passionate love. In a handsome, elegant chamber painted with scenes of Narcissus and Echo, showing how self-love had led him to his death, I eagerly sat down among the ladies. They seemed very much at ease: I found them bare-headed, with kerchiefs and mantles removed; and in carefree spirit they were immersed in conversation about the feats of prowess they'd seen before their very eyes, and the fear they'd felt at the mayhem of the hot and frenzied mêlées, the violence and the injuries, the broken arms and slashed faces, the mighty blows of fist on nose! That's what true lovers are forced to endure if they seek to win honour and praise and the joys and rewards of love: it's what Love demands in return for the pleasures He sends! That's what I found the ladies discussing when I joined them.

After the wine I took my leave. I bade them good night by the deity who confounded the Devil and they wished me the same, and I left on the sweetest terms. Friday now had almost dawned – the night had been snatched away from me by the lovely faces, words and actions I'd been treated to! It seemed to me that Friday had arrived much faster than usual: how time flies for the man who seeks life's joys! [4504]

And early on the Friday, that most high of days, the exalted, sacred mass was sung by the priest with all the authority bestowed on him by God. To hear the service the knights came most willingly and properly and in all humility, the ladies likewise.

And when they'd heard the mass the joy and celebration began anew! They were all wearing white sashes and cords as a special token, and sporting these they entered into a dance, and wove their way past the stands before they all sat down to eat.

Once they'd eaten and made merry at their leisure, the servants delayed no longer: they prepared the carts and harness and boys got the packhorses loaded. Great credit to whoever was ready first! They were all heading homeward. Hearty leave was taken then, with much bowing and embracing, and promises and fair words exchanged. And the observant would have seen lovers and their sweethearts talking intently, weeping tenderly, but hiding it from all the rest, and parting with heavy sighs. As they spoke these couples clasped each other by the hand, and it was plain from their faces that parting was a great sorrow.

The side-saddles were ready and the ladies promptly mounted; the knights followed suit. They all had their belongings packed. No drum or trumpet sounded; instead Waléran of Luxembourg struck up a merry song; standing tall in his stirrups so that everyone could see him, he sang:

'You who know the ways of love, am I taking the right path?'

When the song was done they all rode from the castle, commending one another to God. They took leave of each other most courteously, with warm embraces, hearts and bodies burning with the grievous, clamouring torment felt by those who truly love. [4558]

Amen! May the king of heaven ever grant lovers joy – and finally Paradise! – and bring the one who's written all this to a good end. Amen.

Index to
The Romance of Le Hem

Aiglentine, *maiden in the story of the Knight of the Lion* 10, 12, 13, 16
Aigre, *knight* 28, 48
Alise, the lady of Hebrison, *damsel in the story of Soredamor* 8, 9
Alixandrine, *maiden in the story of the Knight of the Lion* 10, 12
Amoises, Nicole des 55
Annois, Guillaume d' 27
Antoing, Wautier d' 44, 47
Arras: see Baudouin, castellan of
Arthur, King 5, 7, 9, 11
Artois 3, 22
Artois, Robert II, count of 15–17, 36, 38, 50, 58, 59
Autrêches, Gaucher d' 55
Auvergne 5, 29n, 53n, 55
Avaine, Muis d' 31
Aveluy, Baudouin de Beauvoir, lord of 33

Baillet, Bridous de 58
Bailleul, Enguerran de 28, 34
Bailleul, Jehan de, *John Balliol, future king of Scotland* 28n, 41
Bailleul, Pieron de 29
Balliol, John: see Bailleul, Jehan de
Barbançon, Nicolas de 32
Barres, Jehan de 43
Baudouin, castellan of Arras 20–1
Bauffremont, Pierre de 50–1
Bazentin, Huart de 3–7, 26–7, 51–2, 59
Beaujeu, Louis de 56
Beaumetz, Robert de, castellan of Bapaume 33
Beauvais, Guillaume II, castellan of 23–4
Béronne, Simon de 29
Berry 5
Blémur, Adam de 46

Blosseville, Guillaume de 29
Bois-Guillaume, Jehan au 46
Boisset, *knight* 22–3, 56–7
Bos, Jake du 42
Bosquel, Jehan de 43
Boubers, Gérard de 42
Bourg, Dagart de 29
Boves, Enguerran de 46
Brabant 5
Brien of the Isles, *Arthurian knight* 8
Brienne, Erart de 54
Brimeux, Jehan de 45
Britain 5, 7
Burgundy 57n
Burnel, Robert 55, 58

Carbonnel, Pierre 44–5, 54
Cardonelle, *maiden in the story of the Knight of the Lion* 10, 11, 12, 15, 17, 36
Cardonnoy, Adam de 44
Carduel, *Arthurian city* 8
Careu, Willaume de 41
Carrois, Jehan de 33
Castenai, Jehan de 38
Cautens, Jehan de 46
Cayeux, lady of: see Longueval, Marguerite de
Cayeux, lord of 6n, 47
Champagne 5, 33n
Charles of Anjou, *king of Naples and Sicily* 1
Châtillon, Gaucher de 56
Chaulnes, Gerard de 33
Chaulnes, Jehan de 32, 48
Chennevières, Gilles de 34
Chennevières, Pierre de 31
Chevreuse, Anseau de 44
Chrétien de Troyes 6n, 7, 8n, 21n, 24n

124 *Index to* The Romance of Le Hem

Clères, Gieffroy de   23–4
Clères, Jehan, lord of   22
Clermont, Robert count of   26–7, 38, 54, 58, 59
Compiègne   2
Conflans, Huon de   28
Corbiois, *a herald*   19
Couin, Jehan de   43
Coulogne, Jehan de   31
Coupigny, Robert de   39
Coupliau, Mikel   43
Courtemanche, Gui de   34
Courtesy, Lady, *abstract personification*   4–6
Cramaille, lord of   47
Creil   2

Dompierre et Montel, Jehan de   53
Donchart, Nicoles   32
Donsele, Guillaume   38
Douai, Jehan de   53

Écaillon, Gérard d'   43–4
Edward I, *king of England*   5
Englos, Robert d'   58
Englume, Rogier d'   57
Épagny, Jehan d'   43
Épagny, Mahieu d'   45
Estrées, Raoul d'   38, 48

Fampoux, Pierre de, 'the Horrible'   49–50
Fay, Jehan de   42
Fignières, Jehan de   32, 42, 55
Flanders   5, 34n, 49n, 57n
Forteche, *one of Guinevere's maids*   24, 36, 50, 51, 53
Fosseux, Ernoul de   50
Foucaucourt, Pierard de   28
Foucaucourt, Robert de   45
Fouilloy, Gautier de   37, 54
Francières, Jehan de   57
Friaucourt, 'the Uncle of'   46

Gannes, Jehan de   47
Gawain, *Arthurian knight*   5
Ghistelles, Guillaume de   57
Gillart, *a dwarf*   8–9, 24
Goeulzin, Enguerran de   58
Gourlé, Adam   46
Grail   5, 6, 7
Granges, Willaume des   41
Guînes, Arnoul III, count of   29

Guînes, Baudouin, son of Count Arnoul   33
Guinevere, Queen   5, 6n, 7–9, 11, 18–27, 35–42, 44–8, 50–2, 54–5, 57–9

Hainaut   5, 23n, 27n, 32n
Haitiel, Tolart du   53
Halluin, Gautier de   38, 57
Halluin, Hue de   54
Hamelincourt, lord of   28
Hangest, Aubert de, lord of Genlis   56
Hangest, Jean III, son of Jean II, the lord of   22, 55
Harcourt, Jehan de   44
Hardecourt, Wautier de   39–40
Hargicourt, Jehan de   56
Henri 'li Bascle' ('the Bastard') of Meudon   55
Heule, Guillaume de   49
Heule, Wautier de   56
Hodenc, Pierre de   46, 57
Hoteri   47
Houdancourt, Bretoul de   53–4
Hyencourt, Mahieu de   41

Jestes, Jehan des   25
Jumel, Jehan de   29, 49

Kay the seneschal   7, 8–9, 18–19, 21, 24–6, 34–5, 40–1, 44, 47, 48, 51, 56, 58, 59
Knight of the Lion, *role played by the count of Artois*   6, 10, 11–18, 34–7

La Couture, Jehan de   34
Lalaing, Simon de   23, 58
Lancelot, *Arthurian knight*   5, 21n, 24n
Lières, Guillaume de   48
Lindebeuf, Jehan de   56
Locres, Guillaume de   57
Long, Jehan de   49
'Long–Suffering', *damsel mocked by Sir Kay*   34–5
Longueval, Aubert de   3–7, 20–1, 25, 26, 36, 47–8
Longueval, Marguerite de, *Aubert's sister, the lady of Cayeux*   6
Lorraine, Ferry (or Frederick) III, duke of   36, 37–8
Lunes, Jehan de   34
Luxembourg, Waléran de   45

Maignelay, Raoul de   30

Malmaison, Pierre de la   31

Mametz, Enguerran de   53
Manicourt the Younger   46
Melles, Jehan de   34
Mequelines, Boursaut de   57
Merlin   5
Milly, Gieffroy de   45
Moislains, Gérard de   34
Moislains, Nevelon de   33
Mons, Flamenc de   32
Montaigu, Garin de   58
Montaigu, Pierre de   53
Montauban   4
Montauban, Renaut de, *known familiarly as* 'Basin'   30
Montigny, Robert de   27
Montmorency, Mathieu IV, lord of   29–30
Montmorency, Mathieu de, *son of Mathieu IV*   32
Moreuil, Bernard V, lord of   29–30, 58
Moreuil, Jehan de   32
Moreuil, Robert de   33
Morlaine, Dreux de   23
Morlaine, Pierre de   29, 43
Morlaine, Sollars de   43–4
Moyencourt, Le Foisseux de   31

Neuville, Aimer de   34
Neuville, Gilles de   20, 22, 27, 33, 51
Neuville, Guy de   23, 48
Neuville, Jehan de   52–3
Neuville, Ridel de   27
Normandy   5
Northumberland   9
Noyon   6

Oisy, Gilles d'   43
Olhain, Jehan d'   44–5
Onival, Robert d'   28

Perceval, *Arthurian knight*   7
Philip III, *king of France*   2
Picquigny, Jehan, vidame of   44
Piere, Jehan de   32
Pierremont, Jehan de   48, 55
Plaissier, Bernard du   50
Plessier, Dreux du   28
Plessier, Gui du   49
Préaux, Dreux de   28

Raineval, Raoul des Préaux, lord of   19, 51

Reninge, Boissart de   57
Ribécourt   4
Rogy, Enguerran de   49–50
Roizy, Gilles de   30
Ronssoy, Robert de   1
Roye, Dreux de   45
Roye, Mahieu de, lord of Guerbigny   41–2

Saint-Aubin, Gossuin de   45
Saint-Cler, Amaury de   33
Saint Louis, *King Louis IX of France*   2n
Saint-Martin, Jehan de   32
Saint-Nicolas, Bauduin de   32
Saint-Pol, Gui de   42
Saleri, Gui de   30
Salives, Dreux de   57
Sarrasin, *author of* The Romance of Le Hem   1, 7, 50, 59
Scotland   9, 28
Seninghem, Alenard de   43
Seuni, the Deaf Knight of   21–2
Sisi, Wistasse de   27
Soiri, Henri de   45, 52–3
Soiri, Jehan de   41–2, 57
Soredamor, *damsel in a performed story*   8–9
Sorel, Gérard de   42
Sorel, Wautier de   29
'Sueffre-Paine': see 'Long-Suffering'
Suzanne, Fauvel de, *Lord of Provence*   1

Tournelle, Jehan de la   43
Tours (–en–Vimeu), Wistasse de   28
Trie, Mahieu de   30

Varesnes   6
Vaudricourt, Mahieu de   38
Ver, Mathieu de   31
Vic, Mathieu de   53–4
Vilers, Jehan de   57

Wailly, Pieron de   32
Walincourt, Buridan de   55
Warlincourt, Mahiu de   22, 38
Wavignies, Daulés de   58
Wavrin, Robert de   55, 56

Ydone, *maiden in the story of the Knight of the Lion*   10, 12
Ytres, Jehan d'   32–3

Index to
The Tournament at Chauvency

Aeneas   119
Alsace   61, 62, 63, 65, 69
Amance, André d'   113–14, 117
Amance, Wichart d'   66, 86
Apremont, Joffroi d'   66, 82–3, 95, 97, 99–100, 104, 108–9
Apremont, lady of   63, 74, 78
Apremont, Mahaut d'   63, 78
Auberchicourt, Baudouin d'   87, 100, 107, 113
Avesnes, Béatrice d', countess of La Roche and Luxembourg   63, 67, 77–8, 81, 103, 116–18
Avesnes, Jehan de, count of Hainaut   106, 114
Avillers, Jehanne de   93–4

Baissi, Raoul de   77, 108
Baptisiéz, *herald*   109–10, 114–15
Bar, Jeanne, de, countess of Chiny   62, 73, 78–9
Bauffremont, Pierre de [also called Perart de Removille]   67, 88–90, 108–9
Bazentin, Huart de   68
Beauvais   62
Bergheim, Conon de   65, 69–70
Bergues, castellan of   109–10
Blâmont, Count Henri of, advocate of Vic, known as 'Maucervel'   76, 84–5, 97, 99, 103, 107–8
Boinville, Hable de   94–5
Boinville, Jehannette de   95–6
Briey   64
Briey, Henri de   66, 72–3, 74, 113, 118
Briey, Ourri de   66
Bruiant, *herald*   65–7, 77, 80

Champenois, *herald*   83
Chardogne, Ferri, lord of   68–9

Chiny, count of: see Looz, Louis de
Chiny, countess of: see Bar, Jeanne de
Commercy, Agnes of   63, 78, 79, 104
Conflans, Eustache de   66
Coquasse, *name applied to a herald*   70
Creuë, Renier de   80, 100, 113
Cumières, Nicolas de   66, 108, 113

Dammartin, Renaut de, count of Boulogne   84n, 91n
Dido   119

Echo   120
Esch, Joffroy d'   65, 96–7, 100, 104, 113–15
Esch, Perrine, d'   95

Faucogney, Aymon de   66, 69–70
Fauquemont, Waléran de   66, 81, 97, 106, 111–12
Fildor, *herald*   97
Flanders, Guy I, count of   91–2
Fléchin, Simon 'Boulet' de   109
Florenville, Agnes de   63, 95

Garnier, *herald*   77
Grehei, *herald*   97
Grilly, Perart de   65, 71–2, 104, 111–12
Guinevere, Queen   119

Hainaut, Florent of, *son of Count Jean of Hainaut*   65, 78, 87, 97, 99, 106–7, 113–14
Hainaut, Count Jean of: see Avesnes, Jehan d'
Haussy, Sandroi de   107, 113
Helen of Troy   119
Henri, *herald from Looz*   75
Hondschoote, Gautier de   65, 113
Huvelle, *herald*   97

Kaherdin, *character from the Prose Tristan* 119

Lalaing, Cymar de 113
Lalaing, Simon de 107, 120
Lancelot, *Arthurian knight* 84, 119
La Roche and Luxembourg, countess of: see Avesne, Béatrice d'
Leiningen, Emich von 65–6
Leiningen, Friedrich von 65–6
Ligne, Fastré de 94, 107
Ligny, Waléran de (also 'Waléran de Luxembourg'), *brother of the count of Luxembourg* 65, 86, 97, 106, 111, 121
Looz, Gerart de 66, 91, 98, 105, 115
Looz, Louis de, count of Chiny 62, 66, 73, 97, 99, 103, 113
Lorraine, Ferry (Frederick) III, duke of 80
Louppy, Aëlis de 94
Luxembourg, Béatrice, countess of: see Avesnes
Luxembourg, Henry V ('Blondel'), count of 63, 86
Luxembourg, Henry VI ('the Lion'), count of 63, 65, 78, 85–6, 97–9, 106, 110–12

Maignien, *herald* 75–6. 97–8
Maizey, Beckart de 66, 80, 108–9
Malparlier, *herald* 91–2
Margot, *sister of Henry VI of Luxembourg* 63, 103
Maucervel: see Blâmont, Count Henri of
Miriessai, Rogiers de 66
Mirouat, Jehan de 81–2
Moncler, Simon de 66, 79, 115
Montigny, Robert de, 'Le Blond' 107, 113
Montmédy 81, 97–8, 102, 105

Narcissus 120
Negréz, Hugues de 66
Neuve–Vile (Neuville?), Aëlys de la 95
Neuville, Espaulart de 88
Neuville, Joffroi le Roux de 66, 87–8, 115

Nuefvile (Neuville?), Guiart de 113

Oiselay, Étienne d' 66, 79, 115
Oiselay, Jehan d' 94
Ornes, Aubert d' 113
Ouren, Conon d' 71–2

Palamedes the Saracen, *character from the Prose Tristan* 119
Paris, *son of King Priam of Troy* 119
Philip the Fleming, *son of Count Guy of Flanders* 65, 107
'Pikart' 89n
Porrés, Jehan 80–1
Prie, Jehan de 66

Rainouart, *character from La Chanson de Guillaume d'Orange* 111
Removille, Perart de: see Bauffremont
Ronchamp, Miles de 66
Rosières, Jehan de 67, 89–90, 108, 113

Saint-Remy 66
Salm 61, 64
Salm, Henry IV, count of 61, 64
Sancerre, Étienne II, count of 66, 82–3, 111–12
Sierck, Ferci de 70
Sotin, *picks a fight with the herald 'Coquasse'* 70–1

Til, Miles de 70
Trie, Renaut de 66, 90–1, 93, 105, 110–11
Tristan, *Arthurian knight* 119

Valenciennes 106
Venus 119

Waléran, *brother of Henry VI of Luxembourg*: see Ligny
Warnier, Conrad 61–4, 65, 73, 75, 100, 106, 115
Warnier, Conradin 73, 75
Watronville, Robinet de 75–6
Wauterel, *herald* 77, 81

Yolant, *sister of Henry VI of Luxembourg* 63

www.ingramcontent.com/pod-product-compliance
Lightning Source LLC
Chambersburg PA
CBHW070808230426
43665CB00017B/2531